WALLPAPER

in Interior Decoration

WALLPAPER

in Interior Decoration

GILL SAUNDERS

V&A Publications

First published by V&A Publications, 2002

V&A Publications
160 Brompton Road
London SW3 1HW

Designed by Yvonne Dedman
Photography by Dominic Naish, V&A Photographic Studio

Printed in Hong Kong

ISBN 1 85177 356 8

A catalogue record for this book is available from the British Library

V&A Publications
160 Brompton Road
London SW3 1HW
www.vam.ac.uk

Acknowledgements

I would like to thank all those who have contributed to the production of this book. In the course of my research and writing I have benefited from the ideas, advice and support of a great many people, not least my colleagues in the Department of Prints, Drawings and Paintings. I am especially grateful to Margaret Timmers for reading and suggesting improvements to the first draft, and to Liz Miller for unearthing some splendid quotes from literary sources. I must also thank colleagues in the National Art Library, particularly Katie Swann and Sarah Cox, for helping me to access vital research material. The clarity of the text owes much to the careful editing by Rachel Connolly, and any remaining errors of fact or infelicities of expression are my own.

I am most grateful to the V&A Publications team, in particular Jennifer Eiss and Nina Jacobson for their work in tracing and acquiring the illustrations, to Dominic Naish of the Photo Studio for the excellent new photographs of material in the V&A collections, and to Ken Jackson and Ruth Cohen for their help in organising the photography. The staff of the Picture Library have, as always, been efficient and expeditious.

Finally, I must acknowledge an enormous debt to all those whose work I have drawn upon in the writing of this book. Most are cited in the Bibliography, but special thanks must go to the late Eric Entwisle, whose many books on the history of wallpaper were a rich source of evidence. I must also single out Jean Hamilton, Lesley Hoskins, Catherine Lynn, Treve Rosoman, Mark Turner, Anthony Wells-Cole and Christine Woods – writers and curators whose work in this field has been especially useful.

Front cover illustration:
Wallpaper in the chinoiserie style; English, *c.*1700
See plate 60

Back cover illustrations:
A bourgeois interior; possibly French paper, mid-19th century
See plate 41

Sample book of wallpaper; English, 1836–41
See plate 26

Half-title:
Decorator's specimen panel; English, *c.*1875–8
See plate 100

Frontispiece:
Queen Victoria's Bedroom, Royal Pavilion, Brighton
See plate 58

Title-page:
Wallpaper for Liberty & Co.; English, *c.*1975
See plate 128

Contents page:
Floral wallpaper; French, *c.*1850–60
See plate 83

Contents

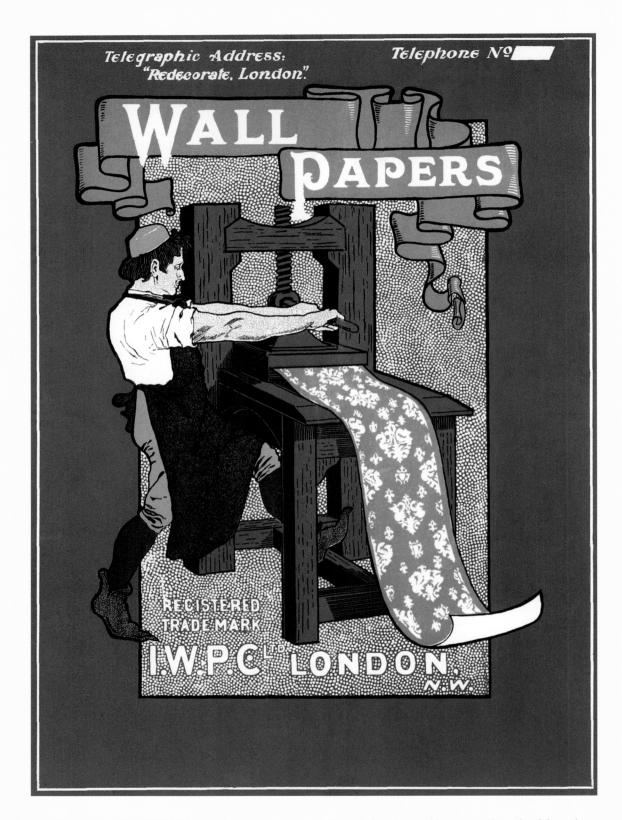

1. Advertisement for wallpapers from I.W.P.C. Ltd; London,
c.1890–1910
Colour lithograph
E.1007–1919

Though the printer is shown in pseudo-medieval dress, the process of block printing is accurately represented. The wood block, with the pattern cut into its surface leaving raised areas for printing, has been inked and registered with the previous impression. It is then impressed firmly and evenly onto the paper, using additional pressure via a foot-operated lever.

Introduction

Wallpaper has long been considered the poor relation of the decorative arts: fragile, ephemeral, easy to replace – it has often disappeared from the historical record. A history of wallpaper has been recovered piecemeal through the various collections and archives in museums, and the papers that survive in historic buildings and in pictorial records of interiors. As a museum of the decorative and domestic arts the Victoria and Albert Museum began collecting wallpapers from its foundation in 1856, and today has one of the finest collections in the world. Inevitably this account of wallpaper in interior decoration will draw extensively on the material evidence in the V&A, but it will also set the use and choice of wallpaper in the context of contemporary opinion, taste, income and social status.

Wallpaper has generally been thought of as background rather than foreground (with some notable exceptions such as the Chinese painted papers and French scenics). Nevertheless, its role in the overall decorative scheme is a vital one, and the choice of wallpaper affects the mood and style of a room, and may influence the choice of other furnishings. The wallpaper itself may point to the function of a room, and will often reflect the age, status or gender of its inhabitants or habitual occupants. William Morris recognised the importance of wallpaper when he advised, 'Whatever you have in your rooms think first of the walls for they are that which makes your house and home, and if you do not make some sacrifices in their favour you will find your chambers have a kind of makeshift, lodging-house look about them … .'[1]

Yet divergent opinions about wallpaper were apparent from the beginning. Where some found it to be 'very pritty, clean … [and] lasting'[2], others saw with regret 'the historical painter' supplanted by 'the paper-hanging maker' in the decoration of interiors.[3] This widespread and continuing ambivalence towards wallpaper can, to a large extent, be attributed to wallpaper's essentially imitative character. It is always pretending to be something else – tapestry, velvet, chintz, silk drapery, linen, wood, masonry, a mural. For much of its history wallpaper has appeared (at least at first sight) to be something other than merely printed paper, and as a cheaper substitute for more costly materials it has never quite thrown off the taint that comes from faking it.

Several nineteenth-century novelists have employed the motif of wallpaper to characterise those who reject honesty and integrity for sham and show. In Hardy's *Far From the Madding Crowd*, set in the 1840s, the handsome, vain, flashy Sergeant Troy, newly married to Bathsheba Everdene and thus in possession of Weatherbury Farm House, explicitly rejects the honesty and integrity that the unmodernised house represents. He complains:

> A rambling gloomy house this … I feel like new wine in an old bottle here. My notion is that sash-windows should be put in through-out, and these old wainscoted walls brightened up a bit; or the oak cleaved quite away and walls papered.[4]

Likewise, the new Mrs Gibson, in Mrs Gaskell's *Wives and Daughters* (1866), tries to impose her own values in the home of her husband and stepdaughter, Molly. Eager to pet and please her daughter, Cynthia, who will shortly be arriving from 'pretty, gay France', she determines that she will 'new-furnish' her bedroom, and Molly's too, though the latter objects to her much-loved familiar furnishings with their associations of a happier past being ousted by 'a little French bed, and a new paper, and a pretty carpet'.[5] The author makes explicit Mrs Gibson's concern for appearances above all else when she explains to Molly that her room must be redecorated, even against her will, so that people will not say that her stepmother has slighted her and indulged only her own daughter.

Thus both Gaskell and Hardy articulate a view of wallpaper as inherently meretricious. In both these instances a new wallpaper is advocated by those who are shallow and false, in-comers with no attachment to the past and the concomitant values cherished by other morally superior characters. These literary details confirm wallpaper's long association with deception and illusion, and with the rejection of tradition and integrity. In France too we find wallpaper implicitly associated with those who discarded history and tradition: Madame de Genlis (in 1760) bemoaned the frivolous ephemeral fashion for English wallpapers which had driven the Gobelins tapestries out of style. Wallpaper itself comes to stand for a decline in values, both moral and social:

> In the old days, when people built, they built for two or three hundred years; the house was furnished with tapestries made to last as long as the building; the trees they planted were their children's heritage; they were sacred woodlands. Today forests are felled, and children are left with debts, paper on their walls, and new houses that fall to pieces![6]

Wallpaper becomes a metaphor for dishonesty and dissembling, for the ephemeral as opposed to the secure and lasting, and for the valuing of appearance over substance.

It is perhaps no surprise that arguments around the morality of ornament – especially on wallpaper – came to prominence just at the time when machine printing and the repeal of duty had put wallpaper within the reach of quite modest households. Wallpaper, which had by the early nineteenth century established itself as a luxurious and elegant decoration, was suddenly commonplace. It therefore became important to differentiate between the chaste, 'honest' and proper on the one hand, and the cheap gaudy excesses and vulgar shams of popular taste on the other. As wallpaper became a standard decoration in working class homes it became less fashionable in wealthier households, and even those who designed wallpapers – notably Morris and Voysey – themselves preferred other kinds of wall covering, or none at all.

Even now, wallpaper is considered a sure signifier of class in a so-called 'classless society'. Writing in *The Daily Telegraph* in response to a poll commissioned by Radio 4's *Today* programme which asked people which class they considered themselves to be, Tom Utley dismissed the findings (55 per cent had described themselves as working-class) and launched into a vicious attack on the 'idle' remnants of the proletariat, that dwindling few with their hideous clothes, revolting food, trashy newspapers, filthy children, disgusting manners, vile wallpaper and violent, dishonest dispositions'.[7]

And yet wallpaper has proved to be a most durable fashion, and has been appreciated as a costly and luxurious decoration, as well as a 'make-do' substitute. It is often associated with cleanliness and comfort, and has become a kind of short-hand symbol for home and domesticity, readily co-opted by writers, artists and advertisers. In her story *The Yellow Wallpaper*, Charlotte Perkins-Gilman memorably employed wallpaper to symbolise the claustrophobia and repressive control that a creative woman might experience within the confines of her home and family.[8] Artist Susan Hiller used wallpaper in certain works because she saw it as 'evoking the fearsome embrace of the nuclear family'.[9] Akiko Busch's book, *Geography of Home: Writings on Where We Live*, uses for its endpapers a sepia tinted photograph of an empty room characterised only by its floral wallpaper, though wallpaper itself is not mentioned in the text. Similarly, a number of artists wishing to recreate or explore aspects of home and identity within the context of the art gallery or museum have taken wallpaper as their medium because of its inherent associations with domestic life.[10] Even charities have employed wallpaper to represent traditional ideas of homeliness. Shelter, a charity that helps the homeless, featured wallpaper in its latest fundraising mailshot as an emblem of a happy, well-housed childhood. For many of us, as Shelter suggested, a wallpaper with 'trains or toy soldiers' in a child's bedroom defines a home, a place that is 'warm and dry…where you felt safe and secure'.[11]

This book does not set out a conventional chronological design history for wallpaper[12], although inevitably some aspects of that account are necessary to underpin the story I do wish to tell. What is central here is how, why and when people used wallpaper, what they chose, where they bought it, how they selected it, how much it cost, where they hung it, what they thought of it, and how we now regard it. Museum collections and historic houses can tell only part of the story. Wallpaper is inherently an ephemeral material. Whereas furniture and textiles often survive, and pass from one generation to the next, wallpaper is frequently obliterated, covered over or removed altogether. Wallpaper has generally been the easiest and cheapest aspect of interior decoration to replace, and thus although it is the most eloquent feature in terms of changing fashions, the most immediate evidence of an individual's taste, and the fundamental framework of any new scheme of decoration, it is the least likely to survive.

The serious academic study of wallpaper, and by association the collecting and preserving of historic papers, did not begin in earnest until the early twentieth century. Inevitably, museum collections and the papers that have been preserved in situ tend to be the best of their kind, and therefore in many respects the least typical. The cheaper papers are almost always even more ephemeral. Thus we have more evidence – material, documentary, theoretical – for the tastes of the monied few than for the lower classes, but the paucity of evidence for the latter's use of wallpaper and their decorative preferences should not be allowed to lead to false assumptions about the use of wallpapers, prevailing tastes, the frequency with which redecoration was undertaken, and so on.

Many museums have themselves emphasised this unbalanced record of wallpaper production and consumption. Even those which have rich collections of wallpapers of all kinds seldom exhibit or publish anything but the examples of élite design and consumption. Rare or unique papers and papers by named designers are shown in preference to the products of the mass-market. Wedded to its original aim to raise the standard of design and manufacture in the decorative arts, the V&A has, until recently, ignored or actively shunned any history of material culture which investigated the marketing and consumption of these more modest products, and their design and production were discussed only as examples to avoid. The popular pictorial wallpaper patterns of the nineteenth century were displayed as a 'Demonstration of False Principles in Design', yet they are a large and vital part of the history of wallpaper, which by the middle of the nineteenth century was perhaps the most democratic of the decorative arts, found in all but the very poorest homes.

The V&A (as other museums) has an extensive archive of papers, but where many of the fine eighteenth-century flocks, the Chinese papers and French scenics come with all the paraphernalia of provenance, with references in inventories, tradesmen's bills, letters and diaries, the humble flower-sprigged paper from a cottage bedroom, or the ubiquitous machine-printed 'sanitaries' (washable wallpapers) of the late nineteenth century are by and large anonymous in terms of both their makers and their purchasers. Though price and practicality will have played a part in their selection (as indeed they will for the élite products, too), we know little more about the factors which guided their purchasers' choices. We have only the superior judgement of design critics such as Charles Eastlake and his acolytes, casually condemning the tastes of the lower classes.

Museum displays of wallpaper also tend to distort or misrepresent the nature, purpose and impact of the material. The wallpaper sample, whether it is a small fragment retrieved from an interior, or an unused length, is isolated. Often it is framed like a picture; always it is enclosed, for its protection and continued preservation. Thus presented, it is automatically foregrounded and its relationship to other furnishings is either ignored or only imperfectly represented. In this context wallpapers become works of art divorced from their original function, and they are analysed by often inappropriate criteria. It becomes inevitable that attention falls on the detail rather than on the overall effect. It is this, I would argue, which has skewed the history of wallpaper and contributed to a disproportionate focus on the unique, the costly and the products of named designers, at the expense of the more modest papers which were more widely used. This may be why wallpaper history has tended to focus on production and pattern rather than consumption, reception and use. Of course, this observation applies not only to wallpaper, but to the whole history of interior decoration, where accounts of the subject have tended to privilege creation and production, often ignoring the role of the consumer and the preferences of individuals.[13]

The artist/curator Fred Wilson[14], artist Hans Haacke and others have been active in uncovering or highlighting the histories that museums have ignored or suppressed, or simply failed to acknowledge or represent. The aim of this book is to do something similar for wallpaper, drawing on material from a variety of sources – in particular papers from public collections and from buildings open to the public – and bringing in other evidence from literary sources. Using both the anecdotal and the academic, I hope to uncover a more inclusive history of wallpaper.

Who Used Wallpaper and Where?

Any account of who used wallpapers, what they used, and where, is inevitably based on partial evidence. Wallpaper, by its very nature, is the most ephemeral feature of interior decoration, and this is compounded by the fact that it is often impossible to remove intact, and may well be obscured or obliterated by successive decorations. Naturally, unique or expensive wallpapers are the most likely to survive, and the use of wallpaper is more likely to be recorded in the houses of the wealthy and/or educated than in the homes of the lower classes. Though inventories, so valuable to furniture history, are of little use when studying wallpaper, there are many other sources: decorators' accounts and order books, letters, diaries, and the memoirs of travellers and visitors are all valuable sources of information about the usage of wallpaper and how it was regarded. The evidence for the decorating choices of the mass-market are more often found in the scornful and dismissive comments of those who saw themselves as arbiters of taste than in any record, textual or pictorial, by those who had chosen them. This does not really change until the twentieth century, when documentary photography, oral history and television began to record the lives of the many rather than the few.

The history of wallpaper, and especially its social history, is therefore full of holes, and seriously distorted by selective survival of material evidence and context. It has always been the poor relation of the decorative arts, often omitted entirely from histories of interior design, or mentioned only briefly in passing. The following account must be read with these provisos in mind. The focus is necessarily on British wallpaper and interiors, and there is no attempt at a comprehensive geographical coverage, although significant examples from France, the USA, China and Australia are represented or discussed.

From the evidence available it would seem that wallpaper was first used not in the grand houses of the aristocracy but in the town houses of the merchant class. Writing a brief account of wallpaper in 1699, John Houghton describes it as being available in 'a great Variety, with curious Cuts [woodcuts] which are Cheap, and if kept from Wet, very lasting'. He explains that these printed papers are

2. (*opposite*) ***Le famille de jug Lecoq, Arras*** [Judge Joseph Lecoq of Arras with his family], **1791**
Dominique Doncre (1743–1820)
Oil on canvas
Musée de la Révolution Française, Vizille, Isère, France

This portrait was painted on the occasion of Lecoq's appointment to a new post under the Revolutionary government. His drawing room is hung with arabesque wallpapers which imitated painted wall decorations in the same style and were then the height of fashion. Arabesque papers were a speciality of the Réveillon workshop, and were an exclusively French product. Most of the designs consisted of tiered motifs – vases, antique figures, festoons and flower garlands – arranged symmetrically around a vertical axis (see plate 4).

designed to serve instead of hangings, by which he means tapestry and other textiles. These qualities – variety of pattern, durability, and cheapness – recommended wallpapers to a class of relatively wealthy but not aristocratic householders. Houghton specifically commends wallpaper as making 'the houses of the more ordinary people look neat'.[1]

However, the fashion for wallpaper was certainly given added impetus by its use in a royal residence. William Pyne, the historian of Kensington Palace, recorded that William Kent, the architect commissioned by George I to redecorate the place, had the King's Great Drawing Room papered, an unusual choice at the time. The result was greatly admired, and 'the new art of paper-hanging, being both cheap and elegant, was generally adopted in preference to the old-style velvet flock hangings'.[2] By 1752, the *Covent Garden Journal* could claim: 'There is scarcely a modern house which has not one or more rooms lined with this furniture [i.e. wallpaper].'[3] In due course wallpapers became fashionable, elegant decorations, even preferred for grand houses in the first half of the nineteenth century.

Some of the earliest papers to survive on walls rather than as linings to chests, cupboards and deed boxes have been found in houses in areas such as Epsom, Surrey, and

King's Lynn, Norfolk. Epsom was a spa town, and a number of wealthy merchants from London made their homes there. It has been suggested that wallpapers might have been manufactured in the area: Houghton makes specific reference to Ebbisham (Epsom) where, he says, paperhangings were known as 'paper tapistry'. King's Lynn, as a port and an important provincial trading centre, also had a population of well-to-do merchants and traders.

In France, it seems that wallpapers (both domino papers and *papiers de tapisserie*)[4] were first adopted by the less well-off and only later moved up the social scale as they improved in quality of design and manufacture. Jacques Savary de Bruslons wrote in the *Dictionnaire universel du commerce* (completed in 1713, published in 1723):

> this kind of paperhanging…had long been used only by country folk and the lower classes in Paris to decorate and, so to speak, 'hang' certain parts of their huts, shops and rooms; but at the end of the 17th century [it] was raised to such a peak of perfection and attractiveness that, apart from the large consignments sent to foreign lands and to all the principal cities of the kingdom, there was not a house in Paris, however magnificent, that did not have somewhere, be it in a dressing room or an even more secret place, which was not hung with paper and quite pleasantly decorated.

The use of wallpapers was to an extent influenced by their price, which in turn was affected by taxes. In Great Britain from 1712, paperhangings were classed as luxury goods and subject to tax, which of course increased their cost. Duty was levied on all paper 'Printed, Painted or Stained in Great Britain to serve for Hangings and other Uses…' at 1d per square yard, raised to 1½d in 1714, and to 1¾d in 1787.[5] Duty was charged on imported paper from 1712, and raised to the same rate as English-made papers in 1773, but the Chinese papers were exempt until 1792. This tax was not abolished until 1836 (imports were taxed until 1861).

The definition of wallpaper as a luxury coincided with the development of more lavish and expensive papers, such as flocks, and the import of the hand-painted Chinese papers. Paperhangings of this kind were introduced into the houses of the nobility, and wallpaper enjoyed a new status as an elegant decoration in its own right rather than as a counterfeit or substitute for a more costly material. Cheaper, simpler papers were also produced – the ubiquitous 'flower sprigs', diapers and stripes – and designs also mirrored changing architectural styles.

Certainly by the mid-eighteenth century wallpaper was widely used. The anonymous *General Description of All Trades* (London, 1747) refers to paperhangings, 'the making and dealing of which has now become a considerable Branch of Trade'.[6] Thomas Mortimer's *The Universal Director* (1763) includes the following under the heading 'Paperhanging Manufacturers': '…for we annually export vast quantities of this admired article; and the home consumption is not less considerable, as it is not only a cheap, but an elegant part of furniture and saves the builders the expense of wainscotting: for which reason they have bought

3. Fragment of wallpaper; English, late 17th or early 18th century
From a house at 6 Castle Street, Dorset
Print from woodblocks with colour stencils
E.259–2000
Given by H.C. Giboud

The building had been purchased in 1698 by a wealthy local yeoman. At that time it was described variously as a slaughterhouse, a little hovel, or a warehouse. The purchaser had it rebuilt for his son, to whom it was transferred in 1700. The wallpaper, which was found behind the wainscotting, would appear to date from this period of refurbishment and gentrification.

**4. Panel of arabesque wallpaper by
Jean-Baptiste Fay (working *c.*1780–90)**
From a house at Longford, Newport,
Shropshire
Printed at Réveillon's works in the Rue
de l'Arbre Sec, Paris, *c.*1785–88
Colour print from woodblocks
E.17–1916
Given by Colonel Ralph Leeke

Arabesque wallpapers were hung as
separate panels, with printed borders or
within architectural frames. Such
papers were popular in France, both
with the aristocracy, and with the ruling
class who succeeded them in the years
immediately after the Revolution (see
plate 2). It is rare to find them in British
houses, though a complete scheme survives at Moccas Court, Hertfordshire.

Arabesque patterns derive from 16th-
century engraved ornament and from
Raphael's famous pilaster designs in the
Vatican Logge, around 1519, and
ultimately from ancient Roman mural
decoration. In the later 18th century the
wealthy commissioned hand-painted
wall decorations in this Pompeian style,
but the wallpapers, though still
expensive, made such designs more
widely available. They came into fashion
with neo-classicism but retain an
element of lightness and vivacity which
is more typically rococo.

it into vogue, and most of the new houses lately erected are
lined throughout with paper'.[7]

The responsibility for furnishing the home and taking
decisions about decorating was in the eighteenth century a
male preserve, in theory, if not in practice. Books illustrating architecture, furniture and suggestions for decorative
schemes were specifically addressed to gentlemen – the
subscribers to such works as Chippendale's *Gentleman
and Cabinet-Maker's Director* (1754) were members of the
nobility and gentry, as well as leading London artisans.
Publications by Hepplewhite and Sheraton were addressed

to the same audience. In practice, of course, women often
initiated and managed decorative schemes. Several eighteenth-century trade cards show men and women choosing
wallpapers together.

In the nineteenth-century home, decorating became the
preserve of women, and this was recognised by the publishers of general interest periodicals and also by the writers of
guides to home furnishing and interior decoration.

By the later nineteenth century wallpaper was widely
used in Europe and America and was regarded as an
essential element of interior decoration. The California

5. *Jasmin* – **No.6 in a pattern book illustrating the use of wallpapers in a range of interiors, *c*.1930**
Probably produced by Paul Gruin, Paris
Colour half-tone
E.2018–1990

The wallpaper, a muted Modernist pattern, has been hung in blocks separated by a matching beige paper, possibly textured. It complements the sleek Art Deco furnishings of this office interior.

6. *Clématite* – **No.15 in a pattern book illustrating the use of wallpapers in a variety of interiors, *c*.1930**
Probably produced by Paul Gruin, Paris
Colour half-tone
E.2018–1990

A bold scheme for a bedroom incorporates a flowered wallpaper hung with a plain red paper, dividing the walls into asymmetric sections horizontally or vertically.

architects Newsom and Newsom wrote in 1885: 'The query "What shall we do with our walls?" has long since been answered … White walls unrelieved by any color are relics of barbarism, and are almost a thing of the past. House-papering is now incorporated into building contracts, and a house is considered incomplete without these adornments.'[8] But by the 1920s leading architects were advocating white walls: Le Corbusier and others rejected the 'decorative' in favour of the self-evidently functional. Writer Adolf Loos, praising the unornamented achievements in the other arts, such as music, declared that 'whoever goes to [Beethoven's] Ninth Symphony and then sits down to design a wallpaper pattern is either a rogue or a degenerate'.[9]

Since then wallpaper has moved in and out of fashion. Though it has continued to sell, the trade has declined considerably from the heights of the late nineteenth and early twentieth centuries, and its status has declined too, despite occasional revivals and the involvement of noted artists and designers (plate 7).

7. *Cat Among Pigeons*, c.1986–7
Edward Bawden (1903–89)
Watercolour
Courtesy of the Fine Art Society, London © The Estate of Edward Bawden, Private Collection

This shows the hall in Bawden's home. The wallpaper, *Church and Dove*, (c.1925), had been designed by Bawden himself and originally printed at home by lino-cut (a popular print medium of the period, which he also used in his work as an illustrator). This and several other of his DIY wallpapers were later produced commercially, using a lithographic process, by the Curwen Press. However they were not a great success. Nine of the designs were sold through Elspeth Little's influential London shop Modern Textiles, but in six years the royalties amounted to only £2 0s 10d.

Which Rooms?

Though conventions grew up about which patterns and colours were most appropriate for different rooms, the earliest makers and sellers of paperhangings rarely specified where their products should be hung. The Blue Paper Warehouse advertised 'Figured Paper Hangings ... for the hanging of rooms and staircases'; James Wheeley offered 'Common Papers for Rooms'; and Matthew Darly made and sold papers in the 'Modern, Gothic or Chinese Tastes for Town or Country', with specific mention only of staircases, ceilings and chimney boards. There are occasional exceptions: Zecheriah Mills of Hartford did specify in 1797 that he had 'a great variety of small figures' which were best 'for lower rooms and chambers [bedrooms]' and claimed that large figures were more suitable for halls.[10] Not until the later nineteenth century, with the proliferation of manuals of household management and the rise of self-appointed arbiters of taste in matters of domestic decoration, is there any prescriptive or proscriptive advice for those choosing to decorate with wallpapers. These authors are firm on the subject of where to hang large patterns, where to use dark papers (dining rooms, billiard rooms) and where to use lighter colours and simpler designs (bedrooms), when to avoid paper altogether, and how to effect an appropriate ambience through the agency of well-chosen colours and patterns.

However, certain conventions were quickly established – the most impressive and expressive papers were preferred for the more public rooms, those used for receiving and entertaining, while cheap papers and simple patterns sufficed for bedrooms and functional spaces. Records relating to the refurbishment of the Proprietary House in Perth Amboy, New Jersey, for the Royal Governor William Franklin and his wife between 1773 and 1775 show these considerations in practice: 'a handsome *Yellow* paper' was wanted for the Drawing Room but in the Governor's Study or Office 'A common *Green* paper will do, as a great Part of the Wall will be covered with Books, Maps, &c.' The only room on the ground floor that 'Needn't be papered' was the Housekeeper's Room.[11]

Though the eighteenth century had seen some differentiation of wallpaper designs according to the function of the rooms for which they were intended – the bedroom and the closet distinguished from the drawing room and the library, and decorated accordingly – and some styles and colours labelled as inherently 'feminine' or 'masculine', it was only in the nineteenth century that these distinctions were codified. This included the division of space – in the home and in public buildings – according to class, gender and age. Wallpapers were increasingly used in recognition of or to reinforce these distinctions – cheap simple patterns (often machine printed, from the 1850s) for servants' rooms, light feminine striped or floral designs in rooms used mainly by women (the morning room, the drawing room, boudoirs) and more assertive patterns in richer, darker colours for rooms associated with men's domestic lives and pastimes (the dining room, the smoking room, billiard room and library). And in due course children's living quarters (nursery and school-room) were distinguished by the use of specially designed wallpapers with pictorial motifs designed to educate and amuse.

Copious evidence of these conventions are to be found in the Cowtan archive: bold naturalistic florals or the ubiquitous white and gold patterns ordered for drawing rooms (plate 26), rich flocks for the library and billiard room, imitation marbling for halls, passages and staircases, floral or tile-patterned sanitaries for bathrooms and sculleries.

Wallpapers in public buildings often refer either to the function of the room, or to the gender of the users. Pictorial patterns were often found in public spaces with specific functions or clienteles. In his short story, 'Madame Tellier's Establishment' (which was a brothel) (1880–1), Maupassant relates that '... The "Jupiter" drawing room, where the local tradesmen foregathered, had a blue wallpaper adorned with a bold design of Leda reclining with the Swan.'[12] Though a scene from Greek mythology, this was a thoroughly risqué subject, with overtones of rape, and as such could only have been used in a room closed to respectable women. Though neither a 1902 American *Gibson Girls* wallpaper (illustrating the popular 'beauty' of the day), nor the similar paper of semi-naked women were

found in situ, the most likely use for both would have been in gentlemen's clubs (plate 8).

An 1870s paper with Highland sporting scenes would have been an apt decoration for a club-house, gentlemen's games room, or a tourist hotel in Scotland. In 1933 the wallpaper hung in the Men's Smoking Room at the Radio City Music Hall, New York, was *Nicotine* by Donald Deskey (b.1894), a humorous design printed in shades of yellowish-brown showing pipes, cigars and tobacco leaves together with other motifs referring to predominantly male amusements – sailing, drinking and gambling (plate 9).

Wallpapers have been used in theatres (the paper decorating the box at Ford's Theatre where Abraham Lincoln was shot was torn away in fragments by souvenir hunters, and has since been reproduced for a reconstruction of the original decoration), in cinemas, especially in their Art Deco heyday, in restaurants and in shops. A recent phenomenon has seen artists designing limited edition wallpapers for exhibitions and installations. One such paper – Sarah Lucas's *Tits in Space*, first produced for her exhibition 'The Fag Show' at Sadie Coles' HQ in London – has subsequently been used in the reception area of the British Council's visual arts department in Portland Place (plate 131).

8. (*above*) **Wallpaper with pattern of semi-naked female figures; probably American, late 19th or early 20th century**
Machine print
E.590–1994
Given by Samuel J. Dornsife

9. (*right*) **Radio City Music Hall Men's Second Mezzanine Lounge, the Nicotine Room, New York, 1932**
Donald Deskey Collection, Cooper-Hewitt.
National Design Museum, Smithsonian Institution/
Art Resource, NY

The aluminium wallpaper was designed by Donald Deskey (b.1894) who was responsible for all the interior decoration at Radio City. This shiny block-printed wall covering with motifs telling the story of tobacco, was designed at the request of a tobacco company which was then looking for alternative uses for one of its new products, aluminium foil.

When selecting wallpapers, the aspect of the room was often taken into account. At Temple Newsam in the early nineteenth century, the north-facing attic rooms were hung with warm tones such as yellows, pinks and reds. When James Burton ordered papers from Cowtan & Son for St Leonard's Hotel, St Leonards-on-Sea, in 1829, he chose greens and blues for the south-facing rooms with sea views and mostly pinks and buffs for the sunless north-facing rooms. The papers for this 'elegant but OECONOMICAL HOTEL'[13] are florals and stripes, much the same as those used in private houses at the same date. For the communal rooms, grander designs with deeper borders were chosen, and this again corresponds with the ordinary domestic practice of using more impressive patterns in reception rooms, and cheaper, simpler papers in private spaces.

It would seem that inns and hotels were often decorated with bolder patterns than might have been used in domestic settings, perhaps because the rooms were larger, and possibly because the oppressive tendencies of a dominant pattern would be of less account to a clientele merely passing through. In Charlotte Brontë's *Jane Eyre*, Jane describes 'a room at the George Inn at Millcote, with such large figured papering on the walls as inn rooms have'.[14] This is confirmed by real-life evidence where French panoramic papers have been found in inns and hotels, notably in Germany, and also in America (as remarked by travellers such as Harriet Martineau), and a bold Gothic 'architecture' paper in the Ostrich Hotel at Swaffham (plate 65). Assertive graphic patterns were often recommended specifically for public buildings. An Art Deco diamond pattern produced by Sandersons in 1933, described as demonstrating dignity and strength, was intended for use in a living room. However, when a more elaborate version was issued in 1936 it was considered 'too telling for domestic work, except on a staircase, but would often be just right for Hotel and Cinema work'[15] (plate 10).

The 1950s and 1960s saw manufacturers making a conscious effort to promote the use of wallpaper in a variety of civic and commercial buildings. Many of the papers in the *Palladio* ranges had large-scale patterns better suited to town halls, hotels, restaurants, shops, offices and corporate

10. 'Art Deco'-style diamond pattern wallpaper, 1933
Produced by Arthur Sanderson & Sons Ltd
Print from woodblocks
Reproduced with permission of Sanderson

Wallpapers in the Art Deco style were considered to be particularly appropriate for large public spaces such as the foyers of hotels or cinemas.

buildings than to the average house (plates 12, 13). An advertisement for the WPM's Service for Architects shows what appears to be a town hall interior with two large-scale wallpapers, one of which is clearly Robert Nicholson's *Columns*, produced for the first *Palladio* range in 1955 (plate 11). The advertising copy makes the point that 'Wallpaper of a suitable design and colour lends character to the formal interior of civic buildings'. Elsewhere, *Palladio* papers, many designed by artists, were recommended for use in a wide variety of post-war building types and interiors, including espresso bars, clinics, car showrooms, motels and local government buildings, as well as private houses.

From the sixteenth century to the present day, wallpaper has been a feature of domestic interiors and some public buildings in Western Europe and North America. Plain and gilded papers have been used in China, but in Africa and India wallpapers have rarely been used, despite the influence of the English colonisers. Accounts of life in India by eighteenth- and nineteenth-century travellers and expatriates often remark on the fact that the interiors of even quite grand houses were 'bare' or 'unadorned'. Everett's *Observations on India* (1853) complains: 'The splendour of the houses does not reach to their inside: we see nothing of English neatness. The rooms were full thrice the size we have been used to, lofty and gloomy, with bare whitewashed walls …'[16] Of course, the heat, humidity and insects made the use of wallpaper impractical, and even undesirable. There is only one known reference to the use of wallpaper in an Anglo-Indian interior, and that is a fictional example: Hartly House, Calcutta, was described as having a closet whose 'walls are covered with pink paper from China, of the softest tint'.[17]

Otherwise the bareness was relieved by painted decoration. Emily Eden, living in India with her brother George, the Governor-General, described the furnishing of her house in Simla in a letter of 1838:

> We bought carpets and chandeliers, and wall shades … from Calcutta, and I have got a native painter in the house, and cut out patterns in paper, which he then paints in borders all around doors and windows, and it makes up for want of cornices, and breaks the eternal white walls of these houses. Altogether it is very like a cheerful middle-sized English country house, and extremely enjoyable.[18]

Nevertheless, a London firm, Allen, Cockshut & Co., produced a series of pictorial papers entitled *Hindoo Gods* for export to India around 1880 (plate 14). However it is thought that these were for use in religious festivals rather

David Gentleman

A SERVICE FOR ARCHITECTS

ARCHITECTS CONCERNED
WITH THE SPECIFICATION OR DIRECTION
OF DECORATIVE SCHEMES
ARE INVITED TO USE THE FACILITIES
OFFERED BY OUR
ARCHITECTS' DEPARTMENT

Wallpaper of suitable design and colour lends character to the formal interior of civic buildings. Though the primary purpose of the ARCHITECTS' DEPARTMENT is to give advice on the use of wallpaper it is also able to deal with enquiries concerning the use and choice of paints and fabrics.

THE ARCHITECTS' DEPARTMENT
THE WALL PAPER MANUFACTURERS LIMITED
125 HIGH HOLBORN LONDON WC1
OR KING'S HOUSE KING STREET WEST MANCHESTER 3

11. Advertisement for the WPM's Service for Architects, featuring a drawing by David Gentleman, 1955
Reproduced by courtesy of The Whitworth Art Gallery, The University of Manchester

The illustration demonstrates the use of bold contemporary wallpapers in large open plan buildings, such as local government offices. The paper on the right hand side is Robert Nicholson's *Columns*, from the first *Palladio* range: fresh, confident, mostly large-scale patterns which helped to revitalise the wallpaper trade.

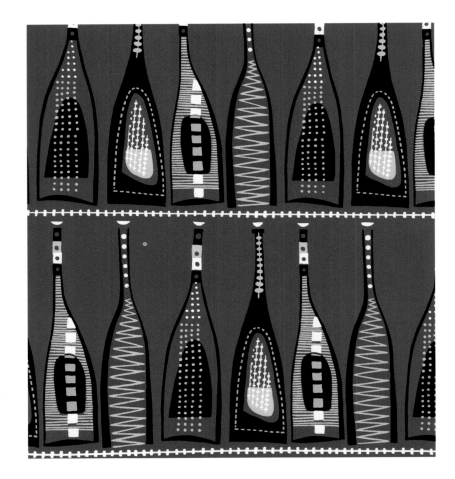

12. (*right*) ***Malaga* – From *Palladio Wallpapers*, a pattern book of screen-printed wallpapers for the architect and interior designer, 1955**
Produced by the Lightbown Aspinall branch of The Wall Paper Manufacturers Ltd
E.444(23)–1988
Given by Arthur Sanderson & Sons Ltd

With the rise of Modernist architecture and design, wallpapers had fallen out of fashion. To counteract this trend the *Palladio* range was designed specifically for the interiors of modern buildings, public and private. Patterns such as *Malaga* and *Bistro* would have been appropriate for cafés, coffee bars and restaurants, as well as the domestic kitchen-diner. The designs reflect the new interest in holidays abroad and in foreign food and wine: Spain was popular with the middle-class and not yet a destination for mass tourism, and Elizabeth David's influential *A Book of Mediterranean Food*, which had appeared in 1950, was reissued as a Penguin paperback in 1955.

13. (*left*) ***Bistro* – From *Palladio Wallpapers*, a pattern book of screen-printed wallpapers for the architect and interior designer, 1955**
Produced by the Lightbown Aspinall branch of The Wall Paper Manufacturers Ltd
E.444(75)–1988
Given by Arthur Sanderson & Sons Ltd

14. (*opposite*) **Wallpaper from the series 'Hindoo Gods', *c*.1880–90**
Produced by Allan, Cockshut & Co., London, for the Indian market
Colour machine print
E.1821–1934
Given by The Wall Paper Manufacturers Ltd

than as conventional domestic decoration. A paper from the 1870s, from an unknown English manufacturer, also has pseudo-Indian scenes, and was reputedly made for an Indian Rajah. And in 1865 Jeffrey & Co. printed a collection of designs by Owen Jones, including some lavishly gilded Moorish patterns, for the decoration of the Khedive's [Viceroy's] Palace in Cairo. But these are rare instances of attempts to translate a Western fashion for a largely unsuitable Eastern climate.

In Australia and New Zealand wallpaper use closely mirrored the tastes and fashions in England and America. Australia had no domestic wallpaper industry to speak of until after World War II. Instead papers were imported first from British manufacturers, and then, particularly from the 1920s when the British industry's output was hampered by post-war shortages of labour and materials, from US companies.

Wallpaper and the Working-class Home

When the Council for Art and Industry produced a report on 'The Working Class Home Its Furnishings and Equipment' in 1937, it set out a list of the essentials needed to furnish and decorate a home to an acceptable standard of comfort and cleanliness at the cheapest price. Carpets and curtains were considered to be basic necessities but no mention was made of wallpaper. This was surprising because wallpaper was available at very low cost and had long been regarded as a cheap and easy way to decorate a house and make it homely.

Even in rented housing (and for the working-class most properties were rented, from private landlords, and later from public authorities, or were tied houses) new tenants saw repapering as the best and cheapest way of making the place look clean and fresh, and of giving it the stamp of ownership, albeit temporary. By 1900 landlords in New York commonly redecorated a vacant apartment simply by replacing the wallpaper before renting it out again, according to a contemporary wallpaper trade journal[19]. Indeed, a view of a New York slum tenement (dated around 1896) shows a cheap wallpaper of a strong diaper pattern, damaged in places, but otherwise a bold counterpoint to the rest of the dingy furnishings (plate 15).

There are plenty of references from the early years of the nineteenth century to the role of wallpaper as an affordable enhancement to modest or run-down accommodation. When Shelley went to London, following his expulsion from Oxford University in 1811, he found lodgings in a house in Poland Street. His friend and companion Thomas Hogg described Shelley's objection to the exterior of the house, but inside they found a back sitting room where 'the walls … had lately been covered with trellised paper; in these days it was not common. There were trellises, vine leaves with their tendrils, and huge clusters of grapes, green and purple, all represented in lively colours. This was delightful,' Shelley declared, 'We must stay here; stay for ever!'[20] A 'light wallpaper which lent an air of gaiety' had also improved the wretched ill-built hovel that was home to journeyman Agricol Perdiguier in Paris in the 1830s.[21]

15. Interior of a slum dwelling, New York, 1896
Photograph by the Byron Collection
Museum of the City of New York, The Byron Collection

At this period wallpaper was the cheapest and easiest way for a landlord
to refurbish a property for new tenants.

Wallpaper was, of course, a cheap way of disguising or concealing faulty construction, such as cracks or uneven plastering, damp and other damage. The Rev. Whitwell Elwin included wallpaper in his schemes to improve the cottages of the labourers in his parish. He wrote to his friend Lady Emily Lytton that he had found a source of pretty printed wallpaper for only 2½d (1p) a roll. Apparently, many workers could not afford to buy wallpapers for themselves, even at this low price.[22] In 1850 the American architect Andrew Jackson Downing asserted that 'The great advantage of papering the walls lies chiefly in the beauty of effect, and cheerful cottage-like expression, which may be produced at very little cost.'[23]

Wallpapered walls represent a certain level of respectability, standards of living which support good character and morality. Moral decline of an individual, or their circumstances, is often mirrored in the deterioration of their living conditions. In *Clarissa* (1748–9), Richardson gives a

minute description of the room in which the eponymous heroine is imprisoned for debt. The room itself has lost its former respectable status, to the extent that it has no wallpaper, only fragments still attached to the heads of rusty tacks.

In cases of extreme poverty, it seems that a desire to decorate or pattern the walls could still stir the inhabitants. Mrs Gaskell, in *Mary Barton*, describes John Barton's home, opening off a squalid slum courtyard but nevertheless neatly furnished, homely, and most importantly, clean: it has 'a washy, but clean stencilled pattern on the walls'.[24] In his *Notes sur l'Angleterre* (1861), Hippolyte Taine compares the typical English workman's cottage to that of the French peasant, and concludes that the former is better furnished and as such indicative of a more respectable character and way of life. In evidence he writes: 'Yet his little house is clean … there is often wallpaper, chairs of polished wood, little framed prints, always a Bible, sometimes some other volumes, devotional books, new novels, how to raise rabbits etc; in short, more useful objects than in our very poor cottages.'[25] And in her story 'The Three Miss Kings', Ada Cambridge describes the characters' impoverished provincial home as 'a poor setting … a long, low canvas-lined room papered with prints from the *Illustrated London News* … from the ceiling to the floor …'[26] A decorated wall here represents a degree of feminine refinement achieved in financially straitened circumstances, but in a practical 'making do' tradition.

Such strategies seem to have been commonplace in real life: Henry Mayhew, in his investigations into the lives of the London working-classes, had found a home in which the wall over the fireplace was entirely 'patched up to the ceiling with little square pictures of saints', and the other walls papered in four different patterns.[27] An 1898 American photograph of two former slaves in their log-cabin shows the walls densely papered with a variety of magazine pages, prints and advertisements in an idiosyncratic display that gives the small room an unmistakable air of homeliness.[27] This practice continued for many years in the homes of sharecroppers and black farmers in the American south and mid-west. Margaret Bourke-White recorded one such in 1937 – a shabby interior entirely papered with sheets of newsprint, their advertisements for a consumer culture an ironic counterpoint to the poverty of the space they decorate. As Jack Delano's 1941 view of a similar scene makes clear, the use of newsprint is only incidentally decorative; its primary purpose is to conceal the rough, uneven boards from which the house is built, and to serve as insulation (plate 16).

It was the introduction of machine printing which did more than anything else to make wallpapers generally affordable. By 1851 the anonymous author of *How to furnish a House and make it a Home* could write that 'paper-

hangings are now so cheap that it is almost as little to paper a room as to whitewash or colour it. A papered room has a comfortable look which no ordinary material can impart …'[29] By the mid-century there were a number of manufacturers in England producing machine-printed papers at a price which placed them 'within the reach of the working classes'.[30] A roll of machine-printed wallpaper

16. Interior of a one-room shack, the home of a black farming family in the vicinity of Bonneau, South Carolina, USA, 1941
Photograph by Jack Delano, March 1941
Courtesy of Library of Congress, Prints and Photographs Division

Newsprint was used in place of wallpaper by the very poorest in society. Here it gives a semblance of homeliness, but also acts as insulation against draughts.

17. Interior of a labourer's flat in rue de Romainville, Paris, 1910

Photographed by Eugène Atget (1857–1927) in 1910

C.399–1974

The room is papered with a cheap wallpaper of conventional floral stripe design. By this date wallpapers were used by all classes in European (and North American) societies. Wallpaper represented respectability and a proper degree of cleanliness and comfort in otherwise modestly appointed homes.

could be bought for as little as sixpence a roll; by 1890 a two-colour machine print cost as little as twopence a roll, whereas a hand-printed paper from Jeffrey & Co. might cost as much as 25s.

Many lower income households were furnished with old-fashioned pieces, family cast-offs, and things bought second-hand. Often the only aspect of their furnishings which such families could afford to replace or to have new was the wallpaper. A view of a working-class kitchen around 1935 shows old-fashioned ornaments and a Victorian wash-stand, but the room has been papered with a contemporary wallpaper and a frieze, in watered down versions of so-called 'modernist' styles. Anecdotal evidence suggests that

wallpapers in working-class homes were renewed regularly; the downstairs rooms would be papered every two years, and the bedrooms every four years or so.[31]

Several rooms of this kind were recorded by Bill Brandt in his series on the lives of Northumbrian coal mining communities. A 1937 scene of a miner at his bath shows an assertive 'Modernist' pattern in stippled tones, almost certainly printed in the beige porridge-like colours typical of such designs (plate 18). In another view of a miner at his evening meal the wallpaper is a mottled floral pattern, again typical of the period. Brandt's photographs were used by journals such as *Picture Post* to illustrate articles about social conditions for both rich and poor. In 1943 an anony-

18. Detail from a wallpaper sample; English, *c*.1920–30
Colour print from woodblocks
E.2996–1930
Given by Arthur Sanderson & Sons

An example of 1930s wallpaper in the style then known as 'modernist'. It is characterised by abstract forms distantly inspired by Cubist painting, and from French decorative styles of the 1920s. Autumnal shades of brown and orange were preferred for sitting rooms; blues and greens were thought more suitable for bedrooms.

mous bedroom with a modernist-style paper was used in a feature about the Beveridge Report, a proposal for a universal social insurance scheme intended to offer protection from absolute poverty through the introduction of family allowances and unemployment benefit. Brandt's photograph shows a dilapidated, barely furnished room; that it represents the lives of the deserving poor is suggested by the picture of Jesus above the bed, and by the wallpaper, which is relatively new and still clean and neat, though the mattresses and pillows are worn out, an unemptied chamber pot is in view and the floor flecked with litter.

Set against these contemporary styles were more traditional styles reminiscent of the mid-Victorian enthusiasm for bold florals and revival patterns. Edwin Smith photographed the interior of a cottage in Crewkerne, Somerset, in the late 1920s (plate 19). The furniture is distinctly shabby, but the wallpaper is typical of the contemporary 'cottage' style – a simple stripe enlivened by a vivid floral border pre-cut in festoon shape.

The fashion for wallpapers in middle-class homes underwent a gradual decline in the early twentieth century, but it remained popular in working-class homes throughout this period. In a review of the 1945 Wallpaper Exhibition at the

Suffolk Street Gallery, designed to raise the profile of good design and revive the market, H. Goodhart-Rendel noted that the class of people whose homes were featured in *Country Life* had more or less abandoned wallpaper. He goes on to observe that in fact:

> Wallpaper was still made and used in great quantities, but not in houses likely to be illustrated in art publications. Its patrons were undiscriminating but vastly numerous, and although we may regret the large amount of rubbish which they joyfully accepted, we should be grateful to them for refusing to be bounced by the more sophisticated people into unnatural puritanism. It was the patronage of people who had never heard of Shaw, or of Lutyens or of Voysey that kept wallpaper alive, of people with a natural healthy taste for the ornamental which no highbrow forms could quell.[32]

19. *(right)* **Interior of a cottage at Crewkerne, Somerset, 1936**
Photograph by Edwin Smith (1912–71)
Reproduced by permission of the Estate of Edwin Smith

The room has been decorated with a cheap striped wallpaper and a cut-out floral border, in a style typical of the 1920s.

Shopping for Wallpaper

The earliest makers and sellers of wallpapers were stationers, thus the trade cards of late seventeenth-century London stationers George Minnikin and Edward Butling (c.1690) both specify that they sold paperhangings in addition to 'other sorts of Stationary Wares' (plate 21). Much of our information about the wallpaper trade in the seventeenth and eighteenth centuries is derived from trade cards, bill-heads and invoices. These list, and occasionally illustrate, the various kinds and styles of wallpapers they sold, and in some cases manufactured. Thus the Blue Paper Warehouse sold the imported Chinese papers alongside a range of papers locally produced; these included imitations of 'Irish Stitch, Marble and Damasks'. The card also shows papers hung in the shop behind a counter at which an assistant is showing samples to a customer (plate 22). A more familiar scene is represented both in James Wheeley's card (c.1754) (plate 23) and in that for Richard Masefield's Manufactory (c.1760s), where the rolls of wallpaper can be seen stacked on shelves, end on like bolts of cloth in a draper's. A roll of wallpaper is unfurled for the customer to inspect the full length of the pattern.

Many advertisements show not just examples of the patterns for sale but the premises too.[1] A lithograph of the 1840s represents Finn & Burton's Paper Hangings Warehouse in Philadelphia[2]: men, women and children are shown looking in at the front windows where panels from Pignet's scenic wallpaper *Les Huguenots* are hung. Other customers are seen seated within, where an assistant shows them a succession of papers. Framing this scene are examples of many different wallpaper patterns on a background of rolls of wallpaper stacked in 'diamond shelving' (plate 24).

French scenic wallpapers, which were popular in America, seem to have been favoured as dramatic and enticing window displays. In an 1847 lithograph showing John Ward's Paperhanging Warehouse, panels from Dufour's *Monuments de Paris* can be seen in the window.[3]

Given the fact that several late seventeenth- or early eighteenth-century papers of the same design have survived in different localities and in different houses in the same locality, we must assume that there was a fairly limited

20. *(opposite)* **Poster for an American wallpaper showroom, c.1895–1900**
Printed in Cleveland, Ohio
Colour lithograph
Reproduced by courtesy of The Whitworth Art Gallery, The University of Manchester

New wallpaper patterns were issued every year. Here the customer has a choice of Art Nouveau, Rococo Revival, Adamesque and conventional floral styles. The multi-directional design top right is a ceiling paper.

choice at this time. It also confirms that London was the main centre for the production and trade in wallpapers, until demand had increased sufficiently to support provincial manufacturers. Recent research has established a provisional list of more than 500 stationers, paperhangers and paperstainers in London in the period from around 1690 to 1820.[4] It has been plausibly argued that 90 per cent of the 255,731 pieces of wallpaper produced in Britain in 1800 were manufactured in London.[5]

It seems that at this date wallpapers were often made to order, although many customers were quite content with 'off the peg' designs. Frances, Countess of Hartford, was among the latter. In a letter to a friend in 1741 she explains:

> Yesterday I was busy in buying paper, to furnish a little closet in that house, where I spend the greatest part of my time within doors ... The perfection which the manufacture of that commodity is arrived at, in the last few years, is surprising; the master of the warehouse told me that he is to make some paper at the price of twelve and thirteen shillings a yard, for two different gentlemen. I saw some at four shillings, but contented myself with that of only eleven-pence: which I think is enough to have it very pretty; and I have no idea of paper furniture being rich.[6]

At first customers purchased paperhangings direct from the manufacturer, but gradually the craft of paperstaining (printing wallpaper) was divorced from that of stationer to

21. Trade card of Edward Butling, Southwark, London, *c.*1690
Woodcut
© British Museum

The card illustrates two typical examples of Butling's stock-in-trade. The pattern on the right appears to be a crude representation of an English-made paper in the Chinese style, similar to the paper from Ord House (see plate 60).

22. (*above*) **Trade card for Abraham Price's Blue Paper Warehouse, Aldermanbury, London, *c.*1715**
Engraved by John Sturt
© British Museum

A selection of fashionable paper-hangings are incorporated in the representation of the shop-front. At the top left is a scene showing wallpaper being printed using woodblocks. In the 18th century, papers were mostly printed to order once the customer had made a selection from the samples displayed in the warehouse.

23. (*left*) **Trade card for James Wheeley's Paper Hanging Warehouse, *c.*1754**
Engraving
© British Museum

A fashionable couple inspect a length of chintz-style floral wall-paper. Behind the counter are shelves stacked with rolled papers.

24. Advertisement for Finn & Burton's Paper Hangings Warehouse, Arch Street, Philadelphia, 1840s
Lithograph by W. H. Rease
Courtesy of the Library Company of Philadelphia

A selection of the currently fashionable patterns is illustrated. Panels of Pignet's *Les Huguenots*, a scenic wallpaper issued in the 1840s, can be seen in the shop windows. French papers sold well in the US, and this is obviously one of the latest imports.

become a branch of the upholstery trade. By the middle of the eighteenth century fashionable upholsterers such as Thomas Bromwich and Thomas Chippendale were selling wallpapers. These businesses, which dealt in furniture and furnishing textiles, were very like present-day interior decorators. As described in Robert Campbell's *London Tradesmen* (1747), an upholsterer was 'a Connoisseur in every Article that belongs to a house'.[7] They not only supplied the materials for furnishing and decorating, they would also design the rooms, if required, and supply the labour to hang the paper, and so on. According to Sheraton in 1803, 'Paper-hangings are a considerable article in the upholstery branch, and being occasionally used for rooms of much elegance, it requires taste and skill rightly to conduct this branch of the business.'[8]

Many sellers of paperhangings stressed that they could produce wallpapers to match fabrics: in 1787 John Colles, a New York paperstainer, told customers that they could order 'any kind of Paper-hanging agreeable to their fancy' in a 'colour to suit their furniture'.[9] It seems that paper was generally printed to order once the customer had made their selection at the warehouse, from a pattern book or from samples sent out. One customer buying wallpapers at Bromwich's in London for a friend wrote to explain: 'They do not keep any quantity by them (only samples of each sort), but promised they shall be finished in a week.'[10] On 8 May 1819 the London decorators Duppa, Slodden & Co. wrote to Thomas Coulthart of Pully-wrath near Cowbridge, Wales, as follows: 'We have selected a few patterns for your inspection … and beg to say that any of them can be made in a week or ten days.' And although they were a London firm, their letter continues 'we shall be happy to send a workman to put up the paper'.[11]

In Britain the trade was centred in London. For those living at a distance, samples were sent out. Others entrusted friends, relatives or agents with their purchases. The poet Thomas Gray shopped for wallpapers for his friend Dr Wharton of Old Park, Durham, when he was visiting London. He wrote to Wharton on 8 September 1761: 'I am just come to town where I shall stay six weeks or more and (if you will send me your dimensions) will look out for papers at the shops.' He was not successful, writing six weeks later: '… after rumageing Mr Bromwich's and several other shops I am forced to tell you there are absolutely no papers that deserve the name of Gothick or that you would bear the sight of. They are all what they call *fancy*, and indeed resemble nothing that ever was in use in any age or country.' He continues: 'one of 3d. a yard in small compartments thus [a drawing inserted] might perhaps do for the staircase, but very likely it is common [i.e. readily available] … therefore I would not send it alone.'

After further correspondence Wharton seems to have persuaded him that what was on offer was quite acceptable, for Gray's letter of 13 November lists all the papers he has now ordered for his friend, including the Stucco paper for the staircase mentioned previously, a crimson paper of unspecified design but the 'handsomest I ever saw', a pretty 'spiral scroll' border, a small-patterned blue 'mohair flock paper' at a shilling a yard which was 'so handsome and looked so well I could not resist it' and a 'cloth colour' library paper.[12]

Though wallpaper production developed in a number of towns around the country, provincial upholsterers and dealers – in Leeds, for example – promoted their stock by advertising its London origins. William Armitage advertised in *The Leeds Mercury* [29 May 1770] that he had 'just returned from London with a fresh assortment of the following articles, viz Paper hangings of all sorts, …'[13] Again in 1773 he announced he had 'just returned from London where he has laid in an elegant assortment [of paperhangings] which are of the newest construction and the genteelest Taste …'[14] But in due course paperstaining manufactories were established in the region, notably in York, and later (around 1782) in Leeds, and advertisements for paperhangings began to compare their own products to those from London: Hargrave & Plowman in Leeds claimed they were '… now manufacturing a collection of new and fashionable patterns in flock, mock flock and inferior papers which will be sold considerably under the London Prices, and equally as good in quality'.[15] In Norwich, Samuel Best advertised his new business as 'Cabinet and Chair Manufacturer, Plain and Ornamental Paper-Hanger, Appraiser and House Agent' in the local press. He claimed he would be able to execute commissions 'tastefully' because, in addition to his experience 'in some of the first houses in London' he would 'constantly receive fresh fashions from London … [including] A new assortment of paper-hangings … not to be excelled for quality by any house in Britain.'[16] Even in America, 'Printed Paper for Rooms lately imported from London'[17] remained fashionable and desirable into the nineteenth century, despite a flourishing native trade.

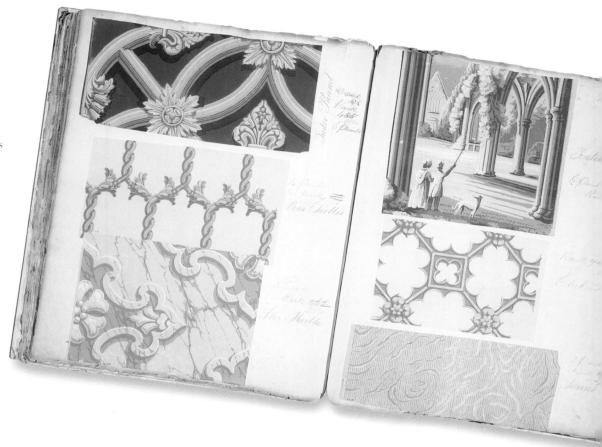

25. Wallpaper samples in a pattern book; English, *c.*1837–44
Colour prints from woodblocks
E.431–1943 (p.22)
Given by Mrs F.E. Warner

This shows the range of patterns available at this date, including papers representing tracery and mouldings, others designed to imitate marble or woodgrain, and a pictorial paper with scenes of Gothic architecture.

Papers were also exported, though cost seems to have been a discouraging factor for some prospective purchasers: Lady Mary Wortley Montagu wrote to her daughter Lady Bute from Italy on 22 August 1749: 'I have heard the fame of paperhangings, and had some thoughts of sending for a suit, but was informed they are as dear as damask here which put an end to my curiosity.'[18] From the later eighteenth century onwards, trade cards for manufacturers additionally specify their involvement in the export trade. Messrs Crompton & Spinnage announced 'Paper Hangings of all Sorts for Home Trade & Exportation', and in the early nineteenth century Ballard & Co. of Finsbury Square, London, claim 'Export Orders Speedily Executed'.[19]

Of course, papers were also imported, notably from France. The Rev. Sydney Smith wrote to his wife from Paris on 26 April 1826: 'Dearest Kate, I went yesterday into a great upholsterer's shop. Nothing can exceed the magnifi-cence and beauty of the furniture. Their papers are most beautiful so that I think I shall bring some over.'[20] By 1839 French papers were being more widely imported, and an English writer in the *Art Union* journal acknowledged their artistic excellence and superiority. In the 1840s the fashion for French papers was widespread in England: the Leeds shopkeepers Trumble & Cooke, and Joseph Wood & Son, both offered papers from Paris in their advertisements in the local press.[21] At Uppark one of the best bedchambers, the Yellow Bedroom, was hung with a lavish French paper, *c.*1850, block printed with 17 colours.

French wallpapers stood for luxury and elegance across Europe and beyond. In Tolstoy's *Anna Karenina*, Dolly Levin visits Anna in the house she shares with her lover Vronsky, and finds it furnished to give 'an impression of wealth and sumptuousness, of the new kind of European luxury which she had read about in English novels, but

never seen in Russia…before. Everything was new, from the French wallpaper to the carpet …'[22] In America too, French papers became more popular than the English (especially when duty was removed in 1861). The commissioners in charge of decorating the White House for the first time in 1800 discussed 'the fitness of pattern, preferring French papers, or second best, those made in England'.[23]

Pictorial trade cards were supplemented by other forms of advertising. The manufacturers of the lavish panoramic wallpapers publicised their new designs with promotional brochures, and with coloured lithographs showing the whole design on a single fold-out sheet. A good example of the latter is the lithograph issued by Dufour around 1818 for *Télémaque*; the story reads from left to right and the division of the scene into the individual lengths of wallpaper is indicated by numbered division running along the lower edge of the print (plate 75).

From the early nineteenth century onwards we have surviving examples of sample books from which customers would choose their papers. The name of the pattern, and

26. (*above*) **Pages 25–6 in**
Cowtan & Son's order book covering the years 1836–41
Colour prints from woodblocks

27. (*opposite*) **Pages 139–140 in Cowtan & Son's order book covering the years 1836–41**
Colour prints from woodblocks, with pen and ink inscriptions
E.1864–1946
Both given by Mr A.L. Cowtan in memory of his father,
Arthur Barnard Cowtan, OBE

Cowtan & Son was a decorating firm with premises in Oxford Street, London. They supplied wallpapers to clients all over the country. Each order was recorded by date under the customer's name and address, and small samples of the papers purchased (and in some cases fabrics and trimmings) were pasted in. These volumes comprise a valuable record of what people were actually buying, and show that many resisted the changing fashions, and ignored the advice of design critics and decorating experts, in favour of bright florals, stripes, 'satins' and trellis patterns.

sometimes its price, are noted beside each sample. Further insights into the wallpaper trade, changing tastes and decorating styles can be found in the order books of the London decorators Cowtan & Sons. The V&A holds the archive consisting of records from 1824 to 1938. Each order is detailed under the name of the client and the name and/or address of the house, with small samples of the papers (and some fabrics) pasted in below, each annotated with an indication of the room for which it was intended. Repeat orders for the same house show us how often people redecorated, and how tastes had changed, or not, in the intervening period. It is clear that by the mid-nineteenth century, with the growth of the industry and the mechanisation of production, wallpaper was used by all but the poorest in society. In the Cowtan order books the customers range from queens and dukes to clergymen and hoteliers (plates 26, 27).

From the late nineteenth century, bound pattern books containing samples of all the patterns and colourways in a manufacturer's current range were being produced. These would be consulted in the showroom (plate 103). Eastlake makes the point that 'Nothing is more difficult than to estimate the value and intensity of colour when spread over a large surface from the simple inspection of a pattern book.' He suggests that the purchaser should 'suspend several lengths side by side *in the room* for which it is intended' to get a proper sense of the effect.[24] Walter Shaw Sparrow, writing in 1909, also warned 'large patterns printed in gay colours, however attractive in a shop window, are (as a rule) too vivid for home use … such patterns are like advertisements'[25] (plate 83). The problem continues to the present, with the customer having only a pattern book to consult, though that pattern book can often be borrowed and taken home. Some suppliers are now using computer simulations to get an impression of the finished room, but inevitably local conditions, such as the aspect of the room, the light and other furnishings, will alter the effect.

By the later decades of the nineteenth century there were many companies producing wallpapers, ranging from Heywood, Higginbottom & Smith, who specialised in machine prints, especially pictorials and 'sanitaries', at the cheaper end of the market, to Jeffrey & Co., self-advertised as manufacturers of 'Art wallpapers', mostly hand-block printed, and designed by names such as Morris and Walter Crane. Prices ranged from a few pence for simple patterns printed by machine on cheap paper, to 24s or more for elaborate embossed wall coverings, or hand-block prints using many colours (plate 28). However, the number of retail outlets open to the public was limited. Larger manufacturers such as Essex and Co., and Jeffrey's, had imposing showrooms in which the range of their products was displayed, but these were in London, and existed primarily to serve the trade.

Sandersons' new showroom at 53 Berners Street opened to the trade in January 1895. There were panels of paper on the walls, and moveable hinged screens; in the centre of the room was a selection of standbooks, with smaller pattern books on tables. A visitor to the showroom in 1901 was moved to rapture by the sight:

> The suite of chambers in which we found ourselves were top-lighted, so as to display their wall-space to best advantage, and those walls were covered with papers of a magnificence, of a beauty, such as we had never imagined even in our wildest dreams of marble halls. Each panel here contained a sample covering specially selected for its charm or novelty…Here were papers light and papers dark: papers suitable for the walls of drawing room, for bed-chamber, or of sober library; papers stretched on screens, and papers displayed in handsome pattern books where every page you turned gave up a specimen more graceful in conception, more original in style and treatment, than the one you looked at last.[26]

Elsewhere wallpapers were sold direct to the public by firms such as Liberty's and Morris & Co., both of which sold a complete range of household furnishings in addition. Generally the ordinary customer purchased wallpapers from their decorator who kept a number of pattern books in stock for the purpose. This situation tended to give dispro-portionate power to decorators to direct customer choice, and the decorator was likely to be more concerned with the profit margin than with the artistic quality of the papers he sold. Amongst those who objected was designer and critic Lewis F. Day (who designed for Jeffrey & Co., amongst others): in an article in the *Magazine of Art* in 1897 he advised readers to 'find out the names of the best paper-stainers and insist on seeing their books'[27], suggesting that this was the best way of ensuring they enjoyed a full choice of the many designs then available.

Gradually, wallpapers became more widely and generally available, with the rise of department stores as well as those which specialised in the full range of house-furnishings, such as Maples.

The many publications – books and periodicals – which addressed the subject of interior decoration and household management in the later decades of the nineteenth century were a further source of advice and information for the ordinary consumer. They were addressed to 'that large borderland between the very rich who can hand over their houses to one or other of the high class decorators of the present day, and the very poor, who have neither taste or ambition, and whose taste is not as conspicuous as it might be'.[28] The *Journal of Decorative Arts*, a trade magazine, acknowledged that it was 'forced to notice the power wielded by those 'Home Art' writers who, in the pages of high-class society papers … write for the decorative education of our lady clients themselves'.[29] The writers of these guides and articles were often specific in their advice on choice of wallpaper, recommending the products of particular manufacturers – Jeffrey's, Woollams and Essex & Co. are frequently mentioned as dependable sources of good wallpapers – and on occasion naming designers and even patterns – Morris and Walter Crane designs are the most commonly illustrated or described.

Where the earlier trade cards and advertisements had shown both male and female customers, often shopping together, the examples from the turn of the century suggest that the choosing of wallpapers had become the responsibility of the woman alone. From the late eighteenth century we find examples of men abdicating responsibility to

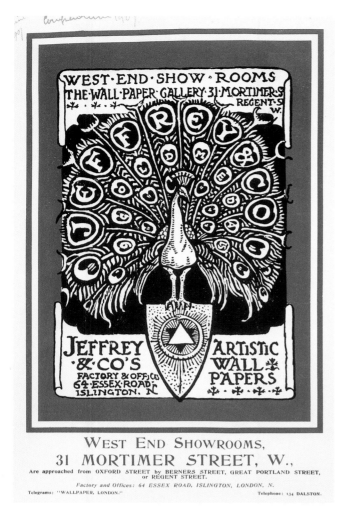

28. Advertisement for Jeffrey & Co.'s Artistic Wallpapers, *c*.1907
Lithograph
E.42A(3)–1945 (p.52)
Given by Mrs Margaret Warner

The peacock was an established symbol of the Aesthetic movement, and around 1900 Jeffrey & Co. adopted it as their logo to emphasise their association with the highest artistic standards in design. From 1864 they had printed Morris's papers and under the guidance of sole proprietor Metford Warner (from 1871) they employed some of the best designers of the day – including Walter Crane, Lewis F. Day, B.J. Talbert and C.F.A. Voysey. The firm's products regularly won medals and prizes at the International Exhibitions.

women in the matter of choosing wallpaper for the home. In 1787 David Spear asked the advice of his fiancée Marcy Higgins about buying wallpaper. Although he had some knowledge of current tastes he admitted, 'There are a great variety of fashions. I am totally at a loss what to get.'[30] Indeed, a typical advertisement of the time claimed a stock of more than 200 patterns.[31] When John Gale married Sylvia Lyon of Colchester, Vermont, in 1858, he had given 'Sylvia the money to get the paper and she got it to suit

herself'.[32] An American poster from *c*.1900 shows a fashionably dressed woman gazing at a wall of samples under the guidance of a male assistant (plate 20). The patterns on offer include the up-to-the-minute Art Nouveau styles as well as more traditional florals. A colour lithograph view of the interior of a wallpaper showroom has a female customer seated beside display stands offering a range of revival styles.[33]

The majority of the later nineteenth century writers on home decorating assumed their readers were women, and that the home was a woman's creation. As John Ruskin wrote, a woman's '…intellect is not for invention or creation, but sweet ordering, arrangement and decision'[34], exactly the qualities needed to furnish and decorate a home. This view prevailed well into the next century: Elsie de Wolfe wrote, in *The House in Good Taste* (1913): 'It is the personality of the mistress that the house expresses. Men are forever guests in our homes, no matter how much happiness they may find there.'[35] By the 1920s and 1930s the manufacturers were addressing the 'lady of the house' directly, flattering her taste and discernment and playing on her desire to have the best for herself, and most importantly, for her family.

Now both men and women involve themselves in decisions about home decorating. Home improvement (DIY) has become a major leisure activity, and redecoration is undertaken on a regular basis. Wallpaper is no longer sold in the vast quantities that it was in the nineteenth and twentieth centuries, but it remains a popular choice amongst a range of other wall coverings and wall treatments. Indeed, many wallpapers now imitate effects such as stippling or rag rolling. Papers can be purchased from the DIY stores to be found in every city and in out-of-town warehouses, as well as from decorators and the manufacturers themselves. Catalogues, swatches and sample books are used by customers to select the style, finish and colourway, but much inspiration comes from the plethora of magazines devoted to interiors and home decoration, and the home decorating and make-over shows that have become a television staple.

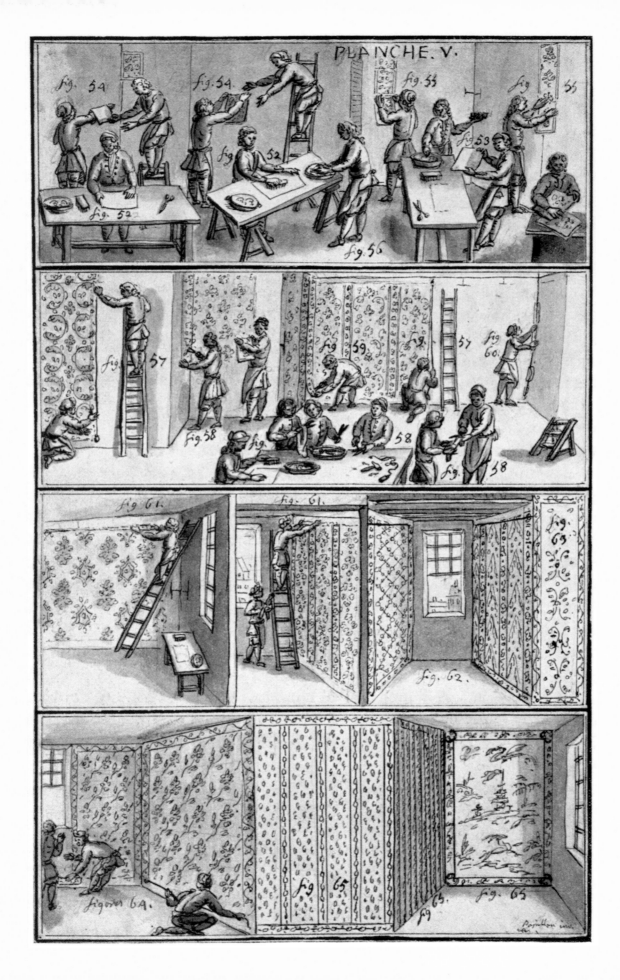

Paperhanging

From the time that printed papers were first used to decorate walls, they were generally described as 'paperhangings', to distinguish them from other materials hung on the walls, such as leather, tapestry, silks, printed cottons and so on. The same term was used as a verb to describe the process of putting up these wallpapers. In fact, wallpapers were hung in much the same way as textile wall coverings. An advertisement for the Blue Paper Warehouse, Aldermanbury, London, of around 1700, gives detailed instructions for paperhanging:

> You may observe the following method in the putting up of the said figured Paper Hangings. First Cutt your Breadths to your intended heights then tack them at the top and bottom, with small Tacks and between each Breadth leave a vacancy of about an inch for the borders to Cover, then cut out the borders into the same lengths and tack them strait down over the Edges of the Breadths and likewise at the top of the room in imitation of a Cornish [cornice] and the same (if you please) at the bottom as you see described in the figure below without borders and with borders.
>
> But if you will putt up the same without borders, then cutt one of the Edges of each piece or breadth smooth and even, then tack it about an Inch over the next breadth and so from one to another.
>
> But whether you putt them up with or without Borders gently wett them on the back-side with a moist spunge or Cloth which will make them hang the smoother.[1]

At this date no mention is made of gluing or pasting the paper to the walls. The method, as described here, closely resembles seventeenth-century methods of hanging rich fabrics in panels (or 'panes') with contrasting borders.[2] Hangings of this kind, dating from the 1670s, can be seen at Ham House (near Richmond, Surrey), in the Antechamber to the Queen's Bedchamber, and in the Queen's Closet. The use of a border, with textiles and with paper, was necessary to cover the heads of the tacks and give a neat finish. Border papers, introduced from necessity, soon became decorative features in their own right (plate 30). Their extensive use is recorded in bills and accounts, where they are listed separately from the wallpapers. In the eighteenth century, in England, borders were generally made en suite

29. *(opposite)* **Drawing illustrating methods of paperhanging; mid-18th century**
J.M. Papillon (1698–1776)
Private Collection (Reproduced from H. Clouzot, *Histoire du Papier Peint en France*, Paris, 1935)

The diagram at the top shows individual printed sheets being pasted up. Until continuous rolls of paper were produced in the early 19th century each length of paper was made up of smaller sheets joined together. Sometimes the sheets were pasted together to make a length which was then printed, but it was also common to print the sheets separately and then paste them up, as we see here. There are also several examples of the use of printed paper borders, either to cover the joins between each length or to give a neat finish to the outer edges. Various floral designs are illustrated, and at bottom right, a landscape paper in the Chinese style.

(i.e. to match) with the wallpaper itself (plates 35, 39). It was only in the following century that the fashion for contrasting borders developed. In the 1780s John Walsh in Boston had complained to his agent in France: 'do let the borders match better – the grounds ought to be alike'[3], implying that wallpaper and border were made as part of the same order, and colour-matched. The importance of borders in eighteenth-century decoration is apparent in a letter from a Rhode Island (USA) firm to their English supplier in 1784: 'The paperhangings came without border, and are now laying useless.'[4]

Hanging wallpapers by tacking rather than pasting continued well into the eighteenth century. As mentioned previously, Richardson, in his novel *Clarissa* (1748–9), describes a room where fragments of the wallpaper are still attached to rusty tacks. And as late as 1784, George Washington ordered wallpaper borders but wrote: 'I do not know whether it is usual to fasten it with Brads or Glew; if the former I must beg that as many be sent as will answer the purpose.'[5]

The practice of gluing papers to the walls was also commonplace from the earliest days of wallpaper. A 1734 receipt from Robert Dunbar, proprietor of a paperhanging

30. Wallpaper borders; English, c.1800–40

Colour prints from woodblocks

E.49,61,66,70–1939

Given by Mr A.L. Cowtan in memory of his father Arthur Barnard Cowtan, OBE

Some border papers were designed to match the design of the wallpaper (examples can be seen in plates 35 and 39) but many were printed to resemble a gilt wood fillet or an architectural moulding and were used in the same way, to cover the heads of tacks or rough edges and joins between lengths of paper.

warehouse also in Aldermanbury, gives alternative instructions for paperhanging:

> Please to observe the following Method of putting up the said Hangings in any Room, Viz.
>
> First, Cut one Edge of each Piece or Breadth, even to the Work, then nail it with large Tacks to the Wall and paste the Edge of the next Breadth over the heads of the Tacks and so on from one to another, till the Room be perfectly hung, observing to make ye Flowers Join.
>
> N.B. Damp the Paper before you put it up, and begin next the window, and make stiff Paste of the best Flour and Water.[6]

Dunbar's advice is still relevant today, at least for the hanging of hand-block printed papers. The paperhanger must still trim off one selvedge (the unprinted margin), and should work from the window outwards so that the shadow caused by the overlapped joints will be less apparent. The evidence of the papers discovered in situ shows that the method described by Dunbar was widely used. Until 1914, all wallpapers were hung using an overlap join, rather than the butt-joint which is most common today. This change is due largely to the different printing methods employed for modern wallpapers. Block-printed wallpapers always had selvedges because it was impossible to print right to the edge of the paper using hand-held blocks – the selvedge was needed for the pins which allowed the printer to register each block with the previous impression.

As Dunbar indicates, the glue used was normally a simple flour and water paste. The furniture designer Thomas Sheraton gave a recipe for this paste:

> … a preparation of wheaten flour, boiled up and incorporated with water. The flour should be mixed with the cold water so as to leave no lumps, which should be little thicker than milk before boiling it; and if the paste be wanted of a very tenacious quality, gum arabic should be dissolved and mixed with it. When this mixture is boiling, it should be constantly stirred about, till it thicken and become like a strong jelly, which then, after this degree of boiling, is fit for use.[7]

As this suggests, a heavier paper required a stronger or more 'tenacious' adhesive; this was achieved by adding substances such as gelatine, gum arabic or animal glue. For the heaviest papers, such as flocks, a pure scotch glue made from animal hoof and horn would generally have been used.

Papers were either pasted directly on to the plastered wall, once the plaster was thoroughly dry, or hung over a lining paper, linen or hessian. A note in George Washington's hand gives clear instructions for hanging wallpaper by the former method:

> If the walls have been whitewashed over, [hang the paper] with glue. If not, simple paste is sufficient without any other mixture, but in either case the Paste must be made of the finest and best flour and free from lumps. The Paste must be made thick and may be thinned by putting water in it. The Paste is to be put upon the paper and suffered to remain about five minutes to soak in before it is put up, then with a cloth press it against the wall until all parts stick. If there be rinkles anywhere, put a large piece of paper thereon, and then rub them out with cloth as beforehand.[8]

However, as Mrs Delany observed in 1750, the use of a lining had its own drawbacks: 'whenever you put up paper the best way is to have it pasted to the bare wall: when lined with canvas it always shrinks from the edges'.[9] There were other common problems with canvas: in *Madame Bovary* (1857), Flaubert describes 'wallpaper of a canary yellow, relieved along its upper edge by faded swags of flowers [which] trembled perpetually over its whole extent because the canvas on which it was hung had been imperfectly stretched'.[10]

There seems to have been little consistency in methods used. The crimson flock hung in Sir William Robinson's house at 26 Soho Square in 1760 was for the most part pasted directly on to the plastered walls, but a small area was lined first: Chippendale charged £2 11s 9d for 'Size Paste & Hanging the first floor wt paper part upon canvas'.[11] The floral paper hung at 29 Sackville Street around 1732 was glued to boards. By the early nineteenth century, lining paper, often a coarse cartridge-like paper, was widely used.

Pasting paper to the walls was the cheaper option. In 1786 Thomas Hurley of Philadelphia advertised wallpaper 'put on … at the usual moderate price of 1s6 per piece on plain walls, or 3s for pasting paper and canvas, which he warrants to execute so as that no damp can long after affect his paper'.[12] Damp was a common problem that often damaged or discoloured a paper pasted directly on to the wall.

An American letter from around 1800 specifies the use of a lining: 'With the paper I have sent some suitable lining – that is such as should be first well pasted all over the wall of the room and the paper put over it – this is to prevent any stains from the wall soaking thro to discolour the paper or injure its appearance and is always done in this country where a room is intended to be well papered. Great care should be taken to lay the first paper fair and smooth … '[13] An expensive paper such as a flock or a Chinese would often be protected by a lining of stout paper or canvas; this might then be pasted to the wall, or stretched on wooden battens which could then be fixed to the walls.

James Arrowsmith, in *The Paper-Hanger's and Upholsterer's Guide* (1851 edition; probably first published in the 1840s), recommends the use of battens and canvas as a protection against damp, '… one of the worst adversaries the paper-hanger has to contend with'.[14] This method created an airspace, protecting the paper from contact with the wall. The other great advantage of this method was that the papers were portable and could be taken down and removed at a later date. For the hand-painted Chinese papers, which were too valuable to paste over, this was a desirable option. But however the paper was hung, the paste itself might damage it, especially if poorly mixed or too watery. The redecoration of Benjamin Franklin's Philadelphia house took place while he was in London in 1765; his wife wrote to him that in 'The Blewroom … I think the paper has loste much of the blume by paisteing of it up.'[15]

Though Dunbar's instructions had included advice about making 'ye Flowers join', in practice little care was taken to make patterns join up neatly from one sheet to the next, and the task was made more difficult when papers were put up, as they often were, on uneven walls. Sometimes, this mismatch could be disguised – for example, the floral paper at 29 Sackville Street has flowers cut from surplus paper stuck on over the joins so that they were less obviously faulty. Mismatched joins were naturally less discordant in floral patterns than in figurative or pictorial designs. The American writer James Fenimore Cooper suggests the unintentionally comic effects that could result from poor paperhanging in a passage in his novel *The*

Pioneers (1823), where he describes a paper with representations of Britannia weeping over the tomb of General Wolfe: 'The hero himself stood at a little distance from the mourning goddess, and at the edge of the paper. Each width contained the figure, with the slight exception of one arm of the General, which ran over on the next piece ... some difficulties occurred that prevented a nice conjunction; and Britannia had reason to lament, in addition to the loss of her favourite's life, numberless cruel amputations of his right arm'[16] (plate 69).

Wallpaper designers, such as Charles Voysey (1857–1941), were often concerned with the way in which the pattern might help or hinder the paperhanger. Voysey recognised that 'small repeats and simple patterns are apt to show the joints' and that 'the figures may be mutilated in turning a corner'. His solution was to conventionalise the natural forms that are typical of his designs (plate 104). As he saw it, 'a real bird with his head cut off is an unpleasant sight ... but if the bird is a crude symbol and his facsimile appears complete within ten and half inches distance, although he may have lost a portion of his body, it does not violate my feelings'.[17]

The whole process of paperhanging, from preparing the walls and trimming the paper, to the use of lining papers and stretched canvas supports, is shown in illustrations by J.M. Papillon to accompany articles commissioned for Denis Diderot's *Encyclopédie ou Dictionnaire Raisonné des Sciences, des Arts et des Métiers* (1751–7) (plate 29). Although the drawings were never published, they not only describe the different stages in the process, but also illustrate the different styles of hanging, including the use of vertical borders around each panel and the alternatives. Floral and chinoiserie papers are pictured, but the scenes are not captioned so it is not clear whether these methods are also appropriate to flock papers.

Today, old paper is usually removed by scraping, stripping or steaming, before a new paper is hung. But in the eighteenth and nineteenth centuries it was commonplace to paste new paper over the old, often accumulating many layers; for example, in the Nathan Beers house in Fairfield, Connecticut, 13 layers were found, dating from the 1820s to the turn of the century. In some English houses as many as 22 layers have been discovered. It was both quicker and cheaper to simply paper over the existing decoration than to strip back to the walls or panelling (plate 49). Paperhangers charged extra to strip and prepare the walls before putting up the new paper.

The flock papers, which were usually pasted up using the 'tenacious' animal glues, were very difficult to remove and were also often simply pasted over. For instance, the red flowered flock in the first-floor front room of 6 St James's Place, London W1, was covered over around 1795 by a sprig and stripe paper.

The suppliers of wallpapers often provided the workmen to hang the papers. Certainly Chippendale's men often prepared and hung the papers he supplied, and his bills detail the costs of paste, tacks, lining paper, canvas and so on, as well as the labour. For example, the accounts of Chippendale, Haig & Co. list the materials and the procedures involved in paperhanging at the house of the actor David Garrick in Adelphi Terrace, London, in 1772:

> Back room ... Battens. Nails & preparing the Room with proper fastenings for Hangings; 72 yds. Canvas to hang the Room; 7 Quires cartridge paper; hanging the canvas and paper, Tacks, Paste etc. included; ditto [i.e. hanging] the Room with your own India paper, paste etc.
> April 1st, 1772: scrapeing the paint of the Walls in passage; hanging the Canvas & paper & afterwards the India ...[18]

A bill from Joseph Smith dated 24 April 1753 shows that he supplied a Mrs Massingberd with papers, including a 'New Flock' and also hung them.[19] The trade card (c.1770s) of John Sigrist of Piccadilly, London, concludes the list of papers supplied with the claim that he has 'People always ready to put up and hang the same.' London firms of paperstainers and upholsterers often sent their workmen out of town. In 1768, Bromwich, Isherwood & Bradley of Ludgate Hill sent men to Audley End, near Saffron Walden, where they spent one day stripping off the old paper, at a cost of 3s 6d. In July 1769 they spent 12 days on preparation work, and charged 5s for their 'Lodging Expenses'. When they were sent out again in 1770, 2 guineas were charged for

**31. *The Dutton Family in the Drawing Room of Sherborne Park,
Gloucestershire*, 1771**
Johann Zoffany (1733–1810)
Oil on canvas
Private Collection with Guy Morrison 2001

The walls appear to have been hung with green verditer paper. Plain
green papers were often chosen as a background to paintings in gilt
frames. At Luton Hoo, Lady Mary Coke noted that 'almost all the rooms
are hung with light green plain papers, which show the pictures to great
advantage' [2 September 1774, quoted in *Literary History*, 50]. A similar
interior decorated with green verditer – the library at 19 Arlington Street,
the London home of Sir Lawrence Dundas – had been painted by
Zoffany in 1769.

travelling from London to Audley End.[20] The method of
hanging the papers was often treated as a selling point:
advertisements by Thomas Fuller in Dublin[21] describe his
stock of new flock and Chinese papers from London, and
claim he can put up the latter 'in a newer and better Taste
than was ever done before'.[22]

Upholsterers such as Chippendale also supplied and put
up plain papers which were then coloured by hand either
as a uniform wash or in stripes. This seems to have been
popular because it was a means of evading the duty levied
on printed papers. The letter book of Duppa, Slodden &
Co. for the period 1817–22 contains many references to the
putting up and colouring of lining papers. These plain
papers were usually coloured green or blue, and were
known as verditer papers (plate 31). Sir Rowland Winn
ordered 'plane green paper' and 'blue Verditure' for Nostell
Priory; elsewhere, 'verditer' papers were often used for print
rooms – a well-preserved example can be seen at Rokeby
Park, County Durham. However, it appears that clients
were not always happy with the standard of workmanship.
One of Chippendale's customers, Sir Edmund Knatchbull,
complained 'As to the Man who putt up & colourd the
Green paper he was not above two days at work & did it
extreamly bad.'[23]

32. (*above*) **A bedroom – Plate 17 from**
***The Decorative Use of Wallpapers*,**
a volume of illustrations showing
wallpapers in a variety of domestic
interiors; British, *c*.1910
Colour half-tone
E.2017–1990

A cut-out floral frieze and borders have
been applied to a paper described as 'a
simple diaper in satinette', framing each
section of the wall. The ceiling border is
a high relief Anaglypta.

33. (*right*) ***Azalée* – No.24 in a pattern**
book illustrating the use of wall-
papers in a range of interiors, *c*.1930
Probably produced by Paul Gruin, Paris
Colour half-tone
E.2018–1990

This grey Art Deco-style wallpaper is
hung in panels with a narrow border,
and with a plain paper in a contrasting
shade, as was the fashion at the time.
The room is an office or study.

It seems that paper could also be flocked after hanging: Duppa Slodden & Co. wrote to the Duke of Rutland on 6 December 1820 to explain that 'the usual manner of doing plain flock rooms [presumably all-over rather than patterned flock], is to paper the walls first, and apply the flock upon them afterwards, as plain flock papers cannot be put up without the joints being seen'.[24]

When cheap wallpaper became available in the mid-nineteenth century, working-class householders usually hung it themselves, and this continued in the twentieth century. In the north of England it was apparently considered to be one of the housewife's chores. Certainly by the 1940s manufacturers' pattern books assumed that women could and would hang wallpaper themselves. The cover to *Colour-Perfect Wallpaper* put out by Sears, Roebuck & Co. in 1942 shows a woman hanging wallpaper, helped by her small daughter, and an advertisement inside takes the form of a letter from a 16-year-old girl explaining how she papered her room herself. Since then, paperhanging has become ever simpler and manufacturers have encouraged it with the production of ready-pasted papers (plate 34).

34. *The Practical Householder,* **cover, October 1957**
© MODA/Middlesex University

DIY magazines promoted the idea that wallpaper-hanging could be an easy, pleasant pastime for the whole family. The illustration shows the contemporary fashion for using contrasting patterns in a single room, and making a feature of one wall, such as the chimneybreast.

Textile Influences on Wallpaper

35. *(opposite)* **Chintz-style wallpaper, with matching border; English, second half of the 18th century**
Colour print from woodblocks
E.797–1969
Given by Mrs Jean Meade-Fetherstonhaugh

Part of the paper has been patched in at the lower left corner, probably to make good a damaged area.

Textile wallhangings of various kinds were the precursors of paperhangings, so it is not surprising that the earliest and most consistent influence on wallpaper design has come from textiles. It is important to make a distinction, however, between wallpapers made to match fabrics, and vice versa, as is common practice now, and wallpapers which derived their patterns from textiles and were intended to imitate them. There are odd examples of the former in the eighteenth century, for example Horace Walpole (in a letter dated 12 June 1753) describes a sitting room 'hung with a blue and white paper in stripes adorned with festoons, and a thousand plump chairs, couches and luxurious settees covered with linen of the same pattern'.[1] John Sigrist's trade card from the 1770s[2] also offers to make papers to match fabrics, but generally speaking wallpapers were designed to imitate the styles, patterns and textures of fabrics, and effectively to represent textile wall coverings.

In *Holinshed's Chronicle* (1577), Sir William Harrison's 'Description of England' includes an account of the kinds of wall coverings then in use: 'The walls of our houses on the inner sides in like sort be hanged with tapestry, arras work or painted cloths … or else they are ceiled with oak of our own, or wainscot brought hither out of the east countries, whereby the rooms are not a little commended, made warm and much more close than otherwise they would be.'[3] In consequence, wallpapers were designed to look like the materials they were substituting. What is thought to be the earliest known wallpaper in England was found in the Master's Lodge in Christ's College, Cambridge, and has a formalised pomegranate design derived from a contemporary Italian velvet or damask. Although traditionally dated to around 1509, it is more probably late sixteenth century. A number of the earliest wallpapers are described in advertisements as being 'after the manner of real Tapestry'[4]: in the early eighteenth century the Blue Paper Warehouse was offering 'Forest-Work … after the Mode, of real Tapestry'.[5] The term 'forest-work' implies a pattern of foliage. In France, *papiers de tapisserie* – single-sheet pictorial papers, each part of a larger design imitating a tapestry – continued in use into the 1760s. These decorations, with their landscape subjects, hunting scenes and so on, were the precursors of the panoramic papers which appeared around 1800.

Tapestries themselves were already being imitated by painted cloth hangings, and these were in turn imitated by printed sheets for wall decoration. Several of these latter designs survive, all from the period c.1680–1700 and all very similar in style, with block-printed outlines, some plain, some with stencilled or hand-painted colour (plate 36). Each of these surviving designs is pictorial: a stag hunt, a house and garden with a robed figure, a woman in a garden beside a fountain, and a seated woman fishing in a pond, with a house beyond. The papers have been discovered in various locations – in the drawer of a chest, lining a deed box at Clandon Park, and at Colonial Williamsburg; only one example has been found in use as a wallpaper – the Stag Hunt design in a first floor front room at The Shrubbery, Epsom.

The 1738 edition of *Chambers Cyclopaedia of Arts & Sciences* has no entry for paperhangings but has the following comment under 'Tapestry': 'Some use "Tapestry" as a general name for all kinds of hangings whether woven or wrought with the needle; and whether silken, woollen, linen, leathern, or of paper (in which they are countenanced by the etymology of the word formed from the French: tapisser; to line, Latin: tapes, a cover of a bed etc.).'[6]

36. *(above)* **Portion of lining paper found on an early 17th-century box; English, late 17th century**
Print from a woodblock
E.405–1968; Croft Lyons Bequest

37. *(opposite)* **Sheet of wallpaper with formalised floral design on lattice-patterned ground, imitating lacework; English, late 17th century**
Print from woodblock
E.1003–1976
Given by Boots the Chemist, Kingston upon Thames, Surrey

This paper has a fleur-de-lis watermark that suggests a possible date of around 1680. The design is very similar to the border of a later 17th-century cotton printed with a lace pattern, in the Textiles Collection at the V&A (no. 1605–1872). One of only a handful of pre-1700 papers to survive, this design has been found in several different locations including houses in Kingston upon Thames (this piece) and Epsom (both Surrey), and in Newcastle, as well as in a wooden box.

Other textile wallhangings included embroideries, chintzes, silks, cut-velvets and damask. The first trade cards advertising paperhangings offer imitations of textile wall coverings such as 'Irish stitch' [flame stitch], 'Damask' and 'Turkey work' [English imitations of oriental pile carpets], and others 'after the mode of real Tapistry', and by the later eighteenth-century 'chints'. The early wallpaper designs are directly imitative of their textile source, to the extent of attempting to reproduce the characteristic stitching of black-work embroideries, the angular patterns of flame stitch, and the delicate filigree of lacework. In almost every case the motifs were floral.

A number of sixteenth- and early seventeenth-century lining papers and wallpapers were direct copies of the contemporary embroidery known as 'black-work', in which patterns – usually of flowers and fruit – were stitched in black and silver thread on a white ground. This was easy to reproduce by woodcut printing. The various stitches which

38. Fragment of wallpaper imitating crewel-work embroidery; English, probably *c*.1715–30
Stencil with details printed from woodblocks
E.517, 517A–1964
Given by the Colchester and Essex Museum

This paper was found in the west wing (built around 1730) of The Holly Trees, a house next to the castle in Colchester (Essex). The design is a crude approximation of the 'flowering tree' class of Chinese wallpaper, but printed in blocks of stencilled colour to resemble late 17th-century embroidered panels and bedhangings. A matching border was also found.

made up the in-fill and the different textures of the pattern were carefully simulated by cross-hatched lines. Although the style seems to have been popular, to judge by the number of embroideries and related papers which have survived, few examples of black-work papers have been found on walls. The majority of extant examples have been found lining drawers and boxes. However, a fine example of a single-sheet design resembling lacework and dated *c*.1680 came from 14 Market Place, Kingston upon Thames (plate 37), and a version with some stencilled colouring was also found at the Shrubbery, Epsom, around 1680. The same pattern, with the background omitted, was also used to line a wooden box.[7]

The distinctive zigzag pattern of flame stitch in embroidery was also copied by the makers of paperhangings, who advertised it as 'Irish stitch'. It seems to have been commonplace for the makers of paperhangings to copy their textile sources as closely as possible, even to the extent of using a single graduated colour for each element of the pattern, as in the textile original. The surviving flame stitch patterns, for example, are printed in warm reddish tones.

A handsome paper dating from around 1730 is block printed and stencilled in direct imitation of crewel work, a kind of wool embroidery with a design based on Indian printed cottons characteristic of such textile hangings (plate 38). The paper is on a similar scale to the embroidery it copies; the latter would probably have been used as a bedhanging.

Calicoes and chintzes were often used as wall coverings. Pepys records (5 September 1663) that he had bought his wife 'a chinte … that is paynted Indian callico for to line her new study, which is very pretty'.[8] Upholsterers and sellers of paperhangings such as Thomas Bromwich (*c*.1740) advertised that they would hang rooms with 'Chints, Callicoes, Cottons, Needlework & Damask', all of which could be 'Matched in Paper to the utmost exactness'.[9]

By the early eighteenth century the paperstainers were producing chintz-style floral wallpapers. An early example survives as a fragment with pink and blue flowers from Hampden House, Buckinghamshire. A finely detailed, delicately coloured piece, dating from around 1730, was found at 29 Sackville Street, London, in a back room on the first floor which had probably been either a closet or a bedroom. Sackville Street was redeveloped in 1730 and the houses occupied by prosperous members of the professions and minor nobility; No. 29 was taken by William East, a barrister who also had a country house in Berkshire. Very similar large-flowered papers are pictured in the trade cards of both Edward Butling (*c*.1690) and James Wheeley (*c*.1754), and were clearly both popular and fashionable (plates 21, 23). At Paxton House, Chippendale supplied '16 pieces of fine Chintz paper for the Bedchamber and Closet the pattern made on purpose to match the Cotton £6. 8. 0'.[10] Amongst the many papers found at Uppark (Sussex) was a late eighteenth-century paper, with a spare and delicate pattern of trailing blue flowers, with a simple cable-pattern border, more closely resembling embroidery or Spitalfields silk patterns of the mid-century (plate 35). By the mid-nineteenth century the full-blown naturalistic floral patterns found on glazed cottons were replicated as wallpapers (plate 82).

Papers imitating brocaded damasks ranged from formal designs such as a green and yellow design from Wichenford Court, Worcestershire, around 1730–40, to vivacious rococo styles exemplified by a blue-ground paper of 1755–60 with a design of flowers, vases and rococo scroll-work, with matching border, from a house in High Street, Brentford (plate 39).

39. Portion of wallpaper with matching border; English, *c*.1755–60
From a house in the High Street, Brentford, Middlesex
Colour print from woodblocks, and stencilling
E.2296, 2296A–1966
Given by Mr John B. Fowler

A lively floral pattern in the rococo style, this paper was designed to imitate the look of contemporary silk damask fabrics.

40. (*right*) **Wallpaper with pattern of flower sprigs on pin–print ground; English, *c*.1870–80**
Colour print from engraved rollers
E.159–1925
Given by Mr H.C. Andrews

This is typical of the style of paper which might have been used in a bedroom or a servant's room of the period.

41. (*below*) **A bourgeois interior, mid-19th century**
By an unknown German or Austrian artist
Watercolour
E.876–1982
Given by P. J. Gordon, Esq.

This decorative scheme has many of the characteristics of the Biedermeier style, notably the light colours and the overall simplicity of the decorations, as exemplified by the pretty, unpretentious flower-sprigged wallpaper, which is in the French style, and may have been of French manufacture.

42. Fragment of wallpaper imitating festooned fringed drapery, with matching border; French, *c*.1800

From La Haute Ville, Vaison, France, formerly the home of the Marquis de Taulignan
Colour print from woodblocks
E.1042–1925

This is an early and relatively unsophisticated version of the fashion for imitation draperies, a fashion which continued into the 1830s with ever more lavish and convincing *trompe l'oeil* effects.

Textile patterns of all kinds provided inspiration to the paperstainers. Stripes, flower-sprigged patterns, and combinations of the two were perennially popular. Chippendale supplied '13 pieces of Blue Stripe and Sprig paper @ 6/-' to Sir Ninian Home for a bedchamber at Paxton House, Berwickshire, in 1774.[11] A similar pattern was pasted over the red-flowered flock at 6 St James's Place, London w1. Sprigged patterns are amongst the simplest designs derived from textiles and have never lost their appeal. Derived from printed cottons and sprigged muslins, the eighteenth-century block-printed examples were succeeded by machine-printed designs in the mid-nineteenth century (plate 40), and are still a staple of middle-market wallpaper design today. By the 1830s and 1840s these light, simple, pretty patterns were commonly used in bedrooms, but in Germany and Austria the Biedermeier style also favoured this kind of decoration for more public rooms (plate 41).

French manufacturers, notably Réveillon, produced designs imitating Lyons silks. Lyons, capital of silk weaving, was also the most important provincial centre for the French wallpaper trade, so a cross-fertilisation of ideas and influences was perhaps inevitable. Réveillon used multi-coloured flocks to copy silk patterns, in contrast to the largely monochrome English flock papers. He also copied silks in distemper-printed papers, mixing the colours with varnish to give the finished paper a silken sheen. Irisé (a method of blending colours to give a subtly shaded effect) was also used for papers which were designed to reproduce the effects of a silk wall covering. These *trompe l'oeil* techniques reached their high point in the early nineteenth century, when the French excelled at producing papers which effectively imitated drapery (plate 42). It became the fashion to decorate the walls with papers that appeared to be panels of silk, velvet or satin, pleated, in vertical folds,

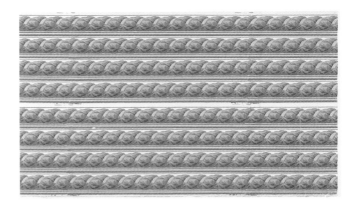

looped, tied or swagged, and trimmed with cords, tassels and braid. The effect at a little distance was startlingly realistic. Paper borders in similar styles were also produced (plate 44). These could be used, to less lavish but equally convincing effect, with a plain or lightly patterned wallpaper. The drapery panels were almost exclusively French and were more commonly used in Continental houses.

A watercolour of the drawing room of the Villa Christine in Nice (then Nizza, part of Savoy), painted around 1830, shows walls hung with swagged 'drapery' that is almost certainly a wallpaper from Dufour & Leroy of Paris, produced in 1825–6.[12] By the mid-nineteenth century English manufacturers were also producing borders of pleated and swagged 'fabric', often using flock to simulate velvet (plate 44). Subsequent illusionistic styles included all-over fabric patterns such as lace.

A number of rooms furnished with textile-patterned wallpapers were recorded by amateur watercolorist Mary Ellen Best who painted views of her various homes in England and on the continent. For her drawing room in

43. Sheet of uncut wallpaper borders, printed to represent ruched fabric; French, c.1840–50
Colour print from woodblocks
E.80–1965
Given by Sir Gerald Kelly, KVCO, PPRA

Today wallpaper borders are produced as rolls, but at this date they were printed as a repeat on larger sheets to be cut up and joined.

44. Wallpaper border printed to imitate velvet drapery with fringing; English, c.1820–30
Colour print from woodblocks with flock
E.2156–1913
Given by Mr Alexander Reynell

Papers printed in *trompe l'oeil* to imitate fabrics were popular in France and England in the 1820 and 1830s. This sample comes from the stock of Thomas Avery, a builder and decorator in Tenterden, Kent. In the 18th and 19th centuries decorators or upholsterers, who dealt with all aspects of the house-furnishing business, often supplied and put up wallpapers.

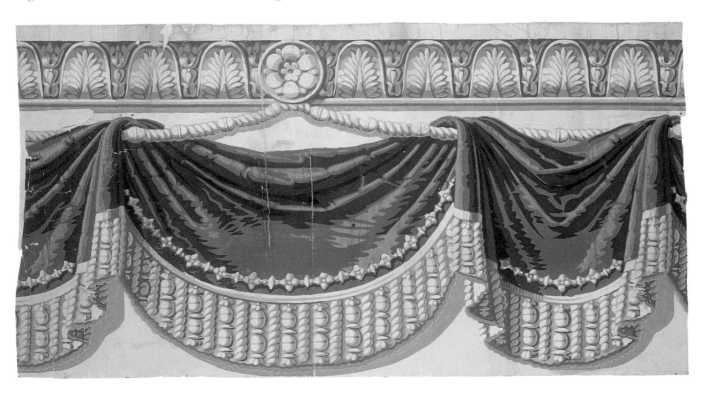

York she chose a paper with a design of tasselled braid (plate 45); a few years earlier she had depicted her room in a new hotel in Rotterdam, with a wallpaper imitating the newly fashionable buttoned, padded upholstery. The effect was comfortable and cosy, in a richly furnished room.[13]

Later in the nineteenth century, papers imitated everything from carpets and tapestries, to watered silks and woven fabrics. The embossing and stamping techniques first introduced in the 1840s allowed French manufacturer Paul Balin to produce convincing paper imitations of silks, gold-threaded embroidery, and other Renaissance textiles – examples of technical virtuosity and elegant luxury. Some of the finest were exhibited at the Vienna Exhibition of 1873.

45. *Our drawing room at York*, c.1838–40
Mary Ellen Best (1809–91)
Watercolour
Private Collection/Bridgeman Art Library

The design of the paper here appears to imitate swags of braid with silk tassels. A white and gold wallpaper was a popular choice for the decoration of a sitting room or drawing room of this period. The writers of guides to interior decorating make regular disparaging references to this ubiquitous taste of the preceding generation – Rhoda and Agnes Garrett's *Suggestions for House Decoration* implies that this was the result of leaving the choice of decoration to a fashionable decorator. Certainly the Cowtan & Son order books show that white and gold patterns were regularly chosen for these rooms in the middle decades of the century. This room is in the house Ellen rented at no.1 Clifton, following her mother's death in 1837, and where she lived as an independent woman until her marriage in 1840. She had the place decorated to her own taste. White and gold were considered to be feminine colours and this room was the centre of Ellen's domestic life, where she entertained guests and wrote her letters.

Flock Wallpapers

5

The status of flock wallpaper has undergone a dramatic transformation over the space of three centuries. Once a luxury product used by the wealthy in the grandest apartments, it has declined into cliché, most familiar (at least in Britain) as nothing more than a commonplace decoration in Indian restaurants where it is intended to evoke an atmosphere of Colonial grandeur.

Flock paper was originally invented to imitate cut-velvet hangings. Flock – powdered wool, a waste product of the woollen cloth industry – had been applied to cloth in the early seventeenth century. It is not clear when the first flock papers were produced, but trade cards and advertisements show that flock papers were available by the late seventeenth century. Edward Butling's card of c.1690 declares that he 'Maketh and Selleth all sorts of Hangings for Rooms', including 'Flock-work', at his premises in Southwark (plate 21). The advertisement for Abraham Price's Blue Paper Warehouse, Aldermanbury, c.1715, shows panels at the extreme left and right with Baroque-style patterns which are almost certainly flocked (plate 22). However, some of the earliest flocks seem to have employed quite simple linear designs; a green flock of oak stems and lattice from Welwick House, South Lynn, Norfolk, c.1715–20, is typical of this light style.

By the 1730s many flock papers that were direct imitations of damask or velvet began to appear. The range of patterns available seems to have been relatively limited, and one particularly magnificent design has been found in several locations. This was a crimson flock on a deep pink ground, which has faded to yellowish buff on most surviving examples. This pattern was hung in the offices of His Majesty's Privy Council, Whitehall, London, around 1735; it was also used in the Queen's Drawing Room in Hampton Court Palace, and in several town and country houses, including Christchurch Mansion, Ipswich, and Clandon Park, Surrey, also in the 1730s (plate 46). The same pattern in green flock was hung around 1745 in the Picture Gallery at Temple Newsam, Leeds. The design itself has been traced back to an Italian brocade and a damask curtain[1], both in the Department of Textiles and Dress at the V&A.

46. (*opposite*) **Red flock wallpaper in the Speaker's Parlour at Clandon Park, Surrey**
© National Trust Photographic Library/Robin Ross

The wallpaper is a later copy of the original which dated from around 1735. This large-scale formal pattern has been found in several grand apartments, including the offices of His Majesty's Privy Council at Whitehall, London, and at Hampton Court. The original colours – crimson flock on a deep pink ground – have faded, resulting in a stronger contrast between pattern and ground than would have been intended.

The flock papers proved extremely durable – certainly more so than the textile hangings they imitated – and so although they were relatively expensive in comparison to other contemporary wallpapers, they were nevertheless good value for money. The flock papers had an advantage over textile wall coverings in that the turpentine in the adhesive used for fixing the flock kept them free from moths. In the 1740s a green cut velvet for the Drawing Room at Longford Castle, Wiltshire, cost 25s a yard, and a green silk damask for the Gallery 12s. A flock paper supplied to the Duke of Bedford in 1754 cost only 4s. Even allowing for the fact that there were several qualities of flock available, and that 4s probably represented the cheaper end of the scale, a handsome, richly coloured, long-lasting flock paper compared favourably with the alternatives.

The designs themselves also proved to have a long life, with several of the large-scale formal patterns – notably the so-called 'Privy Council flock' (now usually known as 'Amberley', the name given to Cole's reproduction of the pattern) – continuously available to the present day. Although flock papers have been produced in every passing style, the designs of the early eighteenth century have survived as a sort of gold-standard for good taste and for an approach to decorating which stands outside fashion.

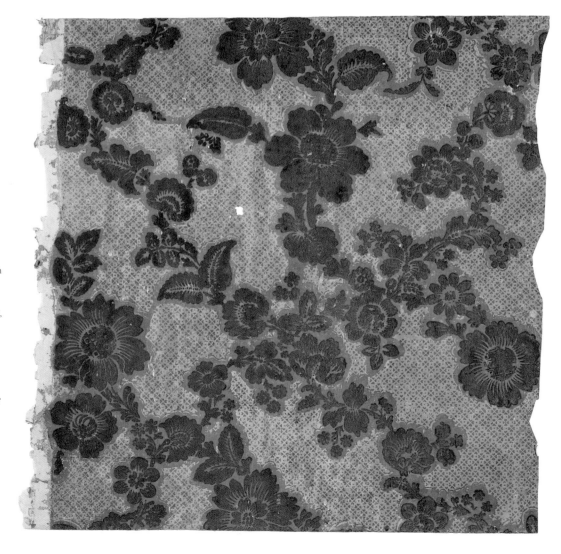

47. (*above*) **Portion of flock wallpaper from Clandon Park, Surrey; English, *c*.1735**
Flock and stencil on stained paper
E.31–1917
Given by Mr John B. Fowler

This paper, one of several impressive flock papers hung at Clandon in the 1730s, comes from the south-east side bedroom. This kind of small-scale informal asymmetric design was considered most appropriate for private apartments such as bedrooms and dressing rooms in contrast to the more formal decoration in the public rooms (see plate 46). The same pattern has been found at Christchurch Mansion, Ipswich.

48. (*right*) **Portion of wallpaper with rococo floral design in flock on a diapered ground; English, *c*.1760**
Print from woodblocks with yellow flock
E.1961–1934
Given by the Arthur Sanderson & Sons branch of The Wall Paper Manufacturer Ltd

**49. Portion of
two flock wallpapers,
one pasted over the other;
English, *c.*1760–70**

From 26 Soho Square, London

E.596A, 596B–1985

Given by Mr Robert Weston, on behalf of the G.L.C. Department
of Architecture and Civic Design

The paper underneath, a red flock with a formal pomegranate and
pineapple design on a gold diaper ground, has a large repeat pattern in
the style of damask fabrics and cut velvets. It is also similar to the
Spitalfields silk designs of the 1740s by Anna Maria Garthwaite. Papers
with an identical design but printed in a single colour have been found in
Eagle House, Bathford (yellow flock), and at Doddington Hall,
Lincolnshire. The paper was supplied to Sir William Robinson by
Chippendale, and recorded in a receipt dated May 1760. It was hung in
both the front and rear rooms on the first floor, between dado rail and
cornice. The second paper, with a smaller pattern of trailing flowers and
foliage on a blue-grey ground of formalised floral motifs, probably dates
from around 1770. Flocks were heavier than other papers and required a
stronger glue to fix them to the wall, so it was not uncommon to paste the
new paper on top, rather than go to the trouble and additional expense of
removing the previous paper.

The grandest flock papers have a large pattern repeat,
often 6 or 7 feet in length. Papers on this scale were
intended for large formal spaces – the public and semi-
public rooms of great houses. Sometimes, papers like
Réveillon's were flocked in more than one colour which
produced a richer, more luxurious effect. Large-scale
Baroque patterns symmetrical around a vertical axis were
appropriate in formal settings and large rooms but were not
used in more modestly sized private rooms. For these
rooms small-scale flocked patterns were available, ranging
from simple diaper patterns to asymmetric floral designs
similar to contemporary silks. A paper of this kind, with a
yellow ground, blue-stencilled colour and dark-blue flock,
was used in a bedroom at Clandon (plate 47).

The designs of flock papers were swiftly adapted to
changing fashions. The earliest known flock paper, from
Saltfleet Manor, Lincolnshire, had a formalised design with
architectural elements and typical seventeenth-century
decorative motifs; the same paper was hung at Ivy House,
in the Worcester Cathedral precincts, in panels alternating
with lengths of embossed leather, another wall covering
fashionable at the time. Chinoiserie designs were also produced in flock – a red-brown flock on a cream ground with
a double-width repeat, from Hurlcote Manor, Easton
Neston, is a fascinating melange of Indian, Chinese and
English motifs. From the 1740s onwards the informal asymmetric style of French rococo was translated into flock. A
particularly fine example with crimson ground, block
printed in white, with mica, and flocked in crimson, was
hung in a parlour chamber in the Sarah Orne Jewitt House,
South Berwick, Maine, *c.*1775–80.

A number of these small-pattern flocks were hung in
bedrooms – a blue flock was used in a bedroom at the
Chateau of the Bishops of Dax at St-Pandelon, France, in
the mid-1770s; and a formal diaper pattern, crimson flock
on a pink ground, in a second-floor bedroom at Temple
Newsam, Leeds. Elsewhere they were used in parlours and
drawing rooms. A popular formal pattern with rococo elements, blue flock on a lighter blue ground, was hung in the
Drawing Room at Doddington Hall, Lincolnshire, between
1760 and 1765. A version flocked in red and yellow on a pink
ground, with diaper filling in white, was hung in two first-
floor rooms of Sir William Robinson's house at 26 Soho
Square in 1759–60 – the paper cost 9s per 12-yard piece,
and 414 yards were supplied (plate 49); it is described in
Chippendale's itemised bill as 'Crimson Emboss'd paper'.[2]
The term 'embossed', which often appears on trade cards,
seems to have been another name for flock because, like
embossing, flocking produced a raised surface pattern.

In *A Complete Body of Architecture*, published in 1756,
Isaac Ware specified that the first-floor rooms of a London

house 'better than the common kind' should be for entertaining, and may include the dining and the drawing room. The use of a handsome flock paper would therefore have been appropriate to the probable functions of the rooms in which it was found in 26 Soho Square. However, it is unlikely that either room hung with flock would have been used for dining – flock papers tended to retain the smell of food, as well as gathering dirt and dust, and were therefore generally considered to be unsuitable in this context. This same paper was, it seems, supplied to Sir Rowland Winn for a bedroom at Nostell Priory; Chippendale's invoice for 4 March 1768 specifies '8 Pieces Norfolk Crimson and Yellow Flock'.[3]

Generally speaking, it seems that the scale of the flock pattern was related to the size of the room, although there are occasional examples of over-sized patterns hung to overwhelming effect in small rooms. A bedroom of the Webb house in Wethersfield, Connecticut, was hung with a red flock with a rococo floral pattern in 1781, rather late for the style. Hung from coving to skirting, it has a disturbing effect in such a small, low-ceilinged room. It was supposedly hung in preparation for a visit by George Washington, and it may be that the status of the prospective guest had more influence on the choice of paper than did the size of the room itself. A similarly outsize red rococo flock was hung in a bedroom in the Palazzo Salis Bondo in Switzerland around 1775. In this case its dominance was moderated by framing it in panels, with a lighter decoration below the dado, over the doors, and so on. On the whole, clients, or their decorators, did take room size into account when selecting a paper. Mrs Kenyon, describing the furnishing of her new house in Lincoln's Inn Fields (1774), wrote: 'The entrance is a broad lobby well lighted by a window over the door … it is wainscot painted white. The dining room is 21' x 17' wide and is to be new papered this week. The paper is to be a blue small patterned flock … Our lodging room is hung with a green flock paper.'[4]

Flocks were generally more expensive than other block-printed papers and most surviving examples come from the houses of the wealthy, although some exceptions are known. A paper of *c*.1760 with blue-flocked foliage and

50. Portion of wallpaper with matching border; English, *c*.1750–75
From the Mansion House, Whitchurch, Shropshire
Print from woodblocks
E.528–2001
Given by Michael Bate

This paper was hung on a canvas backing in a first-floor room and pasted directly onto the plaster in an adjoining passageway. The blue distemper ground was brushed on, and then the pattern was block printed. The areas printed in black may have been intended to imitate flock. So-called mock flock papers were a cheaper alternative to the expensive wool flocks.

block-printed white leaves on a light blue ground was found in a house at 80 St John Street, Clerkenwell. The house itself was built in the 1750s and occupied from 1753 to 1790 by a distiller, John Watson. The area was not fashionable, and was inhabited in the latter half of the century mostly by tradesmen conducting their businesses on the premises.

For those who could not afford the real thing, mock flock paper was available; these papers copied the styles and motifs of flock papers with solid block-printed areas in dense black pigment on a diapered or 'mosaic' ground to give an effective illusion of true flock (plate 50). A good example (now in the English Heritage archive) was retrieved from the first-floor back room of 17 Albemarle Street, London. This was a good address, in a fashionable part of town, so it is quite surprising to find a 'cheap' imitation in what would have been one of the public rooms for entertaining guests.

Such papers were usually considered more appropriate for bedrooms – for example, although Sir William Robinson had an expensive double flock made for the whole of his first floor at 26 Soho Square, he had a much cheaper green mock flock hung in one of the second-floor bedrooms at a cost of £3 2s in April and May 1760.[5]

Cost, colour and durability were the key factors in the choice of wall coverings. Lady Margaret Heathcote writing to her father, 1st Earl of Hardwicke, in 1763, when she was choosing a wallpaper on his behalf, found several advantages in the mock flock papers. Having described some of the options, including an 'Indian paper … [at] treble the price' of a flock, she explains:

> a Cloth paper can only with that furniture be Green, or Green & white as now; plain Green I doubt you would find very dark, & there is some difficulty in putting up a new paper of the same colours as the former one to vary the pattern so as it may not seem the very same; I have therefore ordered a pattern in Mosaick, Green upon a cloth colour ground in imitation of real flock (wch. they tell me in that light colour wears better than the real).[6]

Flocks continued to reflect the changing styles in textile design, and remained in demand through a sequence of architectural styles. Imposing formal patterns were still being designed in the 1820s, alongside lighter informal styles. Flocking was used to embellish designs in every style, from florals to borders with Egyptian motifs (plate 52) and *trompe-l'oeil* printed 'draperies' (plate 44).

The nineteenth-century flocks were even more convincing as substitutes for cut-velvet than their predecessors, thanks to a further elaboration of the production process whereby the flocked areas were blind-stamped to give an embossed finish. A crimson flock of this kind with an imposing pomegranate design survives in two of the State Rooms at Lydiard Park, Wiltshire; a similar red flock was hung by Lady Hertford in the Picture Gallery at Temple Newsam in 1826 or 1827, where it remained until 1940.

Red flock has, since the mid-eighteenth century, been a favourite decoration for picture galleries, or for any grand room hung with Old Master paintings. The colour and

51. Wallpaper border in the neo-classical style; English, c.1800–25
From Montacute House, Somerset
Black flock on a dark pink ground
E.2242–1974
Given by Mr John B. Fowler

texture can be a highly effective foil to gilt-framed pictures. In 1748 Thomas Bromwich was paid £45 16s by Sir Matthew Fetherstonhaugh at Uppark, apparently for supplying and hanging a red flock very similar to the 'Flower'd Red Paper' hung at Felbrigg, Norfolk, during Paine's alterations of 1751–6. The original red flock in the Red Drawing Room at Uppark was replaced by another, also in red, during refurbishments in the 1850s[7] (plate 130).

Artists themselves certainly subscribed to the general view that red was the best background to pictures. In 1813 the painter Sir Thomas Lawrence P.R.A. wrote of his house at 65 Russell Square: '… thus I suffer a Yellow Paper to remain that I know is hurtful to my Pictures. I should have suffered it in my Painting Room but … it is now a rich crimson Paper with a Border.'[8]

52. Wallpaper border with Egyptian motifs; English, 1806
Colour print from woodblocks and flock
E.2259–1966
Given by Mr John B. Fowler

This border was made for the Drawing Room at Crawley House, Bedfordshire. The Egyptian style was popular at this date, though it did not meet with universal approval. Designer Thomas Hope (1769–1831) wrote in his *Household Furniture and Interior Decoration* (London, 1807) that 'Modern imitations of those wonders of antiquity, composed of lath and plaster, of callico and paper, offer no one attribute of solidity and grandeur to compensate for the want of elegance and grace, and can only excite ridicule and contempt.'

The eighteenth-century English flock papers were renowned for their superior quality. They were exported to Continental Europe, notably France, where *papiers d'Angleterre* were favoured by wealthy individuals such as Madame de Pompadour, who used English flock papers in her apartments at Versailles and in the Château de Champs. And like other English wallpapers, flocks were exported to America. Advertisements in the American press from the early 1760s included 'Flock', 'velvet' or 'Damask'; both of the latter terms were used to describe flocked wallpapers. However, they did not suit all customers. Lady Skipwith, an émigrée from England, wrote in 1795 from Virginia to her agent in London: 'I am very partial to papers of only one color, or two at most – velvet paper [flock] I think looks too warm for this country.'[9]

The luxurious aristocratic associations of flock papers continued into the mid-nineteenth century. Many of the design reformers (see 'Design Reform') produced flocked wallpaper patterns. Owen Jones produced a number of elaborate papers – an 1867 example in the Moorish style is block printed in bold colours, embossed and flocked. A.W.N. Pugin, whose papers employed Gothic and medieval motifs, often very simple and severe, also designed sumptuous flock papers (plate 87). He believed that flock wallpapers were suitable as a medium for designs in the modern Gothic style because they were 'admirable substitutes for ancient hangings'.[10] Pugin designed all the papers for the Palace of Westminster; a book of samples compiled by Crace & Son, 1851–4, shows the variety of styles, and gives details of where each was hung. The simplest two-colour block prints were used in servants' bedrooms, whereas the flock papers (often embellished with gold) were hung in the state and public rooms, such as the Royal Gallery and the Conference Room (now part of the Members' Dining Room), and in the apartments of senior officials. For example, a red, gold and olive version of the 'Tapestry' design was used in the Queen's Robing Room in the House of Lords and in the Dining Room of the Sergeant-at-Arms in the House of Commons. Pugin made concerted efforts to promote his wallpaper designs to a wider market, and encouraged Crace to advertise his

papers in *The Builder* in 1851. However, the majority of his designs, and in particular the large-scale flocks, were entirely unsuitable to a domestic setting, both in scale and because they were thought by his contemporaries to be 'too ecclesiastical and traditional in character'.[11]

Charles Eastlake's influential *Hints on Household Taste*, first published in 1868, advanced some strongly expressed opinions about wallpaper, and condemned illusionistic and pictorial patterns, however he defended flocks on the grounds that 'at ordinary shops [they] are the best in design, because they can represent nothing pictorially'[12] (plate 53). But by the later nineteenth century flocks were well and truly out of fashion, casually dismissed or roundly condemned by successive writers of guides to interior decoration. Colonel Edis was particularly severe: 'I can conceive of nothing more terrible than to be doomed to spend one's life in a house furnished after the fashion of twenty years ago. Dull monotonous walls, on which garish flock papers of the vulgarest possible design, stare one blankly in the face with patches here and there of accumulated dirt and dust … if the flock paper be red, we had red curtains hung on a gigantic pole, like the mast of a ship …'[13] A writer in the *Art Journal* in 1889 concurred with this pejorative view of flock papers: 'It is seldom now that one encounters the gaudily gilt monstrosities … or the heavily loaded "flocks" shedding everywhere their poisonous dust.'

Cleanliness had by now become something of an obsession with the Victorians, and lighter colours and washable 'sanitary' papers were supplanting the dark velvety flocks. For those who advised on interior design and household management, such as Mrs Beeton, flocks had a place only in the library, conventionally a sombrely furnished masculine room, or as a foil to pictures since they 'throw up oil paintings to a marvel'.[14] This advice is reiterated by the anonymous author of *Artistic Homes, or How to Furnish with Taste* (1880), where Woollams flock papers are specifically recommended.

Dark, gloomy, a hindrance to cleanliness and a hazard to health – the fashion for flock paper was finally in decline, though as a writer in *The Builder* observed in 1877, 'This movement in the direction of good taste is, perhaps, hardly

53. *Past and Present 1*, 1858
Augustus Egg (1816–63)
Oil on canvas
© Tate, London 2001

The scene is an ordinary middle-class mid-Victorian drawing room papered with a Gothick fleur-de-lis patterned flock wallpaper, a simple motif rendered as a flat pattern, of the kind approved by the design reform movement. Eastlake had recommended flock papers because they never attempted pictorial styles and so were less likely to offend against good taste. This painting is the first of three, telling a contemporary morality tale. The husband has just discovered his wife's adultery and we are invited to find the clues to her character in the furnishings of her home; though the backdrop – the wallpaper – is 'honest' and unpretentious, other items – such as the papier mâché chair – were judged by the standards of the time to be shoddy, cheap and sham, and as such were held to be corrupting influences for susceptible minds.

as general as is sometimes supposed … it has hardly reached the mass of the trading classes at all … and perhaps there are not a few among the professedly more cultured classes who are still sublimely indifferent to the design of their tables and chairs, their carpets and wallpapers.'[15] Certainly the prejudice against flocks amongst the design pundits did not result in their immediate disappearance from the market. Designs continued to be produced, including papers by Morris, Crane and other fashionable designers of so-called 'art wallpapers'. And customers at Cowtan & Son continued to order flocks well into the 1920s, in defiance or in ignorance of these critical injunctions against them.

Flocks are still produced today, using rayon flock applied by a flock gun, but the market is more or less limited to restoration projects in historic buildings.

Chinese Wallpapers
and Chinoiserie Styles

The first Chinese papers appeared for sale in London in the late seventeenth century. These hand-painted papers, and the home-grown chinoiserie styles they inspired, sparked a fashion which lasted more than a century. In due course most of the great country houses had at least one room decorated with a Chinese paper, and some – such as Saltram, Devon – had three or four (plate 55). By the end of the eighteenth century they were to be found in more modest houses, too.

London was the centre of the trade in Chinese wallpapers. Around 1680 the stationer George Minnikin offered 'all sorts of Japan & other coloured paper hangings', and in 1695 an auction of 66 pieces or lengths of Japan paper was held at the Marine Coffee House, Birchin Lane, in the City of London. Contemporary accounts commonly but confusingly referred to the Chinese paperhangings as 'Japan' or 'India' papers. There were several reasons for this. The Far East was for most people a mysteriously amorphous geographic entity; indeed, many writers subsumed all the cultures from Turkey to Japan under the heading of 'the Orient'. The use of the term 'India' probably derives from the East India Company (established in 1599) which, with its later Dutch and French counterparts, enjoyed a monopoly of the China trade. However, the use of the word 'Japan' as a description of the paperhangings was not a reference to the supposed country of origin; rather it was prompted by the character of these painted papers, which with their rich colours and use of glazes sometimes resembled lacquerwork ('Japanning' was the term then current for methods of imitating oriental lacquer in Europe). As Lady Mary Coke said in 1766 of the 'Indian Paper in the Great Room' of His Majesty's Lodge in Richmond Park, it 'looks like Japan'.[1]

The Chinese papers were a novelty in many respects – they were supplied in sets of 25 or 40 lengths, each different in design, which could be hung to form a continuous mural decoration around the room; they were generally hand-painted throughout, although some early papers show extensive use of woodblock printing for outlines, foliage and so on[2], and a few later examples had engraved outlines. With their exotic subject matter – scenes of Chinese life

54. (*opposite*) **Detail from a panel of wallpaper showing a hunting scene; Chinese, second half of the 18th century**
Gouache
E.1181-1921
Given by Mr H.B. Darby

The brilliant colours of the hand-painted Chinese wallpapers were unequalled in contemporary wallpapers made in Europe. The Chinese wallpapers were painted by artists in workshops in the trading ports of Macao and Canton, and although there are often similarities in design and subject matter between the different sets, it is exceedingly rare to find two by the same hand. This is one of the few papers where a corresponding design has survived, on the walls of Oud-Amelisweerd, a house built around 1770 in Utrecht, Holland.

and landscape, or flowering trees populated with birds and butterflies – and their rich colours and fine detail, they were quite unlike the wallpapers then available in England. No doubt their rarity and also the long wait for orders to be fulfilled fuelled the fashion and made them even more desirable. Costly in comparison to locally manufactured wallpapers, they were purchased and hung by a monied social élite. The Chinese paper supplied by Chippendale for Nostell Priory in 1771 cost 15s a sheet, but as Chippendale explained to Sir Rowland Winn, the seller 'must have the money down for it, as he lets it go so cheap'.[3]

The Chinese wallpapers arrived in Europe as part of the larger trade in Chinese artefacts – lacquer, porcelain and silks – carried by the East India Company. The Chinese did not themselves use painted papers of this kind. In the 1690s, a French Jesuit missionary to China, Father Louis Le Comte, had recorded the use of silk hangings by the wealthy, but added that 'others only whiten the Chamber or glew Paper upon it'. Later accounts by William Chambers (in his *Designs of Chinese Buildings*, 1757) and Lord Macartney, the British Ambassador (1794) noted that plain papers – usually white, crimson or gold – were preferred as wall coverings in China. However, it was an established

Chinese practice to paste paper over the windows, and in Macao and Canton, both centres of the export trade, such papers were often painted with pictorial decorations. It may be that these were admired by the European merchants, thus prompting the Chinese to produce similar decorations for export.

It seems then that their manufacture sprang from a congruence of three separate traditions – the practice of papering walls with plain papers, the use of painted papers to cover windows, and the long-established style of decorative painting to produce large panels for hanging scrolls or to be mounted on screens. The first papers were probably produced on a speculative basis, but like other export wares they were designed, or adapted specifically for the European market. Unfortunately, remarkably little is known of the precise origins of the trade in Chinese papers, though various theories have been advanced.

It has generally been thought that they were initially given as gifts to European merchants to secure a contract or mark the conclusion of a sale. After the first examples appeared in London, they were imported in increasingly large quantities. Again, however, evidence for this is deduced mainly from the numbers offered for sale and hung in English houses, since there are virtually no references to them in the East India Company's accounts. It seems that the wallpapers were classed as a minor product and thus carried as 'private trade', not separately recorded in inventories and bills of shipment. Those references which do exist occur rather late in the history of the trade – for example, it is recorded that in 1775 one ship of the East India Company carried 2,236 'pieces' of paperhangings (25 pieces were usually enough to paper one room).[4] A figure paper with scenes of rice-growing was brought back on the 'Empress of China', the first American ship to sail to China. The receipt book of the voyage records their purchase from the Canton merchant Eshing: 'recd at Canton Decr 2nd 1784 of S. Molineux for accot. Capt. Green One Hundred dollars for Paper Hangings for Robt Morris, Esq,. [Morris, of Philadelphia, had a half-interest in the ship].'[5] Certainly by the middle of the century they were being imported in large numbers, and as Madame du Bocage noted in 1750,

55. The Chinese Chippendale Bedroom, Saltram, Devon
© National Trust Photographic Library/Andreas von Einsiedel

Saltram has several rooms with 18th-century Chinese wallpaper hung at various dates. Originally this was a general purpose family room where the Parkers took their meals when there were no guests. By 1861 it had acquired a bed, but the present scheme was created by the National Trust, when the wallpaper was discovered in a servant's room and found to fit this room exactly. It was hung in 1962 and the other furnishings – a mix of chinoiserie and rococo styles – were brought in to complement the wallpaper. The chairs have pagoda crestings very similar to designs in Chippendale's *Director*, where they are described as 'very proper for a Lady's Dressing Room, especially if it is hung with India paper.'

eighteenth centuries was derived almost exclusively from the letters and published works of French Jesuit missionaries, which were in turn quarried by novelists and playwrights who presented China as variously exotic or barbarous, opulent or frivolous, or a sophisticated model society to rival Greece or Rome. Indeed, there was a strong tendency amongst English writers in the 1750s and 1760s to claim China as a more worthy model of civilisation than either. James Cawthorne's *Essay on Taste* (1756) declares:

> Of late, 'tis true quite sick of Rome and Greece,
> We fetch our models from the wise Chinese,
> European artists are too cool and chaste,
> For Mand'rin is the only man of taste.[3]

Both the character of the style and its popularity were hinted at by Mrs Montagu when she wrote in 1749, 'we must all seek the barbarous gaudy *gout* of the Chinese'.[4] This enthusiasm for Chinese styles was reflected in the ubiquity of their use in eighteenth-century decoration. They were most commonly used for bedrooms and the associated apartments – for example, in the State Bedroom at Errdig (when it was moved from the ground to the first floor, to a room newly decorated with a green-ground paper) and at Nostell Priory, and the bedrooms and a dressing room at Saltram. These rooms were much less private in eighteenth-century houses than they would be today, and the use of Chinese papers in such situations does not imply that they were solely for private pleasure rather than for a display of conspicuous consumption and fashionable taste. However, there was playfulness and informality about Chinese styles which made them popular decorations in apartments used by women. Indeed, it has been argued that their exotic 'otherness' and informality were seen as infantile and irrational and therefore essentially 'feminine'.[9] So, at Wanstead in 1724, Lord Castlemaine's rooms were done up in brocade and damask, whereas his wife had Chinese paper in her parlour, and Chinese silk in her bedroom, dressing room and closet. Elsewhere they were hung in drawing rooms, parlours and reception rooms.

The Chinese style was often carried through to the other furnishings, as Lady Beauchamp Proctor observed of the

almost every great house, and many smaller ones, boasted a room furnished with 'painted Paper of Pekin … and choicest moveables of China'.[6]

Why did the Chinese papers become so popular, given that they were relatively expensive, and that by the mid-eighteenth century there was a thriving trade in locally manufactured wallpapers, many of them high quality? First of all, they should be seen in the context of the widespread 'Sinomania' and the fashion for all things Chinese. The appetite for Oriental exotica was fed not only by the variety of decorative goods arriving in Europe, but by a succession of written accounts, many illustrated with engravings. European knowledge of China in the seventeenth and

56. The 'Badminton Bed' (Chinese-style bed by Linnell, 1754) on display in the V&A, with mid-18th-century Chinese wallpaper in the background
Bed: W.143–1921
Wallpaper: E.3674–3682–1913
Given by Sir William Ingram, Bart.

lodging rooms at Osterley Park House, Middlesex, in 1772. They were 'furnished with the finest Chintzes, painted Taffatys, India paper and decker work, and such a profusion of rich China and Japan, that I could almost fancy myself in Pekin'.[10]

Contemporary accounts show that these Chinese papers were generally admired in England, from their first appearance and throughout the century. John Macky, on a visit to Wanstead House [demolished in 1822] described Lady Castlemaine's parlour 'finely adorn'd with China paper, the figures of men and women, birds and flowers, the liveliest

I ever saw come from that country'.[11] When Mrs Delany stayed at Cornbury, Oxfordshire, in 1746, she thought that the apartment that she and her husband occupied was 'so neat and elegant that I never saw anything equal to it ... the next room is hung with the finest Indian paper of flowers and all sorts of birds (that is my dressing room); the ceilings are all ornamented in the Indian taste ... the bedchamber is also hung with Indian paper on a gold ground ...'.[12] The diaries of Mrs Philip Lybbe Powys make regular reference to 'India' papers that she saw on her visits: at Mawley Hall, Shropshire, she describes 'a fine India paper on pea-green' in Lady Blount's dressing-room, and she declares the effect 'elegant'.[13] In October 1771 she was at Fawley Court, Buckinghamshire, where the billiard room was 'hung with the most beautiful pink India paper, adorned with very good prints, the borders cut out and the ornament put on with great taste by Bromwich'. She continues, 'The dressing-room … is prettier than tis possible to imagine, the most curious India paper as birds, flowers etc., put up as different pictures in frames of the same.' She concludes that 'both have an effect wonderfully pleasing'.[14]

Her description suggests that the Fawley Court paper was hung in the print-room style, that is with scenes cut from sheets of Chinese wallpaper, framed with printed borders and pasted directly on to the wall or a plain paper. An arrangement of this kind can be seen at Erddig where a paper with figure groups, landscapes and buildings has been cut up to produce a variety of oval or oblong vignettes framed with flowered paper borders. A similarly economical strategy was employed by Emily, Countess of Kildare (1731–1814) in her decoration of Carton House, begun in 1759. She wrote to her husband, then in London: 'My dear Lord Kildare, don't let Louisa [her sister, Louisa Connolly] forget the India paper, and if you see any you like buy it at once for that I have will never hold out for more than three rooms, and you know we have four to do; for I have set my heart upon that which opens into the garden being done, for 'tis certainly now our best and only good living room.'[15] The 'India' paper duly arrived but there was not enough, so Emily improvised, cutting out individual motifs and scenes and pasting them directly on to the walls around larger framed panels of Chinese paper, and thus completed her decorative scheme.

This enthusiasm for 'India' papers was not universal. Lady Mary Coke disparages the 'Indian Paper' hung 'in the Great Room at His Majesty's Lodge in Richmond Park', because although it was expensive ('three guineas the sheet') its dark-blue ground 'makes the room appear dismal'.[16] The taste for Chinese styles was dismissed by Hogarth and as the fashion declined towards the end of the century it was characterised by Johann Gottfried Herder as 'coarse' and 'unnatural'.[17] A taste for Chinese styles in fact

became associated with the nouveaux riches who had made their money in trade. As William Shenstone put it rather bluntly, 'A mere citizen is always aiming to show his riches … and talks much of his Chinese ornaments at his paltry cake house in the country.'[18] Thus Chinese wallpaper became associated with a vulgar parade of wealth, rather than with elegant and refined tastes.

Others had more pressing and personal reasons to reject or criticise Chinese artefacts. The import of textiles from Asia directly threatened the livelihoods of English textile workers and they campaigned against them. *The Weaver's Complaint* (1719) is particularly scathing:

> 'Tis a test of the brains of the nation
> To neglect their own works,
> Employ pagans and Turks,
> And let foreign trumpery o'er spread 'em.[19]

Likewise there were some who saw the Chinese imported wallpapers as a threat to the progress and inventions of the native paperstainers. John Baptist Jackson fulminated against the Chinese papers and their English imitators in a 1754 essay advertising his own papers. He complained that they showed 'Lions leaping from bough to bough like Cats, Houses in the Air, Clouds and Sky upon the Ground, a thorough confusion of all the Elements; nor Men or Women, with every other Animal, turn'd Monsters.'[20] And in 1756, John Shebbeare wrote: 'Almost everywhere, all is Chinese … every chair … the frames of glasses … the tables, the walls, all covered with Chinese figures which resemble nothing in God's creation!'[21] But these perceived faults of design and representation in the Chinese papers – actually a consequence of their not employing Western conventions of perspective, and of not modelling figures – seemed to emphasise their exotic aspect and thus their appeal to European tastes.

In fact, despite their formalised style, the Chinese papers were characterised by a high degree of scientific accuracy in their depiction of birds and plants. Though William Parrat, writing in the London *World* in 1753, described 'the richest China and India paper where all the powers of fancy are exhausted in a thousand fantastic figures of birds, beasts and fishes which never had existence'[22], he seems to have been confusing the fanciful European imitations with the genuine Chinese papers. Certainly the flora and fauna depicted would have been exotic and largely unfamiliar to a European audience at this date – for example, many of the plants would have been virtually unknown in English gardens before the major plant-hunting expeditions in China in the early nineteenth century – but in all except a few late papers they were identifiable species not fanciful inventions (plates 57, 59). Confirmation came from no less an authority than the botanist Sir Joseph Banks, who noted in his journal in 1771 that 'Some of the plants which are common to China and Java [such] as Bamboo, are better figured there than by the best botanical authors that I have seen.'[23]

The Chinese wallpapers were, as we have seen, designed and made specifically for the European market, as were many of the other export wares which flooded into Europe in the seventeenth and eighteenth centuries. But it seems the Chinese continued to pay close attention to the tastes of this large foreign market, modifying designs and introducing new patterns, motifs and colours as required, and thereby preventing the trade stagnating. The earliest papers to arrive in Europe were the figure subjects, with scenes of daily life and industry in China in a variety of landscape settings. Papers of this kind were hung in the hunting lodge at Stupinigi, Piedmont (*c*.1730), in a bedroom at Milton, Northamptonshire, probably around 1754–5, in the Chinese Bedroom at Blickling Hall, Norfolk, in the 1760s, and in the boardroom of Coutts' bank in the Strand, London, sometime after 1794 (a gift from the British Ambassador to Peking, Lord Macartney, and first hung in his own rooms, and later in the bank).

Such papers, with figures in a variety of styles and scales, continued to be produced into the early nineteenth century, with an example of *c*.1790 hung in a corridor at Brighton Pavilion around 1819. Later examples tend to show the artists attempting the single-point perspective of Western art, and the scenes more closely resemble the Chinese export watercolours of the period *c*.1770–90. A good example can be seen in what was the South-west Bedroom at Saltram where individual panels were hung in a patchwork-style with certain scenes repeated in a symmetrical arrangement.

The other main class of Chinese papers was the so-called 'bird and flower'-type characterised by sinuous flowering trees, with birds and insects among the branches, all silhouetted against a coloured ground. The earliest examples are generally in quiet neutral tones such as buff, but stronger colours became popular as the eighteenth century progressed, with examples in pink (said by Mrs Philip Lybbe Powys, in her remarks on Fawley Court in 1771, to be 'uncommon'), yellow, a rich green, and deep blue. Later modifications of the 'bird and flower' design introduced figures in the foreground, or decorative balustrades, flowering shrubs in pots, and birdcages suspended from the branches above (plate 57). As a general rule, the busier and more crowded the design, the later the paper.

It seems that this embellishment of the basic motif was a response to the changing demands from Europe, where a taste for the spare elegance of the early papers had been superseded by a desire for more detail and ornament. It was already common practice for the Chinese to supply extra sheets with each set of papers. Birds and branches could be cut from these and pasted over damaged or discoloured areas, used to fill awkward corners, or simply to embellish the overall effect. Lady Mary Coke recorded in her journal in 1772: 'I called on the Duchess of Norfolk and found her sorting butterflies cut out of India paper for the room she is going to furnish.'[24] Sometimes this was done professionally. A bill from John Chew, dated 12 September 1772, details papers supplied to Earl Fitzwilliam, either for his London house or for Milton, Northamptonshire, and includes an extra 7s 6d for 'cutting out flowers, filling up India paper with Do 1½ Days, Paste etc'.[25]

Lady Hertford hung a Chinese paper, produced around 1800, at Temple Newsam in the 1820s, perhaps inspired by the contemporary redecoration of Brighton Pavilion in the chinoiserie style. She had been mistress of the Prince Regent and the paper was probably a gift from him to her mother, Frances, Lady Irwin, when he visited Temple Newsam in September 1806. She proceeded to impose a

57. Panel of hand-painted wallpaper (detail); Chinese, second half of 18th century
Gouache
E.3944–1915
Given by Mr W. E. Soltau

58. Queen Victoria's Bedroom, Royal Pavilion, Brighton
© The Royal Pavilion, Libraries & Museums, Brighton & Hove

The yellow-ground Chinese wallpaper has a design of exotic birds, and flowering trees and shrubs growing in decorative pots. The paper dates from c.1800, and is almost identical to the paper in the Saloon.

degree of symmetry on the design by the addition of vases, birds, insects, foliage and flowers. But it seems that the spare sheets did not yield quite enough motifs for her embellishments, and she hit on a novel method of elaborating the paper further: she added 25 birds cut from plates in the first volume of J. J. Audubon's *Birds of America* (1827–38). These impostors married well with their new setting, and their source was not finally identified until 1968.[26]

The fashion for Chinese papers lasted more than a century; the recreation of the Brighton Pavilion as a chinoiserie extravaganza for George IV between 1815 and 1821 was part of a late flowering of the style (plate 58). Sir Walter Scott hung a Chinese paper at Abbotsford in the 1820s. He wrote to Daniel Terry on 10 November 1822: 'Hawl [sic] the second is twenty-four pieces of the most splendid Chinese paper ... a present from my cousin Hugh Scott [who worked for the East India Company], enough to finish the drawing room and two bedrooms ...'[27] (plate 59). The order books of Cowtan & Son show orders for Chinese papers continuing into the 1830s and 1840s.

The Chinese papers were relatively expensive, being hand-painted imports, and orders for specific designs or colourways might take anything up to 18 months to arrive. It is hardly surprising that English and French manufacturers sought to capitalise on this new fashion, producing imitations, pastiches and copies almost as soon as the first 'India' papers appeared in London. As early as 1693, a London paperhanging warehouse advertised in the *London Gazette* that it made and sold 'strong paperhangings with fine India figures'.[28] The earliest examples demonstrate a deficient understanding of the conventions of the Chinese designs. One of the earliest attempts dates from c.1700, and was found in Ord House, Berwick-on-Tweed, Northumberland (plate 60). Unlike the Chinese originals it is a repeating pattern with Chinese figures dwarfed by parrots and red squirrels, all set haphazardly amongst crudely drawn branches.

An advertisement for the Blue Paper Warehouse, of around the same date, illustrates panels of paper with Chinese-style motifs; these repeat down the length of the paper, suggesting that it is an English product rather than a genuine 'India' paper. The most convincing attempt to emulate the Chinese can be seen in a paper of *c*.1740 from a house at Wotton-under-Edge, Gloucestershire, which

59. (*left*) **Detail of the Chinese wallpaper in the Chinese Drawing Room at Abbotsford, Melrose, Scotland**
Courtesy Abbotsford, Melrose, Scotland

The paper was hung in 1824. Like most of the Chinese wallpapers it is characterised by its accurate representation of flora and fauna, such as the lemur shown here.

60. (*above*) **Length of wallpaper with a pattern of squirrels, parakeets, peacocks and chinoiserie figures interspersed in the branches of a flowering tree; English, *c*.1700**
Print from woodblock with colour stencil and varnish
E.5311–1958

The length is made up of six separate sheets which have been printed before being pasted together. The black ground colour has been crudely brushed in by hand. A paper of similar design is illustrated in Edward Butling's near-contemporary trade card (see plate 21).

mimics the 'bird and flower' pattern. Although it is hand-painted, delicate and beautifully executed, it betrays its origins in the dull faded colours, a certain naïvety in the drawing, and the crude simplicity of the botanical details, as well as the compressed scale – it sits above a dado rail at the height of a chair-back at half the length of most Chinese papers.

Imitation 'India' papers appear in the lists of the stock in trade of several UK paperstainers. Richard Masefield's trade card (dating from the 1760s) for his Manufactory in the Strand makes much of his 'Original Mock India Paper Hangings … made after a method peculiar to himself, which surpasses every thing of the kind yet attempted and for Variety, Beauty and Duration, equal to the Real India Paper'. From the 1770s, John Sigrist's card lists papers imitating 'India landscapes, Figures, Flowers, Birds &c'. Matthew Darly's card (from *c*.1760–70) not only offers papers in 'Modern, Gothic and Chinese Tastes for Town and Country', but illustrates examples, including two pictorial panels framed with printed borders, and a length with a design of Chinese-style figures.

These panels are remarkably similar to the group of unused single-sheet papers which survive in several public collections.[29] Since Darly had also published *A New Book of Chinese Designs Calculated to Improve the present Taste Consisting of Figures, Buildings & Furniture, Landskips, Birds, Beasts, Flowrs. and Ornaments* (1754), with engravings illustrating a variety of chinoiserie motifs similar, though not identical to the motifs in these wallpapers, it seems very likely that he produced these papers or examples like them. The papers themselves, with their relatively crude drawing and colouring (by hand and by stencil) offer debased and fanciful versions of genuine Chinese flora and fauna, buildings and costumes. Their manufacturers were probably working from pattern books such as Darly's, combining motifs in an incoherent and inauthentic composition which only superficially approximated the Chinese style. Botanical accuracy is one obvious failure – the flowers are fantastic inventions – and animals never seen in Chinese wallpapers, such as camels or dragons, are introduced. Though by this date there was a substantial body of

accurate information about China available to an educated public, the majority view was founded on what has been described as 'a fairyland of stock exotica'.[30] No chinoiserie panels of this kind have been discovered as part of an extant decorative scheme, so conclusions about how and where they were used are necessarily speculative. Some appear complete in themselves, whereas others have motifs which are cut off at the edges of the sheet, suggesting that they were to be hung in overlapping sequence with others, perhaps alternating two designs (plate 61).

Only a few sets of real Chinese papers reached America in the eighteenth and early nineteenth centuries. This was probably because they were ordered through London, and the demand in England was such that there was little available to fulfil orders from further afield. The few advertisements for Chinese papers that appeared in America date from the last years of the eighteenth century when the fashion in England was in decline. Thus in 1782 Jerathmeel

61. Unused sheet of wallpaper with a design of musical instruments and a caged song-bird in the chinoiserie style; English, *c*.1780–1800
Etching coloured by hand
E.937–2000
Purchased with funding from the Julie and Robert Breckman Print Fund

Single-sheet papers of this kind, with fanciful English interpretations of Chinese motifs were produced by English manufacturers in response to the widespread and long-lived fashion for the hand-painted Chinese wallpapers. The composition suggests that panels were designed to be joined end to end to form a frieze-like decoration, possibly for a music room.

62. Wallpaper with pattern of pine branches hung with Japanese lanterns; English, *c.*1925
Colour machine print
E.1–1975
Given by the Dorset Natural History and Archaeological Society

An eclectic 'oriental' style, encompassing both Japanese and Chinese elements, was popular in the 1920s.

Pierce of Salem offered 'An Elegant India Paperhanging of the newest fashion' at his store. An advertisement in the *New York Evening Post* in 1804 lists 'Chinese Papering – A few sets very elegant for drawing rooms'.[31] Even though American ships were trading directly with China from 1784, bringing in 'paperhangings … from the East Indies'[32] and customers such as George Washington had expressed interest in 'sending for India Paper for my new Room' [the Dining Room at Mount Vernon][33], no American houses are known to have had a Chinese paper installed at this time. The paper which had been purchased for Morris himself in 1784 was never used.

In the early years of the taste for Chinese décor, the Americans, like the less wealthy English customers, had to make do with London-made papers in the Chinese style. A full description of such a paper is given in a letter dated 23 January 1737 from Thomas Hancock of Boston to John Rowe, a stationer in London, in which he orders a wallpaper in the style of 'a Room Lately Come over here'. However, he goes on to say that he would like the paper embellished:

> … by adding more Birds flying here and there, with some Landskips at the Bottom…Let the Ground be the Same Colour of the Pattern. At the Top and Bottom was a narrow Border of about 2 Inches wide wh. would have to mine. About three or four years ago my friend Francis Wilks, Esq., had a hanging Done in the same manner but much handsomer Sent over here from Mr Sam Waldon of this place, made by one Dunbar, in Aldermanbury … In other parts of the Hangings are Great Variety of Different Sorts of Birds, Peacocks, Macoys, Squirril, Monkys, Fruit and Flowers, &c.[34]

The taste for Chinese wallpapers had declined by the late nineteenth century, to the point where Mrs Haweis, in *Beautiful Houses* (1882), described the decoration of the drawing room at Ashley Park, Walton-on-Thames, Surrey, as being 'papered with such vast branches and birds of paradise, in harsh colours, which though interesting as a relic of Queen Anne taste, are scarcely more pleasing on walls than on dresses … '.[35] However, Oriental styles did come back into fashion for a brief period in the 1920s. This is reflected by John Galsworthy's heroine, the wealthy and fashionable Fleur Forsyte, who has her drawing room furnished 'a la Chinois', though the walls were set with ivory panels rather than papered.[36] And in 1932 Rex Whistler (1905–44) painted an exquisite panel to replace a missing section for a nineteenth-century chinoiserie wallpaper bought by Samuel Courtauld for a house in Bath. The style filtered down to more modest homes in brightly coloured machine prints with loosely 'Oriental' patterns of birds, flowers and paper lanterns in bold colours, as much Japanese as Chinese in their origin (plate 62).

Architectural Wallpapers

Papers imitating plasterwork appeared in England in the late seventeenth century (plate 64). Some of the early black and white papers seem to derive from plasterwork, particularly on ceilings; these were succeeded by simple patterns printed in grisaille and used on walls and ceilings where they convincingly imitated low-relief modelling in plaster or stucco. The advantages of using paper decorations to imitate stucco and plaster were set out by the Eckhardt brothers of Chelsea, London, in a leaflet issued by the firm in May 1793: 'Eating rooms already stuccoed might, at a small expense, receive additional embellishment' and rooms with bare walls could be given the same beauty and elegance of a stuccoed interior, but without echo (a common complaint about such rooms) and without having to wait for the stucco to dry.[1]

Architectural papers in a variety of styles were available from the mid-eighteenth century, and continued to be popular until the mid-nineteenth century. As well as elaborate renderings of sculpture, architectural features and plasterwork, there were *trompe l'oeil* imitations of masonry and marble, and later, brickwork, tiling and woodgrain (plate 25). As early as 1690 Edward Butling's stock included papers in imitation of 'Wainscot' (wood-panelling) and 'Marble'. By 1795 a Parisian manufacturer, Durolin, was offering an extensive range:

> architectural ornaments in grisaille and highlighted with gold, papers imitating Brazil wood and book spines of all sizes, grillework imitating that of bookcases, open as well as closed, trellising, brickwork, stonework, ashlar, marbles, granites, columns, pilasters, margents, banisters, cornices, architraves, statues, swags, parterres, corners, borders, panelling and overdoors of all kinds.[2]

There were two main styles of 'architecture papers' – the Gothic and the classical, with occasional eccentric mixtures of the two. In 1762 John Gordon, a Dublin paperstainer, advertised papers 'consisting principally of Gothic or Grecian Architecture, in due Perspective, and proportioned agreeable to their respective Orders'.[3] On the whole, classical pillar and arch papers, even those which were English-made, were more popular in America than in

63. *(opposite)* **Nowton Court, 1975**
A reprint by Cole & Son (Wallpapers) Ltd of a flocked block print from *c*.1840
Colour print from woodblocks
E. 642–1976
Given by Cole & Son (Wallpapers) Ltd

This was one of eight wallpapers reproduced from document samples in the V&A and issued in various colourways by Cole & Son. This pattern of neo-Gothic window tracery was reconstructed from fragments found at Nowton Court, Bury St. Edmunds, Suffolk, and had been reprinted for the owner in the 1970s. An order for the original paper (a block print with flock), with sample attached, is listed in the Cowtan & Son records for 1 December 1840.

England. Gothic styles, it seems, appealed rather more to English tastes, although they were also produced in some numbers on the Continent, particularly in France and Germany.

From the middle of the eighteenth century, most paperstainers advertised 'Gothic' papers in their lists of patterns. Amongst the earliest examples of Gothic wallpapers were those at Horace Walpole's house, Strawberry Hill, which was decorated throughout in the Gothic taste in the period 1753–76. In a letter to Lord Dover in 1753 Walpole describes this aspect of his decorations:

> The bow window below leads into a little parlour hung with a stone-colour Gothick paper and Jackson's Venetian prints, which could never endure while they pretenced, infamous as they are, to be after Titian &c., but when I gave them the air of barbarous *bas-reliefs* they succeeded to a miracle; … From hence, under two gloomy arches you come to the hall and the staircase … Imagine the walls, covered with (I call it paper, but it is really paper painted in perspective to represent) Gothick fretwork.[4]

Walpole's papers were chosen with the eye of an antiquary, and were simple, authentically styled representations of Gothic forms. The novelty and the fame of Walpole's

64. Fragment of wallpaper with a design of strapwork borders enclosing a flower spray motif; English, late 17th century
From a house at 8 West Street, Epsom, Surrey
Print from woodblock
E.464–1993
Bequeathed by Dudley Snelgrove

The pattern of this paper is almost certainly adapted from plasterwork. Ceilings with similar designs are recorded at Somerset Lodge, Canonbury Place, London (1599) and Balcaskie House, Fifeshire (c.1665). No 8 West Street was a relatively modest house, probably built for a London merchant. The use of wallpapers to copy or approximate more costly decorative effects tends to confirm the idea that wallpaper was first adopted by an aspiring middle-class in an attempt to emulate the fashions of the rich.

decorations at Strawberry Hill gave an impetus to the Gothic revival style across Europe, and must have helped to create a market for Gothic wallpapers. Visiting Lady Orkney at Taplow, Buckinghamshire, Mrs Philip Lybbe Powys is shown '… a Gothic root-house [summer-house] which hangs over the river … the inside is Gothic paper resembling stucco'.[5]

In due course, the Gothic style was both popularised and debased. Complex elaborate implausible patterns combining a miscellany of fanciful and inauthentic details were characteristic of the 'Gothick' style wallpapers from the 1820s onwards. Such papers, rather than imitating stone and stucco-work in low relief, were more obviously illusionistic and pictorial, with vignettes of ruins, figures and landscapes, often printed in colours. By the mid-century such styles were appearing in machine-printed versions, designed to appeal to the lower end of the market. A typical

example from around 1850 in the Whitworth represents a carved relief of Crusaders fighting Saracens, a sculpture of a monarch, and a complex framework of arches, pinnacles, fretwork and masonry.

Another of these popular Gothic wallpapers was hung in the Ostrich Hotel at Castleacre near Swaffham, Norfolk, around 1820[6] (plate 65). The style was still popular, though hardly fashionable, but the paper may well have been chosen in part for its relevance to local sights and scenes. Castleacre had a number of Gothic remains, including 'The site of the priory church … a venerable large gothic pile … [a] great part of the front or West end of it still remaining.'[7]

At a time when travellers were often interested in ruins and antiquities, a Gothic wallpaper would have been an apt choice of decoration for a hotel. It has also been plausibly suggested that the Gothic style had inherent associations with hospitality, conviviality and feasting. An anonymous writer in the *Gentleman's Magazine* wrote: 'Methinks there was something respectable and venerable in those hospitable *Gothick* Halls, hung round with the Helmets, Breast-Plates and Swords of our ancestors.'[8] Indeed, the paper from the Ostrich even features representations of trophies of this kind in niches.

In fact, this association of the Gothic style with hospitality seems to have been commonplace. In 1841 the architect and designer A.W.N. Pugin was writing dismissively of 'What are commonly termed gothic pattern papers for hanging walls, where a wretched caricature of a pointed

65. Fragment of wallpaper with design of saints and trophies in the neo-Gothic style; English, *c.*1820
From the Ostrich Hotel, Castleacre, Swaffham, Norfolk
Colour print from woodblocks
E.3538–1913
Given by Mr T. Taylor

building is repeated from skirting to cornice, door over pinnacle and pinnacle over door.' He noted that there was 'a great variety of these miserable patterns', and that the style was 'a great favourite with hotel and tavern keepers'.[9] Just as hoteliers in America favoured the French scenic papers for their spectacular character and their obvious references to travel, so it would seem that the Gothic style served a similar purpose for British innkeepers, though at lesser cost and with rather more parochial associations.

The so-called 'pillar and arch' papers of the later eighteenth century employed both classical and Gothic features, often in the same design; they typically represent arcading, or a façade punctuated by sculptures in shallow niches. Dramatic and handsome when considered in isolation, they seem to us rather disturbing and over-assertive when used to paper an entire room – the multiple vanishing points distort the perspective. Generally it seems that papers of this kind were used for halls and staircases, tall narrow spaces where the perspectival problems of the repeat would have been much less apparent. An elaborate pattern of this kind, dated *c.*1760, with landscapes framed by Gothick tracery and figures within a Gothic and classical framework, was found on the staircase of the Ancient High House in Stafford. It was pasted directly to the wattle and daub wall panels, with a ceiling paper representing low-relief plasterwork used on the structural timbers to frame the pictorial scenes of the main design. In the same year Chippendale supplied a 'Cathedral Gothic' paper for the back stairs at 26 Soho Square, London, for Sir William Robinson. A late example of the style – a classical 'pillar and arch' paper – was hung in a newly built house at 370 Commercial Road, Hackney, around 1810, and a 'gothic ruin' paper was used in the hall of a small two-bay terraced house in Waterloo Place on Kew Green around 1815–20.

These 'architecture papers' were popular with American customers. Advertisements placed by Thomas Lee in Boston newspapers in 1764 and 1765, included 'a fine Assortment of Gothic Paper Hangings' from London.[10] As in England, such papers were mostly recommended for halls and staircases: in the 1790s Zecheriah Mills, a Hartford paperstainer, advertised 'Large and elegant Pillar

66. Portion of a classical 'pillar and arch' wallpaper; English, c.1769

Chiaroscuro print from woodblocks

E.964–1926

This is an unused portion left over from the decoration in 1769 of the Old Manor, Bourton-on-the-Water, Gloucestershire.

and Arch figures for spaceways, halls, &c.'[11] Imposing pillar and arch papers survive, or have been replaced in kind in several New England houses, including Hamilton House, South Berwick, Maine, which had an American-made 'pillar and arch' paper of c.1787 in the entrance hall; the paper has been replaced by a reproduction of the original, with the ground colour changed from grey to blue. An elegant large-scale pattern of a similar type, based on an English original of c.1769 (a fragment of which is in the V&A) (plate 66) has been reproduced for the staircase and entrance hall at Gunston Hall, Virginia, to striking effect.

Though such papers worked best in halls and stairwells, they were occasionally used in living rooms. A good example of the way such papers dominated a room can be seen in a painting by Philip Hussey (1713–83), which shows an anonymous family posed informally in their drawing room (plate 67). The room is in fact decorated with *two* pillar and arch papers, one for the walls, and a subtly different design on the chimney breast. The effect is startling, and rather sombre, and this is typical of the eighteenth-century architecture papers which were printed exclusively in naturalistic colours – black, white, buff and shades of grey.

This limited palette is confirmed by Thomas Gray in a letter to his friend Dr Wharton of Old Park, Durham, in 1761: 'You seem to suppose they do Gothic papers in colours, but I never saw any but such as were to look like *stucco* … Lastly, I never saw anything of gilding such you mention on paper, but we shall see.'[12] An equally dark, oppressive design was hung around 1780 in the 'best room' of the early eighteenth-century house built by Timothy Johnson in North Andover, Massachusetts, but the use of architecture papers in these situations was rare.

A much lighter Gothic-style pillar and arch paper was used by Frances Viscountess Irwin to decorate her bedroom at Temple Newsam shortly after she arrived as a young bride in 1758. The paper now in situ is a reproduction of a design similar to the original but copied from a pattern found in the ground floor parlour of No. 1 Amen Court, London. At Temple Newsam the paper complemented white-painted rococo style plasterwork on the ceiling and picture frames (plate 68).

The 'pillar and arch' formula was gradually elaborated to include figurative elements – often in the form of monuments and memorials. A late eighteenth-century American paper frames figures emblematic of the defeat of the British and the declaration of American Independence; another of c.1800, advertised by its maker Ebenezer Clough of Boston as 'An elegant Device in Paper Hangings, suitable for large rooms, especially for Halls, Stair-ways, Entries, &c.'[13] shows a memorial to George Washington

67. *Family in an interior with an architectural wallpaper, c.1760*
Attributed to Philip Hussey
Oil on canvas
National Gallery of Ireland, Dublin

Features such as the distinctive grate and the pattern of the doors indicate that this is an Irish interior. The sparsely furnished room is dominated by the sombre grisaille 'pillar-and-arch' wallpaper.

with figures of Liberty and Justice. As described in Chapter 3, James Fenimore Cooper gives an unflattering description of a similar wallpaper in a house modelled on that of his own father in Cooperstown, New York:

> The walls were hung with a dark, lead-colored English paper that represented Britannia weeping over the tomb of Wolfe. The hero himself stood at a little distance from the mourning goddess, and at the edge of the paper …[14]

Cooper may well have been describing an actual paper of the period: a modern American reproduction of a 'pillar and arch' pattern with Britannia weeping, and the figure of an American patriot with outstretched arm has been based on fragments found in a tavern in Lexington, Massachusetts, and a house in Salem, New Jersey (plate 69).

This kind of chiaroscuro printing was also well-suited to producing wallpapers in imitation of mouldings for frames and cornices, as well as imitation plaster decorations, especially ceiling roses. Some decorations were also made in papier maché, as a cheap alternative to plaster.

In the 1840s and 1850s wallpaper panels were printed in grisaille to represent sculptures; French manufacturers specialised in these grand decorations, but their subjects

68. The Gothick Room, Temple Newsam, Leeds

© Leeds Museums and Galleries, (Temple Newsam House)

This room was redecorated by Frances, Viscountess Irwin, soon after she arrived at Temple Newsam following her marriage. She chose a Gothic-style pillar-and-arch paper in keeping with the style of the other furnishings. Only a small fragment of the original paper survived, insufficient for a reconstruction of the pattern. So when the room was refurbished in the early 1990s the paper was replaced by a reprint of a similar design, dating from the 1760s, which had been found in a downstairs front parlour at 1 Amen Court, London. The new paper was a painstaking reconstruction by specialist wallpaper conservator Allyson McDermott. It was hand-printed using newly-cut blocks, and each length of paper was made up of smaller sheets measuring 23 x 22 inches, with rag edges overlapped and beaten down to form a fine joint, just as the original would have been. This attention to detail gave an unusual degree of historical authenticity to the scheme.

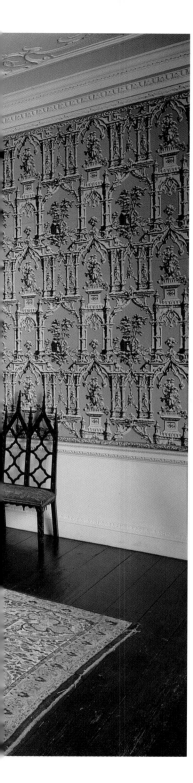

69. *(right)* ***Ipswich*** **wallpaper;**
American, *c*.1950–53
Reconstruction of a late
18th-century original
Produced by the Thomas
Strahan Company, Boston, USA
Machine printed
Gift of the Wallpaper Magazine
Cooper-Hewitt, National Design
Museum, Smithsonian Institute/
Art Resource, NY

This paper, in the 'pillar and
arch' style shows Britannia
weeping over a tomb, beside
figures representing America
and the Declaration of
Independence.

1953–198–15

were often English, including representations of Queen
Victoria and John Milton, as well as French royalty and
allegorical figures. These were probably intended for public
buildings such as town halls and other civic buildings, and
for places of public entertainment such as theatres.

Papers imitating marbling and woodgrain, produced
throughout the eighteenth and nineteenth centuries, were
popular for halls and passageways. As J.C. Loudon explained (in his *Encyclopaedia*, first published 1833), for
entrance lobbies and staircases one of the best designs
was a paper 'simply marked with lines in imitation of hewn
stone' because if it was damaged a piece the size of one of
the stones could be renewed without the repair being obvious.[15] Despite these practical advantages such papers were
frowned upon by the tastemakers of the later nineteenth
century, including Robert Edis, Charles Eastlake and Oscar
Wilde, because they objected to the sham of imitating one
material in another.

Print Rooms

The fashion for print rooms – rooms decorated with prints cut out and pasted directly on to the wall or a plain wallpaper – seems to have originated in Paris. Writing in 1726 Mademoiselle Aïssé described the 'new passion for cutting up coloured engravings' which were then glued to sheets of pasteboard, varnished and used for wallhangings or screens. Costly books were sacrificed to this craze, with some 'women mad enough to cut up engravings each costing one hundred livres'.[1]

In England the print room seems to date from the mid-eighteenth century. Horace Walpole had a room at Strawberry Hill hung with yellow paper and with prints pasted up and 'framed in a new manner invented by Lord Cardigan; that is with black and white borders printed. Over this is Mr Chute's bedchamber, hung with red in the same manner.'[2]

In her account of the lives of the Lennox sisters, Stella Tillyard details Louisa Connolly's creation of a print room at Castletown (plate 70). To carry out this scheme, she assembled prints of suitable subjects and sizes from the early 1760s onwards. At that time prints were sold individually, or in packets of four, six, ten or more. In 1766 she wrote to Sarah [her sister, in London]: 'any time that you chance to go into a print shop, I should be obliged if you would buy me five or six large prints. There are some by Teniers, engraved by Le Bas, which, I am told, are larger than the common size. If you meet with any, pray send a few.'[3] Various members of the family were enlisted to help Louisa build her collection. Her second son, William, while on his Grand Tour, sent a large batch of prints from Rome in 1767, and her own account books record regular purchases of prints in twos and threes throughout the next decade: 'Paid Mr. Bushell for prints £1: 2: 2½' (1766); '£1. 2. 9 for a subscription for prints' (1771) and '3 prints at 15s' (1773).[4]

The trend for creating print rooms was extensive enough to justify printers producing pattern sheets (of the kind referred to by Walpole) with borders, swags, ribbons and bows, to be cut out and pasted around the prints to create the desired illusion of a gallery of framed and beribboned pictures (plate 71).

70. (*opposite*) **View of the Print Room at Castletown House, County Kildare**
Courtesy of Duchas
The Heritage Service

The print room was created by Lady Louisa Connolly, with the help of her sister Lady Sarah Bunbury, whose engraved portrait after Reynolds was included in the scheme. Also included are well-known theatrical portraits of David Garrick and the tragic actress Mrs Siddons. Though Louisa had mentioned her print room plan in a letter of 1762 the decoration was only begun in 1768, and took several years to complete, with friends and family enlisted to acquire prints in London and on the Continent.

This use of pre-printed borders is confirmed in contemporary comments, such as that of Mrs Delany, writing from Ireland in 1751, 'I have received the six dozen borders all safely, and return to you, my dear brother, many many thanks for them. They are for framing prints. I think them much prettier than any other sort of frame for that purpose, and where I have not pictures I must have prints.'[5] The 1775 catalogue of Sayer and Bennett, a London print publisher, described their 'fine prints in sets' as 'proper for the collections in the cabinets of the curious; also elegant and genteel ornaments when framed and glazed, and may be fitted up in a cheaper manner, to ornament rooms, staircases, &c. with curious borders representing frames, a fashion much in use, and produces a very agreeable effect.' They supplied these 'Decorations for *Print Rooms*' too, and advertised:

> … bordering in an infinite variety, festoons of flowers, trophies of various kinds, circles, Ovils of different dimensions for heads, landscapes, &c, &c. Vases, urns, brackets, pedestals, terms, statues, masks, drops, knots and centres. The whole elegantly engraved on upwards of Eight-hundred Copper Plates, containing every ornament necessary for fitting up print rooms.[6]

71. Four examples of decorative borders; English, later 18th century
Engravings
25084.7, 25084.8, 25084.9, 25084.11

Engravers and print-sellers were quick to respond to the demand for printed borders, frames, swags and bows to fit up print rooms, as the fashion grew in the 1760s.

Both men and women created, or designed, print rooms. A gentleman might decorate a closet with engravings acquired on the Grand Tour – an array of mementos from the journey, often depicting the sites visited, or representing the works of the Old Masters. Such a print room was both a reference to his having completed the education proper to his class and position, and a subtle advertisement of the cultivated tastes thereby acquired. Arthur Young, describing the print room at Wanstead in 1769, shows that visitors were sensitive to such matters: 'We entered a breakfast room, elegant indeed, prints pasted on a buff paper, with engraved borders, all disposed in a manner which displays great taste. The prints are of the very best masters, and the ornaments elegant.'[7]

Women's print rooms were often more intimate and personal, with genre scenes as well as classical landscapes, and engraved portraits of friends and relations. For example, Louisa Connolly noted the purchase in 1771 of 'Lady Sarah Bunbury's print (for £1:1:0)'.[8] Sarah Bunbury was her sister (the same to whom she had written for prints earlier) and the print to which she refers here is an engraving after Sir Joshua Reynolds' portrait entitled 'Lady Sarah Bunbury sacrificing to the Graces' (1765). Louisa made this print a central feature of her display, giving it pride of place on the south wall, opposite a print after Van Dyck of the children of Charles I which included the Lennox sisters' great-grandfather. The east and west walls were dominated by prints of Garrick, the actor, in portraits after Reynolds and Zoffany. Other prints were then fitted in around these, to create a pleasing and balanced arrangement. The whole had a strong autobiographical element, consisting of family portraits, alongside images which referred more generally to maternal and filial duties, and made subtle points about morality and mortality.

Lady Clanbrassil, a friend of both Louisa and her sister Emily, Countess of Kildare, had prints of her friends pasted up in her house, Templeogue, on the outskirts of Dublin. Her display also included the engraving after Reynolds' portrait of Sarah Bunbury. While staying at Templeogue, Louisa wrote to Sarah in the summer of 1766: 'I am with Lady Clanbrassil, who desires a thousand loves to you. She has employed me in cutting out a border to go round your print which she has put up in her closet. It was pleasant work for me as I looked at your dear Fiz. [face] all the time.'[9]

The original print room at Uppark (restored after the fire of 1989) was on the mezzanine floor inserted around 1770 during the construction of the Saloon below. The Uppark prints are hung in a severely formal manner, with printed frames but no use of linking swags or other decorative embellishments. This print room was the project of Sir Matthew Fetherstonhaugh. In 1774 he paid £5 15s to 'Mrs

Vivaro for Prints'[10] [she was perhaps the wife of Francis Vivares (1709–80), an engraver who supplied the printed borders and other elements for making a print-room]. The Uppark room is dominated by prints after Italian, Flemish and Spanish Old Masters, including a series showing scenes of witchcraft and alchemy after David Teniers the Younger (1610–90). The most recent print included is Fisher's 1762 engraving after Reynolds' *Garrick between Tragedy and Comedy* (also featured in Louisa Connolly's scheme). The style of arrangement and the subjects depicted tend to suggest this was a man's room; much later (from 1931) Admiral Meade-Fetherstonhaugh used it as a dressing room. At Woodhall Park, Hertfordshire, Piranesi's etchings of the churches of Rome are well represented; while Dr Johnson's friends, the Thrales, had a print room in their house in Streatham, south London, featuring the prints of Hogarth.

Though many print-rooms were put together by amateurs as a hobby, others were the work of professional decorators. In 1767 Thomas Chippendale was responsible for Lady Knatchbull's dressing-room at Mersham Le Hatch, Ashford, Kent, which was hung with verditer paper (plain green, deriving from copper carbonate) and decorated with prints, framed with printed borders and interspersed with cut-out festoons, busts, masks, swags, baskets, and so on. His bill for this scheme includes a charge of £14 10s for 'Cutting out the Prints, Borders & Ornaments and Hanging them in the Room Complete'.[11]

Prompted by this fashion for print rooms, the paper-stainers responded with wallpapers imitating the effect of walls hung with framed prints. The best of these have often been attributed to J.B. Jackson, though no conclusive evidence to support this has ever come to light. Three fine examples were supplied to Doddington Hall, Lincolnshire, in the 1760s, where they were hung in small closets and passages. The most striking of these papers has blue and pink grounds with chiaroscuro representations of the prints (plate 72). The medallion depicting a pair of lovers seated on a garden bench relates to a design by C.N. Cochin the Younger (c.1745) and to engravings by Robert Hancock for use on Battersea enamels and on Worcester and Bow

porcelain. The unused lengths of this paper are vividly coloured and offer a useful corrective to the general view that eighteenth-century papers were sombre or dark. Such assumptions are all too readily drawn from the age-faded evidence of the majority of surviving papers.

Yellow or so-called straw-coloured grounds were very popular in print-room papers and a yellow-ground print room wallpaper was found at Doddington, where it was originally hung in a closet and a corridor, and now survives in two alcoves on the corridor (plate 73). The corridor itself dates from around 1761. The design on this paper features Italianate landscapes and portrait medallions set between vertical bands of flowers, fruit and musical instruments.

A paper of the same type was hung at the Old Manor, Bourton-on-the-Water, in 1769, and a blue-ground version was discovered at Doddington. The borders of this paper, and of a similar paper with architectural scenes on a deep pink ground, resemble stucco or plasterwork rather than conventional picture frames. The 1762 edition of Chippendale's *The Gentleman and Cabinet-Maker's Director* has a page of engraved designs of 'Borders for Paper Hangings etc' which imitate plasterwork mouldings in a rococo style which may well have been used in print-room schemes as well as to frame wallpapers.

Yet another surviving fragment from Doddington features two alternating views of Gothic ruins printed in shades of brown, green and grey. It is thought that it was designed to be cut up and the scenes pasted on to the walls in print-room style.

Print-room papers were also used in America. A yellow-ground paper was hung in the hall in the Lady Pepperell House, Kittery Point, Maine, built around 1760. Some of the scenes were adapted from *The Ladies Amusement*, a magazine published by Robert Sayer in London in 1762, suggesting that the wallpaper manufacturers were quick to adopt new styles and that they took their motifs from the most up-to-date publications available to them.

72. *(opposite)* **Detail of a 'print room'-style wallpaper with design of medallions, framed landscape and figure scenes, interspersed with flowers and insects; English, *c.*1760**
Colour print from woodblocks
E.474–1914
Given by Mr G.E. Jarvis

73. *(right)* **'Print room'-style wallpaper with design of trophies, medallions and framed landscape scenes with floral swags and festoons; English, *c.*1760**
Colour print from woodblocks
E.473–1914
Given by Mr G.E. Jarvis

This paper comes from Doddington Hall, Lincolnshire, and was used in the fashionable redecoration of the house undertaken by Sir John Hussey Delaval around 1760. A blue-ground version of the same pattern also survives.

Scenic Wallpapers

9

The French 'scenic', 'panoramic' or 'landscape' wallpapers (*papiers-peints paysages*) represent the most ambitious phase of wallpaper design and production, and constituted an important statement of confidence and taste in the period following the Revolution, when the abolition of legal privilege in 1789 left wealth as the chief mark of social distinction. It seems they were also conceived as a challenge to the market dominance of English flock wallpapers and were devised as advertisements for the skills and standards of the French wallpaper industry. They were shown at the Expositions des Produits de l'Industrie Française from 1806 to 1849, and then at the international exhibitions.

These landscape papers were printed on up to 30 individual lengths and hung to form a continuous mural around a room. Though printed from woodblocks they were so highly detailed that from a distance they gave the illusion of a painted decoration. Mural painting was obviously an important precedent, but so too were the large-scale figurative tapestries from the Gobelins and Beauvais workshops. Also influential were the painted panoramas exhibited in specially built rotundas; two such 'entertainments' were exhibited in Paris in 1800, one of which – *The Monuments of Paris* – may well have been the inspiration for the later wallpaper decoration by Dufour, *Les Monuments de Paris* (1815).

The design and printing of such papers was very costly and thus the panoramics were considerably more expensive than most repeating patterns. Their representation of exotic landscapes, city scenes and parks, historical events, mythological subjects, and even scenes from contemporary literature were designed to appeal to an educated class, an élite with social influence and probably political power. Most surviving examples are in the houses of rural *notables* [leading citizens]. When used by an urban élite, they rarely survived the vagaries of fashion.

However, within the category of scenic papers there was a variety of styles and prices to suit the tastes and the pockets of a wide range of consumers. A number of designs were printed in grisaille, for example, which made them significantly cheaper than the full-colour designs. In

74. (*opposite*) **Panel of panoramic paper, No.1 from the *Eldorado* series, c.1915**
Produced by Zuber et Cie, Rixheim
Colour print from woodblocks
E.2901–1938
Given by Mr W.L. Wood

The *Eldorado* series was first produced by Zuber in 1849, and is still available today. It pictured a sequence of lush exotic unpeopled landscapes in which each of the four main continents – Europe, Asia, Africa and America – is represented by its native plants and characteristic architecture. El Dorado, a mythical golden city, had come to stand for riches and abundance. To choose such a decoration, which was itself expensive, was an overt display of the owner's wealth. This wallpaper (and similar decorations from Defossé, for example) was a seductive illusory equivalent of the conservatories and winter gardens which were features of the grandest houses at the time.

Balzac's *Le Père Goriot*, the Dining Room of the Maison Vauquer, a modest Parisian boarding house, has Dufour's *Télémaque* on the walls (plate 75). The action of the novel is set in 1819, the date the design was issued, suggesting that Madame Vauquer, for all her frugality in household matters, is nevertheless keen to make a good impression in her public rooms. But the quality of the wallpaper is offset by the other worn and workaday furnishings. With a characteristic prudence where money is concerned, she had the paper 'varnished', to ensure that it would survive the inevitable accretion of dirt and grease.[1]

As befitted the expensive nature of these decorations, chosen to exhibit the buyer's taste and wealth, they seem to have been hung in the most public spaces of European houses – reception rooms, salons and dining rooms – and, in America, in halls and passageways. Sometimes they were hung continuously, as far as windows and doors allowed. The manufacturers had clearly given some thought to the problems of hanging these papers to form a coherent decoration, and thus they were often divided into episodic scenes with features such as trees or rocks as divisions which could be trimmed or sacrificed altogether when the

75. Publicity lithograph for the scenic wallpaper *Paysage de Télémaque dans L'Île de Calypso*; French, c.1825
Produced by Dufour, Paris
Musée des Arts décoratifs, Paris, Photo: Laurent-Sully Jaulmes, all rights reserved

The fold-out promotional lithograph shows the entire sequence of the narrative of Telemachus and Calypso, giving the customer an idea of the effect of the decoration when hung.

paper was hung. Alternatively they were hung as single panels, like paintings or tapestries, often with printed paper borders, or pilasters. A Zuber design of 1815, *La Grande Helvétie*, is shown hung in this fashion in the Drawing Room of the Princesses Sophie and Marie of Bavaria at Nymphenburg outside Munich, in a watercolour of around 1820 (plate 76). This arrangement enhances the illusion that the room opens on to an arcade with views of a landscape beyond. In this illustration it becomes clear that a scenic paper was a very demanding decoration, a dominant element of an interior, not merely a background. All the furniture had to be kept to the height of the dado rail so as not to interfere with the visual unity of the paper views. Pictures, mirrors, lamp brackets and the other paraphernalia of the conventional interior were to be avoided or kept to a minimum.

The earliest *paysages panoramiques* were designed to educate and inform as well as to charm and to entertain. Dufour issued a promotional booklet with his first scenic wallpaper, *Les Sauvages de la Mer Pacifique* (1804), in which he claimed: 'We believed that we would earn the appreciation of the public by bringing together, in a clear and accessible way, the multitude of peoples who are separated from us by the vast oceans.' He appeals to the curiosity of 'the armchair traveller' who may 'experience for himself the journeys that provided the subject matter' without the trouble of leaving his apartment.[2] He was so proud of the precision and accuracy of his paper, and the prodigious research involved in its design, that he went on to suggest that: 'The mother of a family will give history and geography lessons to a lively little girl. The [several kinds of] vegetation can themselves serve as an introduction to the history of plants.'[3] The claims made for other sets also emphasised their accuracy and informative character: the promotional text for *La Grande Chasse au Tigre dans l'Inde* (issued by Velay before 1818) promises that 'the costumes are accurate, and they and the buildings have been copied from drawings made on the spot'. In a less respectful reference to the didactic role of the panoramic papers, the author Théophile Gautier, writing nearly 20 years later in 1834, said that he regarded them as 'a useful encyclopaedia to study while waiting for the soup'.[4]

The scenic papers have been described as 'comic strips on a mural scale'[5], and indeed those which illustrated literary subjects employed a narrative format, either morally improving subjects drawn from French authors such as

Bernardin de Saint-Pierre (*Paul et Virginie*, Dufour, 1824) or episodes from Greek mythology, such as tales from Ovid, or the great sequence in grisaille telling the story of Cupid and Psyche in a neo-classical setting. Papers representing historical events, like the anonymous *Battle of Austerlitz* (*c*.1827–9), offered a sequential account of proceedings, in this case the engagement between Napoleon's army and the allied forces of Austria and Russia.[6] It was not designed by

the wallpaper workshop but consisted of a collage of scenes from printed and painted representations of the battle.

Patriotic subjects such as the Napoleonic campaigns, celebrated in several wallpaper designs, had an obvious appeal in France, with a cult of Napoleon continuing into the late 1820s. However, military subjects were ill-suited to domestic decoration, especially an example as graphically violent as *Austerlitz*. Writer Friedrich Blaul, in 1838,

76. The Drawing Room of the Princesses Sophie and Marie of Bavaria in the Schloss Nymphenburg, with scenic wallpaper *La Grande Helvétie*, *c*.1820
Wilhelm Rehlen (*c*.1795–1831)
Watercolour
© Wittelsbacher Ausgleichsfonds München

To enhance the impression of the room as an arcaded loggia with views onto a landscape, the panels of scenic wallpaper have been framed by printed paper pilasters. There is also a richly-patterned frieze above. Scenic papers were generally hung about 1 metre or 36 inches above the floor level, so that the furniture did not obscure any part of the design, and to ensure that the horizon line in the landscape would appear at eye level.

describes an encounter at the Wittlesbach Hof in Speyer, where he met a lady in tears in the dining room. She explained that the wallpaper was the cause of her distress: 'As I was looking around, a dreadful, magnificent period rose before my eyes from the dead: the hero of the century on his first military campaign in Italy. The wallpaper was printed grey on grey, and the dusk imbued all the figures with a strange life.'[7] The paper she refers to would appear to be a grisaille version of the *French Campaigns in Italy*. Such papers were more commonly used in town halls and other public buildings, where their shocking scenes would have been less affecting for delicate female sensibilities. In other subjects where a death featured in the narrative (such as that of Captain Cook in the *Sauvages de la Mer Pacifique* or the drowning of Virginie in *Paul et Virginie*) it is only hinted at or reduced to a background detail. Military subjects obviously had a limited appeal outside France, but even the more commercial designs were produced in smallish numbers, around 150 sets in most cases, and exported in relatively limited quantities to other European countries.

Though the panoramic papers were admired in Britain, they were rarely purchased for British homes. While Caroline Halstead, for example, described 'whole sides of rooms ... papered with illustrations of one subject drawn from history, travels or voyages. Some of these are most beautifully painted [sic], and few things attract a stranger's attention more ... than the brilliant colours and admirable effects of the French scenic papers'[8], this kind of enthusiastic appreciation did not lead to many sales. No doubt the main obstacle was that Britain was at war with France until 1815 and thus the opportunities for trade in such luxury goods were limited, and scarcely patriotic, unless one had a family connection with France. A house in Oxford built for the exiled heir of the Bourbons, the Duc de Berri, about 1808, apparently had a room papered with 'a gorgeous view of the Tuileries Gardens under the "ancien Régime"' which survived into the Victorian period according to a later reminiscence.[9]

Only a handful of such papers survive in British houses, and of these fewer still were acquired and installed in the

77. Bedroom at Crawford Priory, with *Cupid and Psyche* wallpaper, photographed *c*.1900

Royal Commission on the Ancient and Historical Monuments of Scotland

The *Cupid and Psyche* scenic paper was first produced in a set of 26 lengths, by Dufour in Paris in 1816, and printed in grisaille. It was reissued five times by Defossé & Karth, Paris, between 1872 and 1931. Unlike the majority of scenic papers, this set was not designed as a continuous sequence – instead it comprised a number of discrete scenes and single panels to be framed separately as they are here. The same paper was used around 1911 by Lady Duff Gordon in the dining room of her London house. This house, and her salon, were decorated throughout in historicising French styles, as befitted the image of a successful couturier at that time.

78. View of the dining room at Stonor Park, Oxfordshire, showing *Les Monuments de Paris*, first issued c.1815
Produced by Dufour, Paris
By kind permission of Lord Camoys, Stonor

This was acquired in Paris in the 1930s and is probably a contemporary reprint. Scenic papers enjoyed a revival at this time. However it was not hung in its present location until 1978–9. Scenic wallpapers have been a favourite decoration for dining rooms from their first appearance. They contributed to the general purpose of entertainment and display, and flattered the host's taste and education. Their subject matter would no doubt have been a useful stimulus to conversation.

early decades of the nineteenth century. Doddington Hall acquired a spectacular scenic paper by Dufour – probably *Don Quixote* (c.1819) – which was hung in a bedchamber around 1820.[10] Another scenic survives at Ombersley Court, Worcestershire; a complete set of Zuber's *L'Hindustan* hangs at Attingham Park near Shrewsbury; while Laxton Hall, Northamptonshire, has fragments of Dufour's *Vues de l'Inde* (1806) in a bedroom. Some other examples were hung at later dates, such as the *Cupid and Psyche* panels hung

in a bedroom at Crawford Priory, probably in the 1860s (plate 77), and the *Monuments de Paris* set hung in the Dining Room of Stonor Park, Oxfordshire, in 1978–9 (having been acquired in Paris in the 1930s) (plate 78). Cowtan's decorated a bedroom at Knole Park, Kent, with *Psyche et Cupidon* in 1901 (probably one of the reprints issued in 1873 and 1889); The White Hart Hotel (formerly Rashleigh House) in Cornwall had a set of the *La Baie de Naples* (c.1822), although the date of the installation is unknown.[11]

But a general prejudice against the pictorial illusion inherent in the French panoramic papers grew up, at least amongst the class most likely to be able to afford them. Henry Smithers, writing about Liverpool in 1825, noted: 'A few years since every room in some houses and some rooms in all, were ornamented with paintings and prints … and now, we see the walls decorated with the glare of French or Swiss papers in fresco, illustrative of the history of Don Quixote, or views of countries, in glowing colours, unlike anything in nature. This fashion is in such bad taste that it cannot long continue.'[12] A writer in the *Illustrated London*

News in 1862 praised the technical achievement of *L'Eden* (exhibited in London by Defossé et Karth, 1862) but says 'it must suffer condemnation if regarded as the decoration of a wall ... it is unsuited as a background, both through its obtrusiveness and the fact that it is altogether inconsistent to hide parts with articles of furniture'.[13]

The scenic papers, which found so few takers in England, were purchased in large numbers by Americans. The nineteenth-century Zuber account books record shipments of wallpapers to individuals in the US as well as to dealers and wholesalers. Archives and advertisements make it clear that from the 1820s onwards the major scenic designs were available in several American cities shortly after their production in France. Zuber's *Eldorado* (1848) is displayed prominently in an 1855 pictorial advertisement for the New York store Sutphen and Breed, and the *Monuments de Paris* in an 1847 lithograph illustrating John Ward's Paper-Hanging Warehouse in Philadelphia. Most of the surviving examples of French scenics in the US are in rather grand houses, but this is slightly misleading. It seems that they were purchased by merchants, businessmen and professionals of all kinds. At Prestwould, a prestigious plantation house built in the 1790s by wealthy merchant Sir Peyton Skipwith, three scenics were installed for his son around 1831, including *La Chasse de Compiègne*, and in the hall *Le Parc Français*. An advertisement for a two-storey frame house on Prospect Street, Brooklyn, noted that it had 'landscape paper in three rooms', and in the relatively modest Harper House at Harper's Ferry, West Virginia, a restoration uncovered fragments of Dufour's *Les Fêtes Grecs*, probably hung in 1832–3. Around 1819, prices for scenics ranged from 10 to 40 dollars – by no means cheap, but not prohibitively expensive either, and similar in price to the more luxurious contemporary American wallpapers.[14]

In private houses Americans generally chose to hang scenic papers in entrances and hallways. In 1825 S.P. Franklin advertised 'a few Historical views' as 'well calculated for Halls and Passages', and as late as 1857 a New York dealer was offering wallpaper 'scenery for halls'.[15] Two American presidents had used panoramic papers in their own homes: President Jackson, retiring from the White House to his new home, the Hermitage in Tennessee, chose the Dufour paper *Télémaque* (c.1819) for the entrance hall, where it can still be seen, while President Monroe hung exotic garden scenes from the 1848 Zuber set *Eldorado* in his Virginia home, Oak Hill (plate 74).

French scenics were also popular for inns and hotels in the US. Harriet Martineau saw several examples, irreverently treated by the guests, as she described in her *Retrospect of Western Travel*, published in 1838:

> I observed that hotel parlours in several parts of the country were papered with the old-fashioned papers, I believe French, which represent a sort of panorama of a hunting party, a fleet, or some such diversified scene. I saw many such a hunting party, the ladies in scarlet riding habits ... At Schenectady, the Bay of Naples, with its fishing-boats on the water and groups of lazzaroni on the shore adorned our parlour walls. It seems to be an irresistible temptation to idle visitors, English, Irish, and American, to put speeches in the mouths of the painted personages; and such hangings are usually seen deformed with scribblings. The effect is odd, and in wild places, of seeing American witticisms put into the mouths of Neapolitan fishermen, ancient ladies of quality, or of tritons and dryads.[16]

The élite associations of the scenic papers, and their use in France by those who enjoyed both political and social prestige, were significant factors in their use in American interiors. Two scenic wallpapers by Zuber are now in the White House, Washington D.C., hung by Jacqueline Kennedy as part of the major refurbishment of the house which she undertook between 1961 and 1963. Though the over-arching theme of the White House redecoration was Colonial America, it acknowledged the preference for French styles – and especially for French wallpapers – in American interiors. The *Vues d'Amerique du Nord* of 1834 was chosen for the Diplomatic Reception Room (plate 79). With its idealised scenes of the North American landscape, including Virginia's Natural Bridge (a rock formation), Boston Harbour, and the US Military Academy at West Point, in this setting it was calculated to offer a subtle assertion of America's natural magnificence, its independence, and its military prowess, to representatives of foreign governments. The paper is also an example of

79. A view of the Diplomatic Reception Room at the White House, Washington D.C., hung with *L'Amerique du Nord*, first issued 1834
Produced by Zuber of Rixheim
White House Collection, courtesy White House Historical Association

This room is used primarily for meeting ambassadors arriving to present their credentials to the President. Since 1960 it has been furnished as a drawing room of the Federal Period (1790–1820), though the dramatic panoramic wallpaper is of a later date. Retrieved from an old house, the panels were installed here as part of the refurbishment undertaken by Jacqueline Kennedy. The design – a sequence of American landscape scenes – was modified and re-issued in 1853 as *Scenes of the American Revolution*. This latter version was used more discreetly in the dining room used by the presidential family.

political correctness *avant la lettre* for it shows amongst the travellers and sightseers parties of fashionably-dressed African-Americans, and thus offers a brilliant shorthand for the inclusiveness of American society and its much-vaunted equality of opportunity. With the paper's inherent associations of the elegance and taste belonging to an élite social class, it was perfectly adapted to the Kennedy conception of the White House as backdrop to a mythic Presidency.

The Kennedy decoration of the State Rooms (managed by Stefan Boudin, chief interior decorator with the Parisian company Jansen) was thus designed with a self-conscious debt to stage scenery, as a setting for ceremonies of state. Nevertheless there was some strong criticism in the press, including articles in the *Washington Post* attacking the extravagances of the project. These centred on Mrs Kennedy's decision to purchase the Zuber wallpaper panels, which had been salvaged from a dilapidated house in Thurmont, Maryland, for $12,500, although a modern reprint of the paper was available at a fraction of the cost. When a new private dining room for the presidential family was established on the second floor, a revised version of the same paper design, dated *c.*1853 and retitled *Scenes of the American Revolution*, was chosen: the sightseers and stage-coach passengers that peopled the original were replaced with red-coated soldiers. However there is something

**80. Scenic Beauty For Your Walls; page from
the catalogue of Montgomery Ward & Co.
of Chicago, 1932**

© MODA/Middlesex University

The original 19th-century French scenic decorations
had enjoyed great popularity in the US, and the
revival of mural wallpaper decoration in the 1920s
and 1930s was also largely an American
phenomenon. Montgomery Ward, a mail-order
company, offered cheap pastiches of French
scenic as well as contemporary designs –
predominantly soft focus romantic landscapes
or exotic flora.

faintly incongruous about such grand public themes in
decoration when they become the setting for the prosaic
events of twentieth-century family life (as a later photograph of the Nixon family at dinner makes clear).

Panoramic wallpapers and reprints are still used in certain public and semi-public interiors, such as grand hotels
and embassies. The elegant grisaille panels of Dufour's
Cupid and Psyche series hang in the Finnish embassy in
Stockholm, while the Zuber paper *Vues de Brésil*, originally
produced in 1830, hangs in the library of the Brazilian
embassy in Washington.[17] The design, by Jean Julien Deltil,
was based on scenes from J. M. Rugendas's *Voyage pittoresque dans le Brésil* published in 1827. The ascendancy of
European culture in this South American nation is neatly
encapsulated in this wallpaper, with its representations of
exotic wildlife, jungle landscapes and naked tattooed
Indians – a lavish representation of primitive 'otherness' as
seen through the eyes of European travellers, and translated into an elegant expensive entertaining decoration that
was designed initially for a European audience.

The style of the scenic papers changed significantly
around 1840. Instead of offering a vista on an exotic and
entertaining world beyond the home, the subjects of the
new decorations were unpeopled garden landscapes
(*Eldorado*, 1849) (plate 74) and highly detailed botanical
subjects (*Isola Bella*, 1843) which enclosed the occupants of
the room in a dense, luxuriant flora. The home became a
self-contained paradise when papered with Defossé's *Décor
Eden* of 1861, or Zuber's *Le Brésil*, 1862 [no connection with
the 1827 *Voyage pittoresque dans le Brésil*, mentioned
above]. This change of style and subject reflected a taste
for lush floral patterns in textiles too, and a preference for
the purely decorative as opposed to the improving narrative
character of the earlier scenics.

Scenic wallpaper decorations enjoyed a revival in the late
1920s and early 1930s, but the style of these is very different
from the earlier papers: the drawing and the printing were
no longer characterised by highly detailed realism of the
kind which attempted to suggest an accurate view; instead

they are pleasing soft-focus fantasies in a painterly style with non-specific titles such as *Pleasant Shores* (a German wall decoration of the 1920s). Montgomery Ward & Co. of Chicago produced a number of scenic decorations – a 1932 catalogue includes *Olympia Fields*, *Southern Beauty Frieze* and *November Woods Frieze* – which the manufacturer described as suitable for 'your large formal rooms – reception hall, spacious dining or living room' (plate 80). The *November Woods* design was particularly recommended for the library; no doubt the warm autumnal colours were thought to complement a room of leather-bound books, and by evoking the onset of cold weather, enhance the implied cosiness of reading indoors. Scenics of this kind were widely used in the US, but although they were also available in Britain they were much less popular there.

The dramatic effects of the expensive block-printed panoramic papers were democratised in the mid-twentieth century with the introduction of the photo-mural. Like its predecessors, the photo-mural – a wall-sized picture – was an expression of escapist fantasy, the desire to alleviate the prosaic reality of the home and domestic routines. In particular it bespoke a yearning on the part of an urban class for country life, for a view on to lakes and hills instead of brick walls, factories and monotonous streets. This inarticulate desire for a better life, embodied in an illusionistic picture, was well expressed in the television soap-opera *Coronation Street*, where the charlady Hilda Ogden had a landscape mural on the wall of her living room in her back-to-back terraced house near Manchester. This yearning for a rural past on the part of the displaced urban poor has an earlier counterpart in Dickens' *Little Dorrit*, where Mrs Plornish's shop parlour has one wall painted to resemble a cottage, a rural fantasy in the heart of London.[18]

Photo-murals also supplied the necessary element of fantasy and illusions of exoticism and foreignness in hotels, restaurants and cafés, especially in the 1960s and 1970s. Patrick Caulfield's painting *After Lunch* (1975) shows a photo-mural of a Swiss landscape (the Chateau de Chillon) in what is evidently a London version of a Swiss-themed restaurant, built in the chalet style and with a fondue dish on the table.[19]

More recently, the 1970s revival in fashion and furnishing coupled with a taste for kitsch has encouraged the further use of photo-murals. Habitat's catalogue for 2000 caught the retro mood and illustrated a mountain landscape mural in one of its lifestyle spreads (plate 81). In addition, a news item in *Design Week*[20] promoted original 1970s murals from the Scandinavian company Photomural – at 3m x 4m, the writer suggests that a Swiss mountain view or a Mauritian sunset scene would be the perfect wall decoration for the vast walls of a Shoreditch loft.

81. Interior with photo-mural reproduced in the Habitat catalogue, 2000/2001
Courtesy of Habitat

Habitat's catalogue alternates details of the products with 'lifestyle' pages illustrating the furnishings and accessories in room sets. The revival of 1970s styles is a feature of this issue, with bold geometric wallpapers used to cover screens or framed as focal points, and a typical photo-mural showing a Swiss landscape covering one wall in an otherwise sparely furnished kitchen-diner.

Design Reform

10

The Great Exhibition of 1851 was a triumphant celebration of contemporary manufacturing, and amongst its thousands of exhibits were many wallpapers, the products of more than 50 firms from Continental Europe and the United States as well as Britain. These papers became a focus for criticism by certain designers and educators who were increasingly depressed by the decline of design standards in the industry and the evident popularity of these debased products amongst consumers. Richard Redgrave, RA, then Inspector-General for Art (later Principal of the Government's Schools of Design) wrote an official report on the wallpapers shown at the Exhibition, in which he suggested that judgements of excellence were based on the number of colours used rather than any other aesthetic criteria. Certainly technical achievements within the industry were the primary focus of the displays and the prizes. The *Illustrated London News* meanwhile claimed that the British public was getting the domestic furnishings its lack of discrimination merited, and pictured John Bull sitting in an easy chair, his feet on a double-piled Axminster carpet, gazing vacantly at the crimson flock wallpaper, fully content with his lot.

Indeed the Exhibition was itself commemorated in a wallpaper which embodied so many of the faults identified by the critics that it was selected for the display of 'False Principles in Design' that featured in the Museum of Ornamental Art set up at Marlborough House in 1852 (plate 84). A short story by Henry Morley, 'A House Full of Horrors', which appeared in *Household Words* in 1852, describes a visit to this display. The narrator, Mr Crumpet, is appalled to find his own taste held up to ridicule in 'a gloomy chamber, hung round with frightful objects in curtains, carpets, clothes, lamps and whatnot'. Thus newly aware of 'some Correct Principles of Taste', 'I saw it all; when I went home I found that I had been living among horrors up to that hour. The paper in my parlour contains four kinds of birds of paradise, besides bridges and pagodas …' Distressed by this excess, and accumulated aesthetic shocks, he can only cry 'Horr-horr-horr-i-ble!'[1]

Also in 1852, Wilkie Collins gave a vivid vignette of contemporary tastes in his novel *Basil*. The eponymous hero

82. (*opposite*) **Floral wallpaper with rococo scrollwork motifs, c.1860**
Produced by William Woollams & Co.
Colour print from woodblocks
Reproduced by courtesy of
The Whitworth Art Gallery,
The University of Manchester

This florid naturalistic pattern is typical of the styles deplored by the design critics of the time.

goes to the home of Margaret Sherwin, and there meets her father, a successful draper newly risen to the middle-class. Basil describes his first sight of the décor in the Sherwin household: 'The brilliant-varnished door cracked with a report like a pistol when it was opened; the paper on the walls, with its gaudy pattern of birds, trellis-work, and flowers in gold, red and green on a white ground, looked hardly dry yet; the showy window-curtains of white and sky-blue, and the still showier carpet of red and yellow, seemed as if they had come out of the shop yesterday …' The violent colours and restless patterns affront his self-consciously cultivated taste, and he feels that 'the room would have given a nervous man the headache before he had been in it a quarter of an hour'.[2]

George Dodd, in his *Curiosities of Industry* (1852), was one of many calling for a raising of design standards in the wallpaper industry:

Unless paper ceases to be a material for wall decoration (and there seems no reason why it should so cease) the time has come for a little more artistic meaning in the designs – something like an approach to a principle in decorative pattern. The people, the paper users – will welcome a new infusion of mind in this art: for many of the 'curiosities of industry' in the shape of paperhangings are felt to be very absurd curiosities indeed.[3]

Many other voices were raised in support of this view, then and later. Eastlake, writing in 1868, condemned the examples of 'vitiated taste' which 'lines our walls with silly representations of vegetable life' or gives the impression that 'the drawing room walls are fitted up with a trellis work for training Brobdingnag [sic] convolvuli'. He concluded that 'The *quasi*-fidelity with which the forms of a rose, or a bunch of ribbons, or a ruined castle, can be reproduced on carpets, crockery and wallpapers will always possess a certain kind of charm for the uneducated eye' and these things, though 'ingenious amusing, attractive for the moment', do not 'lie within the legitimate province of art'[4] (plate 82). Manufacturers were blamed – their eagerness to sell wallpapers encouraged 'a public who prefer the vulgar, the gaudy, the ugly even, to the beautiful and perfect'.[5]

The mechanisation of the industry was seen by many commentators as a chief cause of the decline in design standards and the rout of good taste by the vulgar and the gaudy. The very perfection and uniformity which the machine could achieve were perversely held to be symptomatic of degraded taste. It was certainly true that printing from engraved rollers allowed fine detail and shading that were impossible with hand-block printing. Naturally, this capacity was exploited by designers, who submitted more detailed, illusionistic designs which could be accurately reproduced in the production process. The flat forms and blocks of unmodulated colour characteristic of block printing were, to the design reformers, more 'honest' and 'appropriate' as decorations for flat surfaces such as walls, and thus to be preferred to the ambitious, inventive products of the machine. As Redgrave put it (in a passage on calico printing, but equally applicable to wallpaper):

> Printing from metal cylinders has put at the command of the designer all those powers of more perfect imitation enjoyed by the engraver, and, instead of using them as they should be used, consistently with the requirements of manufacture and the principles of ornamental art, they are wasted on the imitation of flowers, foliage, and accidents of growth, quite out of ornamental character and opposed to just principles.[6]

83. Wallpaper with naturalistic floral stripe framed by rococo pilaster motifs; French, *c*.1850–60

Colour print from woodblocks

E.771–1955

Given by the Curator of the City Museum, Gloucester

84. *(above)* **Wallpaper illustrating the Crystal Palace; English, c.1853–5**
Probably produced by Heywood, Higginbottom & Smith, Manchester
Colour machine print
E.158–1934

This was exhibited as No.28 in the display demonstrating 'False Principles
of Decoration' at the Museum of Ornamental Art, Marlborough House,
Pall Mall, London. The catalogue to the display describes the errors of this
design, which include 'falsifying the perspective' by repetition of the
architectural view.

85. *(right)* **Wallpaper from a pattern book, 1853**
Produced by Richard Goodlad & Co., Newcastle upon Tyne
Probably printed from woodblocks
E.1607–1934
Given by The Wall Paper Manufacturers Ltd

This simple pattern is printed in two colours on a thin brittle woodpulp
paper and would have been one of the cheapest papers available at this
date. The pattern book also includes some machine prints and was clearly
aimed at low-income groups. By the mid-19th century, wallpaper
manufacturing had been established in most sizeable towns in Britain
and local retailers and decorators no longer relied exclusively on London
for their stock.

In fact, Redgrave and his peers ignored the fact that many
machine prints were precisely of the kind that they advocated – simple flat forms printed in two or three colours
(plate 85). Perhaps the very modesty and cheapness of such
papers, and the fact that they were unlikely to be advertised or exhibited in the way that the more elaborate and
ambitious designs were, led to them being overlooked.

A further perceived contribution to the low standard of
design was the desire on the part of English manufacturers
to keep production costs to a minimum. John Stewart, writing in *The Art Journal* (1861), compared the status of the
designer in England and in France: 'In the matter of
designs a French maker will spend as many pounds as an
English maker will spend pence … In France the designer
is an artist and treated and remunerated as such … In
England the designer for paperhangings ranks with a writer
of window show tickets … [who] hawks his stock from
door to door, thinking himself fortunate if he gets ten
shillings more or less for the "pick" of his portfolio.'[7] He
goes on to observe that the French also spend more on
their materials, and on the process of manufacture itself,
and value their skilled workmen more highly.

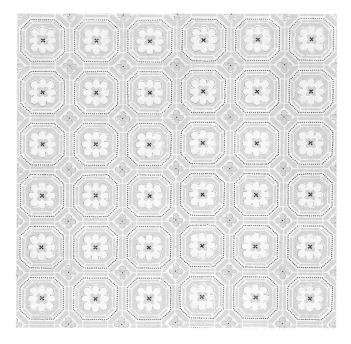

Twenty years later, however, French critics were also complaining about the public's fondness for papers which imitated other materials, particularly those which achieved their effects by *trompe l'oeil* techniques. In *L'Art au Foyer Domestique* (1884), Emile Cardon followed Eastlake in urging a greater discrimination in the choice of house furnishings.

Several of the design reformers in Britain suggested that it was the responsibility of the trade to educate public taste, but this was resisted. A letter from a wallpaper dealer to the *House Furnisher* in 1871 explains why:

> Paperhangings, as you must well know, are perishable goods, and do not improve by keeping like Port wine: and we tradesmen cannot afford to educate public taste, or give up buying and selling our, and the public's favourite pretty bouquets of flowers. My experience is that of all the different classes of goods they are the safest to put into stock. The greatest evil in our trade is the multitude of patterns: we all have shelves and counters loaded with books and patterns from every manufacturer in the trade, and as ladies never tire of looking over samples the selection of papers for a house becomes frequently a very bewildering and tiring business: we are generally too glad to finish the transaction to think of upsetting our customers' choice by any remarks as to incorrectness of taste in the design chosen.[8]

Commentators such as Edis regretted the fact that there were so many patterns to choose from, with new ones issued every season, and blamed the public's appetite for change. Of course, the industry also relied on novelty as the impetus to sales. Diversifying the product to increase demand was a strategy developed in many industries in the nineteenth century, a strategy supported by the mechanisation of production processes. The reformers themselves, with close ties to the industries whose products they criticised, rarely acknowledged this aspect of the argument, however. Only William Morris, as a Utopian Socialist, could openly blame the insatiable demands of the market, 'the great intangible machine of commercial tyranny'.[9]

What was very apparent by the mid-nineteenth century was that an unprecedented eclecticism had led to a proliferation of styles, with the market dominated by revival styles and historical pastiches. Heavy rococo elements, quite unlike the lively lightness of the eighteenth-century originals, were combined with naturalistic floral motifs to produce patterns which were dense with ornament and printed in strong colours, especially the newly-fashionable mauves and magentas (plate 82). Such designs, which complemented the other fashionable furnishings of the period, were favoured by a prosperous, self-confident middle-class, for whom such exuberance and abundance represented comfort, both physical and financial.

Amongst the miscellany of historical periods plundered for wallpaper designs, Gothic and Renaissance featured strongly. Papers with Renaissance motifs, usually printed in dark, rich colours, or as embossed imitation leathers, were used mostly in traditionally masculine rooms – the dining room, the library and the billiard room.

Also popular, particularly amongst the less well-off, were the novelty wallpapers with pictorial designs that were produced in vast quantities from the 1840s, easily outselling more restrained patterns. Their subjects were often commemorative – souvenirs of public occasions and historical events, sports and pastimes, landscape views, *trompe l'oeil* representations of picture galleries, and so on. Condemned by most discerning critics, they were nevertheless seen by some as acceptable decorations for the poorest homes, by virtue of their educational value. A writer in *The Builder* in 1851 recommended 'Historical episodes, or colonial military subjects … the life of our Great Alfred … and many views of the places in our colonies … might be represented on the paper used for covering the walls of the houses of the humbler classes of society'.[10] No doubt such papers were indeed purchased by the class he commends them to, but

86. Sanitary wallpaper commemorating Queen Victoria's Golden Jubilee of 1887; English, 1887
Colour print from engraved rollers
E.791–1970
Given by the Royal Scottish Museum, Edinburgh

Wallpapers commemorating newsworthy events such as military victories, cultural events and royal anniversaries were popular in the second half of the 19th century. This example is a 'sanitary' or washable paper, and was probably intended for use in hotels, public houses or schools.

they might also have been bought for nurseries, and perhaps schools and civic buildings. They would also have been used in inns, as an entertaining and topical decoration, or perhaps in connection with the name; Wellington's victories (in a paper of 1853–5), for example, would have found a fitting home in a public house named in his honour, just as various papers celebrating royal anniversaries and coronations would have been much at home in The Crown or The Queen's Head.

Wellington himself is said to have had a room in which newspaper cuttings concerning his victories were pasted on the walls[11], and it may be that this practice, which was commonplace in poorer homes, inspired wallpaper manufacturers to take up topical events. But prejudice against the

pictorial wallpapers remained – even Walter Crane's design, *National*, with its medallions of knights on horseback and coats of arms, issued in 1897 for Victoria's Golden Jubilee (plate 86), was considered inappropriate as domestic decoration. A writer in *The Ladies Realm* thought it '… might serve for a waiting-room wall at a railway station where her most gracious Majesty was expected, but heaven defend us from it in an ordinary house'.[12]

The subject matter of these pictorial papers may have been educational or inspirational, but the fundamental objection to them was that they violated the central principle of wall decoration, as formulated by the design critics – that decoration of a flat surface should itself be flat rather than giving an illusion of three-dimensional ornament or – worse – a three-dimensional picture. As Eastlake put it, walls should be decorated in a manner which 'will neither belie its flatness or solidity'.[13]

Design reform had of course pre-dated the Great Exhibition; that only served to give added impetus and publicity to the cause. A leading figure in the reform movement was the architect and designer A. W. N. Pugin (1812–52), an ardent campaigner for the Gothic style. He claimed this as the true British style, and promoted it on moral as well as aesthetic grounds. In the design of wallpapers he too deplored the false illusion of depth and the use of *trompe l'oeil* shadows, and argued instead for flat patterns composed of simple forms which would confirm the wall as a flat surface rather than disguising or contradicting it. Pugin was one of the first to promote the idea of 'honesty' and 'propriety' in ornament and design, thus enlisting ornament as a

87. Page from a sample book of wallpapers supplied for the decoration of the Palace of Westminster, 1851–9
Colour prints from woodblocks and flock
E.137:10–1939
Given by Mr A.L. Cowtan, in memory of his father
Arthur Barnard Cowtan, OBE

This gives some idea of the variety of patterns that Pugin designed for the Palace of Westminster, which range from simple two-colour repeats of floral motifs to complex large-scale designs embellished with gilding and flocking.

88. Wallpaper for the Palace of Westminster, 1847
Designed by A.W.N. Pugin
(1812–52)
Produced by Samuel Scott
for J.G. Crace
Colour print from woodblocks
E.150–1976

This is one of more than a hundred papers designed by Pugin for the Palace of Westminster. It exemplifies Pugin's principles of pattern design, combining rich colours with flat formalised motifs. For Pugin, Gothic was the pre-eminent style. He believed that 'All ornament should consist of enrichment of the essential construction of a building' [Pugin, *True Principles*, 1841, reprint, NY, St Martin's Press, 1973, p.1], and for him only the art and architecture of the Gothic period had fulfilled these ideals. He abhorred the debased version of the style promulgated in wallpapers illustrating Gothic ruins or elaborate architecture.

moral influence in society. He practised what he preached, designing wallpapers with flat, formalised geometric patterns such as fleurs-de-lis, quatrefoils, heraldic motifs, and flower and foliage forms adapted from medieval art, architecture and textiles, printed in the rich colours of a 'medieval' palette (plate 87). Such papers, each designed specifically for its setting, were used throughout the New Palace of Westminster (Pugin had won the commission for the interior decoration in 1835) and in his domestic projects.

He also supplied wallpaper designs to Crace & Son from 1844 onwards. Although his papers were thought to be 'too ecclesiastical and traditional in character'[14] for the general domestic market, he did supply papers for many of the houses he built for private clients, and his serious formal patterns were ideally suited to the mix of public and semi-public spaces in the Houses of Parliament; here wallpapers were mostly obviously and aptly emblematic of the moral principles deemed essential to public service and political life (plate 88).

Pugin's principle of historical authenticity in the design of ornament, and his belief that only flat patterns should adorn flat surfaces, became the fundamental tenets of the design reform movement. In the 1850s these ideas were promoted through the Government's Schools of Design in South Kensington, and by several individuals connected with them: the painter Richard Redgrave, Principal of the School; Sir Henry Cole, a civil servant, and later the V&A's first Director; and Owen Jones, a leading designer and architect. All three were keen to raise standards of design in industry and to educate public taste away from the meretricious and debased patterns which dominated the mid-century wallpaper market. Cole was Secretary to the New Department of Practical Art in London which was set up to reform training in schools and colleges across the

89. Wallpaper with design of framed horse-racing scenes, *c*.1870–80
Probably produced by Heywood, Higginbottom & Smith, Manchester
Colour machine print
E.1819–1934
Given by The Wall Paper Manufacturers Ltd

In his novel *Hard Times* Charles Dickens parodied the views of the design reform movement. To illustrate the faults of popular wallpaper patterns to a class of schoolchildren, his fictional official describes a paper with repeated naturalistic pictures of horses. However, it is unlikely that such a paper would have been used in an ordinary domestic context; its subject matter would make it an appropriate decoration for a public house, a games' room or a sportsmen's club.

country. His ideas were the subject of a thinly veiled caricature by Charles Dickens in his novel *Hard Times* (1854), in a scene in which a Government Inspector explains the principles of good taste to a class of school-children:

> Let me ask you girls and boys, would you paper a room with representations of horses? … Of course not … Do you ever see horses walking up and down the sides of rooms in reality – in fact? … Of course not. Why, then, you are not to have, in any object of use or ornament what would be a contradiction in fact … You must use for all purposes, combinations and modifications (in primary colours) of mathematical figures which are susceptible of proof and demonstration. This is the new discovery. This is fact. This is taste.[15]

But the powerful appeal of the patterns he condemns is evinced by Sissy Jupe, one of the children he addresses; raised in a circus family, she *is* used to the sight of horses around her at home, and she plaintively defends flower-patterned carpets as 'pictures of what was very pretty and pleasant'. Sissy spoke for many who would continue to buy wallpapers, carpets and fabrics adorned with 'florid and gaudy compositions … imitative flowers and foliage rendered with the full force of their natural colours'[16], despite the best attempts of Cole and his associates to persuade them otherwise (plate 89).

Owen Jones (1809–74), architect, designer and authority on historic pattern and ornament, had begun to formulate rational and reforming theories in the course of his travels in the 1830s and 1840s. He particularly admired Greek, Egyptian and Islamic (or Moorish) motifs, and adapted them into his own architectural schemes and designs for wallpaper which went into production with various manufacturers from the early 1850s. The fruits of his researches were published as *The Grammar of Ornament* (1856), an important source book for fellow designers of his own and succeeding generations. The design of geometric patterns and the division of interior walls into dado, filling and frieze (an obsessive fashion in the last quarter of the nineteenth century) were both innovations suggested by Jones's work. Though many of his patterns were geometric, reducing motifs from nature to severely ordered mathematical abstractions, his papers seem to have been more popular than those of Pugin for the ordinary domestic interior (plates 90, 91). A number of his designs were produced as machine prints, which helped to disseminate his style more widely.

George Eliot chose Owen Jones to manage the decorating and furnishing when setting up home with G. H. Lewes at the Priory in 1863. An entry in Lewes's journal, dated 13 November, reveals not only the trials of moving house, but also the bespoke design service Jones provided for his clients: '… the drawing room is still uninhabitable. Besides the trouble and vexation incident to moving we have had extra annoyances. The [piano] tuner was sick over our elegant drawing room paper, which Owen Jones had

decorated, and over the carpet! This obliges us to have fresh paper made as there are no remnants of the old, and it was originally made for us.'[17] That Eliot should choose these morally impeccable products of design reform for her own home is in keeping with her admiration of 'that sublime spirit which distinguishes art from luxury, and worships beauty apart from self-indulgence'.[18]

This moral dimension to wallpaper design was repeatedly stressed by writers who addressed themselves to a largely female audience. Women were told that 'the decoration of houses … contributes much to the education of the entire household in refinement, intellectual development, and moral sensibility'.[19] Mothers were urged to consider the injurious influence which 'false' ornament would have on their impressionable children.

By the mid-nineteenth century the home was widely regarded as the counterpoint to the outside world. Home was conceived as a refuge, a place of honesty, authenticity and uncorrupted values, raised above the worlds of business, commerce and politics. Cleanliness and order were central to the making of this happy home, but in due course the furnishings themselves were co-opted to the project of moulding the character of the inhabitants and instilling sound moral values. Decorative strategies involving illusion and deception were condemned: for example, wallpapers which imitated marble or woodgrain were regularly cited as dishonest materials, to be avoided (plate 25). Edis was the most explicit on the dangers of furnishing a home with 'dishonest' design:

> If you are content to teach a lie in your belongings, you can hardly wonder at petty deceits being practised in other ways … All this carrying into everyday life of 'the shadow of unreality' must exercise a bad and prejudicial influence on the younger members of the house, who are thus brought up to see no wrong in the shams and deceits which are continually before them.[20]

For the design reformers, good design was 'chaste' and subtle, expressing a moral rectitude. Their fight was against the kind of ornament which has been described as 'design debauchery'[21] (plate 53).

91. (*opposite*) **Wallpaper with design of formalised foliage, mid-19th century**

Designed by Owen Jones (1809–74)

Colour print from woodblocks

8337.138

Given by Miss Catherine Jones, daughter of the artist

90. (*above*) **Wallpaper with formalised floral motif, mid-19th century**

Designed by Owen Jones (1809–74)

Colour print from woodblocks

8341.57

Given by Miss Catherine Jones, daughter of the artist

Jones was a prolific designer of wallpapers. His designs drew heavily on his anthology of historic decorative motifs, published as *The Grammar of Ornament* (1856). However, unlike Pugin, Jones did not believe that one could simply reproduce past styles in a modern context. He believed that architecture and design should be of its time, but that it should look to the ornamental art of the past for inspiration. Though the forms he used were often naturalistic, he reduced them to flat forms in patterns based on 'geometrical construction' [Jones, *Grammar*, 1868, p.5]. He wrote that 'paper hangings should not call attention to themselves, but remain as a background for the paintings, engravings, and other art works' [Jones, 'Colour in the Decorative Arts', in *On the Manufacture of Glass*, ed. George Shaw, 1852, p.286] yet his wallpapers are characterised by strong colours in uncommon combinations, devised in accordance with his own colour theories.

Design reform initiatives continued well into the twentieth century with the establishment of bodies such as the Art in Industry Movement (AIM), which like its nineteenth-century predecessors was largely concerned with the education of taste amongst designers, manufacturers, retailers and the general public. The moral overtones of previous attempts were also carried forward into these later efforts. Nikolaus Pevsner wrote: '… the question of design is a social question … To fight against the shoddy design of those goods by which most of our fellow-men are surrounded becomes a moral duty.'[22] Nevertheless it was the 'bad' designs which sold in vast quantities, and the artist-designed patterns were mostly produced as smaller, more expensive 'hand-print' ranges. Gradually, however, the design establishment which had been so dismissive of wallpaper, became more accepting as designs which were more obviously contemporary began to appear.

William Morris

11

92. *(opposite)* ***Fruit (or Pomegranate) wallpaper, designed and first issued 1866***
Designed by William Morris (1834–96)
Printed by Jeffrey & Co. for Morris, Marshall, Faulkner & Co.
Print from woodblocks
E.447–1919
Given by Morris & Co.

One of the most enduringly popular of Morris's designs, *Fruit* was used in many artistic homes of the period, and is still available from the Morris & Co. division of Sandersons, who own the original printing blocks.

Morris's name and reputation are indissolubly linked to wallpaper design, but there is a tendency to over-estimate the influence he had in this field, at least in his own lifetime. In fact, despite his much repeated belief in 'art for all', his wallpapers, like most of the products of Morris & Co., were hand-made and expensive, and consequently had a relatively limited take-up. His papers were slow to find a market beyond fellow artists, and were positively disliked by some influential figures, such as Oscar Wilde. However, he has had a long-lived effect on wallpaper design and consumption, creating designs which have enjoyed lasting appeal.

Morris's first wallpaper design was *Trellis*, a pattern suggested by the rose-trellis in the garden of his house in Bexleyheath, Kent. Designed in 1862, it was not issued until 1864, a delay that was due to Morris's unsuccessful experiments with printing from zinc plates. The first pattern to be issued, in 1864, was *Daisy*, a simple design of naïvely drawn meadow flowers. The source was a wallhanging illustrated in a fifteenth-century version of Froissart's *Chronicles*[1], but similar flower forms can be seen in late medieval 'mille-fleurs' tapestries and in early printed herbals. These two designs, and the next pattern *Fruit* (also known as *Pomegranate*) (plate 92), share a medieval character that links Morris's early work in the decorative arts with the Pre-Raphaelite painters, and with Ruskin. However, they are also influenced by Morris's abiding interest in naturalism in ornament. Lecturing on pattern in 1881, he claimed, 'any decoration is futile … when it does not remind you of something beyond itself'.

His sources were plants themselves, observed in his gardens or on country walks, and also images of plants in sixteenth-century woodcuts (he owned copies of several sixteenth- and seventeenth-century herbals, including Gerard's famous *Herball*), illuminated manuscripts, tapestries and other textiles incorporating floral imagery. His designs were not to be literal transcriptions of natural forms but subtle stylised evocations. In *The Lesser Arts* he wrote: 'Is it not better to be reminded however simply of the close vine trellises which keep out the sun … or of the many-flowered meadows of Picardy … than having to count day after day a few sham-real boughs and flowers, casting sham-real shadows on your walls, with little hint of anything beyond Covent Garden in them?'[2] Although he advised those designing wallpapers to 'accept their mechanical nature frankly, to avoid falling into the trap of trying to make your paper look as if it were painted by hand', he also encouraged intricacy and elaboration so that the repeat itself was disguised.[3]

Morris designed over 50 wallpapers, and his firm produced a further 49 by other designers including George Gilbert Scott (usually credited with *Indian*, plate 94), Kate Faulkner (*Carnation*), and J.H. Dearle (*Compton*). Every pattern employs plant form, whether expressed in a luxuriant naturalism (*Acanthus, Pimpernel, Jasmine*) or a flatter, more formalised style (*Sunflower*). In common with many of the writers offering advice on home decorating, Morris maintained that the choice of wallpaper must take into account the character and function of the room. He advised that 'if there is a reason for keeping the wall quiet choose a pattern that works well all over without pronounced lines, such as Diapers, Mallows, Venetians, Poppys, Scrolls, Jasmine etc' (all plural titles of Morris & Co. papers). Alternatively, 'if you venture on a more decided patterning … you ought always to go for positive patterns … the Daisy, Trellis, Vine, Chrysanthemum … Acanthus or such'[4] (plate 97).

93. *Borage* ceiling paper, 1888–9
Designed by William Morris (1834–96)
Printed by Jeffrey & Co. for Morris & Co.
Colour print from woodblocks
E.833–1915
Given by Mr Allan F. Vigers

Though he designed several ceiling
papers Morris rather disapproved of them,
feeling that they created a box-like effect
when used with patterned walls. His
ceiling papers were generally printed in
only one or two colours and the pattern is
multi-directional.

Despite his involvement with wallpapers and his decided
views on their design and use, Morris always regarded wallpaper as a 'makeshift' decoration, a tolerable substitute for
more luxurious wall coverings. Some of the old snobbery
about wallpaper as an imitative material, a cheap option,
still persisted, and Morris, as a wealthy man, preferred
woven textile hangings for his own home. Helena Maria
Sickert described the drawing room at Kelmscott House,
Hammersmith, thus: 'beautiful blue tapestry hangings all
around the big living room … the atmosphere was deli-
ciously homely'.[5]

94. *Indian* wallpaper, first issued 1868–70
Possibly designed by George Gilbert Scott
Printed by Jeffrey & Co. for Morris, Marshall, Faulkner & Co.
Colour print from woodblocks
E.3706–1927
Given by Morris & Co.

Morris was not the sole designer of wallpapers for 'the Firm'. Patterns
were contributed by several others, in this instance, probably the
architect G.G. Scott (1811–78). He was later one of the founders of Watts
& Co., which issued some wallpapers in a similar style. The pattern was
said to be derived from an anonymous 18th-century wallpaper, but the
source for this earlier paper was an Indian chintz. A number of Morris
& Co. wallpapers were inspired by historical textiles and Morris himself
studied the textile collections in the V&A. He believed that a good
designer must look to the past, and claimed, 'However original a man
may be, he cannot afford to disregard the works of art that have been
produced in times past when design was flourishing.'

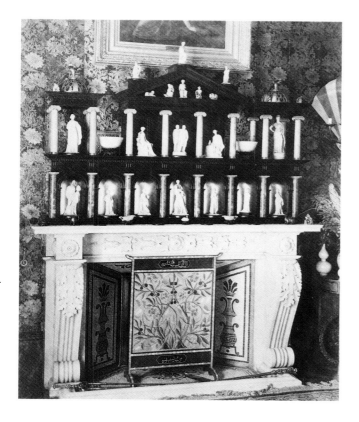

95. The Antiquities Room at 1 Holland Park, London, *c*.1898
Photograph by Bedford Lemere
E.1–1995

The wallpaper is a Morris design, *Chrysanthemum*, first issued in 1877.
The decoration of the house, completed in 1888, was the work of Morris
& Co. It was described by Gleeson White in an article in *The Studio* in
1889 as 'an epoch-making house' and 'a consistent example of the use of
fabrics and patterns designed
chiefly by Mr Morris'. However, by
this date the original effect of the
Morris & Co. scheme had been
subverted by the subsequent
accumulation of *objets d'art* and
domestic clutter.

**96. An interior at 1 Holland Park,
London, *c*.1898**
Photograph by Bedford Lemere
E.1–1995

This room, which appears to be
a morning room or family sitting
room, has been wallpapered with
Garden Tulip (1885). By the
aesthetic standards of the time
this light and relatively simple
pattern was suited to this more
informal setting, whereas heavier,
richer designs were preferred in
those rooms used for entertaining
or for study.

Though Morris himself made little use of wallpapers in
his own domestic surroundings, a number of wealthy clients
commissioned decorative schemes from Morris & Co. An
extensive redecoration of No. 1 Holland Park, for the Greek
merchant A. A. Ionides, included several wallpapers as well
as tapestries, woven hangings and painted wall decoration.
The Antiquities Room, for example, seen in a contemporary
photograph, was papered with *Chrysanthemum* (plate 95).
Other photographs show *Vine*, *Garden Tulip* (plate 96), and
various Morris papers elsewhere in the house. The Ionides
house was considered a showcase for Morris & Co. designs,
and certainly led to further commissions.

The Howard family employed the company in their
London house, and again at Castle Howard, Yorkshire, and
at Naworth Castle, Cumberland, where several Morris
papers still survive. Major country houses such as
Wightwick, near Wolverhampton, and Standen, Sussex
(completed in 1894), built by Morris's architect friend Philip
Webb were furnished extensively with Morris papers. At
Standen the Billiard Room had *Pomegranate*, while the
Drawing Room had *Sunflower* in green, as a background for

97. (*right*) *Acanthus*, **1875**
Designed by William Morris (1834–96)
Printed by Jeffrey & Co. for Morris & Co.
Print from woodblocks
E.495–1919
Given by Morris & Co.

Acanthus was one of a group of papers
Morris designed in the 1870s which are
characterised by heavy large-scale patterns
in deep colours. Thirty blocks were required
for this design making it one of the more
expensive at 16s a roll.

98. (*below*) **Bedroom at Standen, West
Sussex, with Morris's *Willow Bough*
(1887) wallpaper, renewed in the 1970s**
© National Trust Photographic Library/Jonathan
Gibson

When furnishing Standen in the 1890s the
Beale family chose Morris designs, having
already employed Morris & Co. to decorate
their London home. In accordance with
contemporary decorating advice they
preferred simple small-scale patterns in
quiet colours for papering the bedrooms,
though Morris himself believed that a large
pattern, properly designed, was more restful
to the eye.

paintings. Each of the twelve bedrooms had Morris paper,
mostly the lighter patterns (plate 98). At Wightwick, where
the decorative scheme was not supervised by Morris & Co.,
the owners chose the papers themselves and the prevailing
style and colouring was richer and more typically Victorian
than at Standen. Morris papers, such as the large-scale
Acanthus, were used in conjunction with other contemporary wallpapers, and other wall coverings, such as chintz.

Daisy, Trellis and *Pomegranate* were all used in 1867 at
Speke Hall, the house of Liverpool shipping magnate
Frederick Leyland, and he also bought Morris papers for his
London houses in the 1860s and 1870s. But generally speaking, in the early years of 'the Firm', sales of wallpapers were
rather limited, and fashionable taste took a while to accom-
modate Morris's designs. Though naturalistic, they were not
of the over-blown chintzy floral style generally described as

'French', then popular with aristocratic and wealthy customers (plate 83). On the other hand, though many were 'flat' and to a degree stylised, often drawing on medieval sources for their motifs and character, they did not have the severity and the moral overtones of 'reformed' design, typified by Owen Jones, Pugin and their followers.

Certainly Morris's papers did not find favour immediately: around 1865, Lady Mount Temple's London house was decorated in the 'French' fashion with 'watered papers on the walls, garlands of roses tied with blue bows! Glazed chintzes with bunches of roses …' She recalled that Rossetti came to dinner, and 'instead of admiring my room and decorations, as I expected, he evidently could hardly sit at ease with them'. When asked if he could suggest improvements he advised her to 'begin by burning everything you have got'. Shortly afterwards Morris & Co. carried out some renovations, and a Morris paper was hung on the staircase walls, followed in September 1865 by Morris's *Daisy* in grey in an attic room (the paper supplied by Cowtan & Son, their only order for a Morris paper around this time). The result was that 'all our candid relations and friends intimated that they thought we had made our pretty little house hideous'.[6]

Sales of Morris papers continued modestly, mostly to 'purchasers who had acidently [sic] seen some of his [Morris's] wall-papers'.[7] As Metford Warner explained later, most West End decorators dismissed his papers as 'too peculiar'[8] when they first appeared. It was only when Eastlake's book *Hints on Household Taste* (1868) stimulated wider interest in interior design that the trade, and the public, began to appreciate Morris's designs.

By the 1880s Morris papers were being recommended in many home decorating guides, including the affordable 'Art at Home' series (1876–8). Pages of each were devoted to a discussion of wallpapers, with advice on how to select the best of the latest styles. Papers by Crane, and by Morris, were regularly commended, either in the illustrations or sometimes by name (Lady Barker, for example, suggested *Vine* and *Jasmine* as suitable patterns for the drawing room). Mrs Orrinsmith's book shows three designs by Morris (*Jasmine, Rose* and *Vine*), though she does not credit

the designer or the manufacturer, which tends to suggest that she was writing for an educated audience already familiar with such designs. The writers themselves were certainly practising what they preached. The frontispiece of Robert Edis's influential book *The Furniture and Decoration of Town Houses* (1881) shows his own sitting room, with *Pomegranate* wallpaper and other 'Aesthetic' furnishings (plate 99). Certainly Morris's patterns fulfilled the

99. Frontispiece to Colonel R. W. Edis, *Decoration and Furniture of Town Houses***, London, 1881**
National Art Library

This illustration (engraved from a photograph dated *c*.1880) shows the author's own drawing room at 3 Upper Berkeley Street, Mayfair, London. The wallpaper is Morris's *Fruit*, hung below a deep hand-painted frieze. In his text Edis recommends Jeffrey & Co., the printers of Morris designs and other 'Art' wallpapers of the period.

Frontispiece

A·Drawing·Room·Corner·

R.W.EDIS. F.S.A. ARCH^T

demands of these authors for papers in 'quiet' or 'subdued' colours, and designs which were 'rich yet grave' or 'calm yet cheerful'.⁹ Though these publications were aimed at a general readership, most of the authors were themselves personally connected with artists, architects and designers, including Morris's own circle; Mrs Orrinsmith, née Lucy Faulkner, was the sister of Morris's associates Kate and William Faulkner.

By the late 1890s Morris wallpapers were commonly found in 'artistic' middle-class homes. According to the *Daily Telegraph*, 'university dons' were typical of Morris & Co.'s clientele, and 'when married tutors dawned upon the academic world, all their wives religiously clothed their walls in Norham Gardens and Bradmore Road [Oxford] with Morris designs of clustering pomegranates'.¹⁰ In the 1870s the art critic Walter Pater, who lectured at Oxford, lived in one of the newly-built houses in Bradmore Road, opposite Mr and Mrs Humphrey Ward. Mrs Ward, a best-selling novelist, described Pater's 'exquisite' house with its drawing room decorated 'with a Morris paper' and other carefully chosen Aesthetic accessories. The Wards adopted a similar style themselves, though as Mary Ward explained, the average income of married tutors was not much more than £500 a year: 'We all gave dinner-parties and furnished our houses with Morris papers, old chests and cabinets and blue pots … Most of us were very anxious to be up-to-date,

100. Decorator's specimen panel showing dado, filling and frieze wallpaper patterns printed as a single drop, c.1875–8
Possibly designed by Bruce Talbert (1838–81)
Produced by Jeffrey & Co.
Colour print from woodblocks
E.656–1953

Wall decorations divided in this way were first described in C.L. Eastlake's *Hints on Household Taste* (1868) where he recommended such schemes as a way of breaking up the monotony of a single pattern on the wall. They became a popular feature of Aesthetic interiors, printed in muted 'art' colours that owed much to Morris's influence. The rules for designing such papers were set out by a writer in the *Journal of Decorative Art* in 1886: 'the frieze should be light and lively; richer colours should be employed than in the filling, and it should be as striking to the eye as the dado.' The filling – the largest area of the wall – was the background to any paintings hung from the picture rail and so it was generally the least assertive pattern of the three.

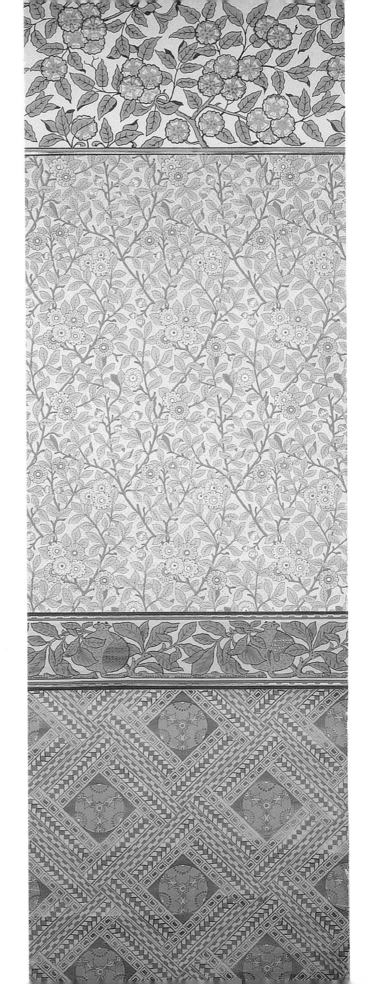

101. *(left)* **Illustration from** *The Building News*, **March 1879, showing wallpaper decorations by Jeffrey & Co.**

29502.D.60

The Building News regularly featured new wallpaper designs because their readers – architects, builders and decorators – were largely responsible for selecting wallpapers on behalf of their clients, or at least directing their choices. This shows two wall-treatments – a deep frieze and a filling by Walter Crane and a bolder scheme by Brightwen Binyon for a hall and staircase. The decoration has been adapted to fit the stair-case wall. Morris's influence is evident in the foliage pattern of the filling and in the *Daisy*-like panels at the bottom of the dado.

102. *(right)* **Illustration from** *The Building News*, **March 1879, showing** *Rose Paper* **wall decoration**

Designed by Walter Crane
Produced by Jeffrey & Co.
29502.F.38

This design (also known as *Briar Rose*) is a reworking of Crane's nursery paper, *Sleeping Beauty*, without the figures. This illus-tration makes the point that a good filling paper was designed with an unassertive 'all-over' pattern, as a suitable background to pictures.

and in the fashion, whether in aesthetics, house-keeping or education.'[11] In John Galsworthy's *The Man of Property* (1922; the first part of the Forsyte saga), Soames Forsyte, the title character, and a shrewd art collector, lives in a London house which is characterised by Aesthetic tastes, with 'inner decoration which favoured the First Empire and William Morris'.[12]

Artists themselves also favoured Morris papers. They were hung in the London home of Edward Burne-Jones, and were used throughout at 18 Stafford Terrace, the home of *Punch* cartoonist Linley Sambourne, where they were deemed the perfect complement to other Aesthetic furnish-ings – dark wood furniture, de Morgan pottery and tiles, oriental screens, fans and peacock feathers. The total cost of Sambourne's wallpaper scheme was £35 5s. In the Dining Room and the Morning Room, *Fruit* was used, with a blue

ground in the latter. The large first-floor Drawing Room was papered in a yellow and white version of *Larkspur*, a light, unassertive background to a dense hang of pictures. When the house was redecorated by Sambourne's daughter Maud in 1912, the original scheme was preserved as far as possible. Maud wrote: 'I have been to Morris's about the papers & they have all our dear old patterns. They sent me a large packet to see, & some chintzes too'[13] (plate 103).

Morris papers were each produced in several colourways, but this range of choice was not always sufficient for demanding clients. Laura Alma-Tadema wrote to Ford Madox Brown, an artist who was closely involved with Morris's firm, complaining that they had refused to supply a paper in the colour she had requested to match a chintz. She reported that the firm had replied to the effect that 'they consider their taste quite complete and they have given shades enough for me to be pleased with'.[14]

Despite the enthusiasm of aristocratic clients and artistic circles, Morris papers were not universally admired as decorations for the ordinary home. A writer in the *Journal of Decorative Arts* in 1892 praised the design and colour of Morris papers, but went on to say, 'many of the patterns are not such as to make them acceptable for general purposes. Mr. Morris is so palpably the decorator of the palace and "grande ville" that his productions are not subject to the same criticisms as those of ordinary folk. The patterns are palatial in scale, and whilst their colouring is very beautiful and soft, the magnitude of the designs exclude them from ordinary work.'[15] Certainly many of Morris's later patterns – notably *Acanthus* and *St James's* (which was in fact designed for the London palace of that name) – are on a grand scale; *St James's* requires two widths of paper to complete the pattern horizontally, and the vertical repeat is 119.4 cm, requiring two blocks to print each colour. He felt that his larger patterns worked well in smaller rooms, but this went against the prevailing view of the tastemakers from Eastlake onwards.

There is no doubt that some of Morris's designs are assertive, an effect exaggerated in certain colourways, and this was further cause for criticism. Mrs Watson, for example, condemned 'that school of mural decoration for which

103. Wallpaper stand-book for Morris & Co. showroom, 449 Oxford Street, London, *c*.1905
Wooden easel stand, with wallpaper samples (block prints and machine prints) in leatherette cover
E.2734–2866–1980
Given by Shand Kydd Ltd

This upright stand-book was typically used in wallpaper showrooms to display the range of patterns to customers. This example is big enough to show a full repeat of all but the very largest patterns. 'Table books', which could be loaned out, were rather smaller. The book includes a small selection of machine-printed papers, though the introduction stresses their inadequacies in comparison to the hand-block printed versions.

the designs of Mr William Morris may be taken as the leading type' because 'it fell into the common error of considering wallpaper as an independent system of decoration in itself, instead of as a portion of the general scheme, a background for the contents of the chamber whose nakedness it is to cover'.[16]

The subdued good taste that most Morris papers represented was not to everyone's liking. In Forster's novel *Howard's End* (1910), Margaret Schlegel comes to prefer the bold, assertive style of furnishing in the home of her friends the Wilcox family to the subtleties of the Aesthetic style she encounters elsewhere: 'After so much self-colour and self-denial Margaret viewed with relief the sumptuous dado, the frieze, the gilded wallpaper, amid whose foliage parrots sang.'[17] She recognises that the paper and the room's heavy furnishings are well matched. And Oscar Wilde, so often associated with the Morris style, in fact disliked Morris papers and preferred the Japanese leather papers which he used in his own London house at 16 (now 34) Tite Street (plate 108). The architect Richard Norman Shaw also disapproved of Morris's delight in 'glaring wallpapers', though several of his clients (such as Wickham Flower at Old Swan House) favoured them. Shaw wrote:

> It is disconcerting, you will admit, when you find that your host and hostess are less noticeable than their wallpapers and their furniture … present day belief that good design consists of pattern – pattern repeated ad nauseam – is an outrage on good taste. A wallpaper should be a background pure and simple that and nothing more. If there is any pattern at all … it ought to be of the simplest kind, quite unobtrusive …[18]

Morris's papers were too expensive for most[19], but by the 1880s their growing appeal had been recognised by other designers and manufacturers who began to produce cheaper papers in the Morris style. The Silver Studio, in particular, was responsible for many wallpapers in the Arts and Crafts and Art Nouveau styles which show clear evidence of Morris's influence and example. Even by the late 1870s machine-printed papers in the Aesthetic style were available for as little as 7d a roll. His success in creating structured patterns from natural forms, with a sense of organic growth controlled by a subtle geometry, was his most important design legacy. Morris designs seem to have satisfied a widespread desire for pattern in a way which the more formal and didactic designs of the reformers such as Jones and Pugin never did. The next generation of designers were conscious of working with Morris's legacy. For example, Charles Voysey, later described by Essex & Co. in advertisements as 'the Genius of Pattern', produced designs which show clear evidence of Morris's influence in the mastery of flat but complex patterns and in the preference for stylised organic forms and motifs from nature (plate 104).

Morris also transformed the way in which people of relatively modest means decorated their houses. By designing and selling all the ingredients of the Morris style in a single outlet, first in the relative obscurity of Bloomsbury, and from 1877 in premises on Oxford Street, he allowed the householder to furnish in a co-ordinated fashion (plate 103). His was thus one of the first 'one-stop shops' for interior decoration. Liberty's, opened in 1875, and specialising in oriental arts, was the other.

104. *The Saladin*, c.1897
Designed by Charles F.A. Voysey (1857–1927)
Produced by Essex & Co., London
Colour print from woodblocks
c.261–1953
Given by Morton Sundour Fabrics Ltd

Voysey was a prolific designer of wallpapers and textiles, many in an Art Nouveau style but clearly influenced by Morris's principles of pattern design and use of plant forms and birds. However in an interview with *The Studio* in 1893 [vol.1, 1893, p.233], Voysey claimed that with good furniture 'a very simple or quite undecorated treatment of the walls would be preferable' and that wood panelling, polished, stained or painted, was a better wall covering than paper. Nevertheless the house he built for his father two years later was decorated with Voysey wallpapers and there is photographic evidence to show that he also used them in his own house, The Orchard.

Embossed Wall Coverings

Gilt leather was widely used as a wall covering in the sixteenth and seventeenth centuries, long before paperhangings became commonplace, though it was costly to produce and was therefore found only in the houses of the wealthy. Decorated leather was first made in North Africa in the sixth century. Following the Moorish invasion of the Iberian peninsula the technique was developed there, and by the ninth century gilt leathers were being made in Spain. There the trade centred on several cities, including Cordoba, Barcelona, Seville and Madrid, reaching a flourishing climax in the sixteenth century. After 1600, Spanish production declined, but the hangings themselves were often known as 'Spanish' or Cordovan leather, even when the trade had moved on to the Netherlands, France and England. The production of leather hangings was established in London by the mid-seventeenth century, when a man by the name of Christopher is recorded as having patented a cheap method of enamelling and gilding leathers for wall decoration. And in 1666 one Hugh Robinson sought to settle in London, having learned 'to make leather more bright than gold in Amsterdam'.[1]

There is plentiful pictorial evidence of the use of gilt-embossed leather wallhangings in Dutch seventeenth-century interiors in paintings of the period; it was used in the homes of the merchant class as well as the houses of the aristocracy. The painter Johannes Vermeer had leather hangings in his own home: his inventory in Delft (dated February 1676) includes '7 *ellen goutleer aen de muyr*' [seven ells of gilt leather on the walls].[2] These paintings, with their precise renderings of interiors, show us exactly how and where leather hangings were used, as well as recording the range of different styles available.

A painting of a couple in *Interior with a Picture Collection* by Gonzales Coques, dated around 1640[3], shows a room which has been decorated throughout with a rich gilt leather. It covers the walls from the floor to the height of the door frame, including a border of a different design at the top edge. The area of wall above is left plain, as the background to a sequence of framed oils. Every other aspect of the furnishings and the dress of the couple

105. (*opposite*) **Panels of embossed, painted and gilded leather, probably commissioned by John Maitland (1616–82) for Ham House, Richmond, Surrey; probably Dutch, but possibly English, c.1672.**
HH.169–1948

These panels were hung in the dining room at Ham before they were replaced in the 1750s (see plate 107).

confirms that this is a wealthy and cultured household. Pieter de Hooch's *Interior with Figures c.*1663–5[4] shows a fine leather wallhanging (plate 106). The pattern of this leather is recorded in a contemporary Dutch engraving, one of a series of published prints which seem to have been produced as advertisements for popular patterns, and were probably sent out to potential clients. This would have been cheaper than sending out gilt-leather samples, though this practice continued through the seventeenth and into the eighteenth century.

The use of leather wallhangings was not limited to domestic interiors. A wallhanging with an elaborate pattern of floral garlands and cupids representing the five senses was ordered in November 1664 by the Brewer's Guild in Antwerp to decorate the main wall of their Guildhall, where it still hangs.

The main centres for the production of leather hangings in the seventeenth century were in fact in the Netherlands. The majority were for home consumption, but some very fine examples were exported. Until the early seventeenth century the patterns on gilt-leather hangings were either painted or stamped, but in 1628 Jacob Dircxz de Swart, a maker in the Hague, patented a new technique for embossing the patterns using engraved wooden printing blocks. Using these on thin French calfskins allowed the craftsmen

106. *Interior with Figures*, c.1663–5
Pieter de Hooch (1629–84)
Oil on canvas
The Metropolitan Museum of Art, Robert Lehman Collection, 1975 (1975.1.144);
photograph © 1990 The Metropolitan Museum

The pattern of the gilt leather wallhangings suggests that they were
probably produced in Amsterdam around 1640. The same pattern features
in the interior of Pieter de Wit's *Portrait of Dirck Wilre* in Elmina Castle,
1669 (Rijksmuseum, Amsterdam).

to produce finely detailed designs with crisp embossing.
When gilded, these raised areas caught the light and gave
a sumptuous and dramatic effect in a candle-lit interior.
Leather was also favoured in the Northern European climate as effective insulation, so these hangings were widely
sought after.

In England, the trade centred on London, and as in the
Netherlands, gilt leathers were used in the well-to-do, but
not necessarily aristocratic houses. For example, on 19
October 1660, Samuel Pepys recorded: 'This morning my
dining-room [in his house in Seething Lane] was finished
with green serge hanging and gilt leather, which is very
handsome.'[5] A gilt leather with a Bacchus and Ceres pat-
tern was installed in Dyrham Park, Gloucestershire, in 1702,
but the same pattern or mirror images of it occur across
Northern Europe: in the presbytery of the church in
Kartuzy, Poland; in a bedroom at Grimbergen Castle in
Humbeek, Belgium; and, as fragments, in the Swedish
Royal castle of Ulriksdal. Around 1756 the 4th Earl of Dysart
acquired a 'Sett of gilt Leather Hangings White and gold,
Mosaic Pattern'[6] which still hang in the Marble Dining
Room at Ham House, Surrey (plate 107). This was the cen-
tral room on the domestic floor where the family lived, and
it was originally hung with a leather patterned with cherubs,
fruit and flowers, dating from the 1670s (plate 105).

A speciality of the English leather workshops was the production of chinoiserie-style gilt-leather hangings and leathers painted with pictorial scenes of Chinese life, in imitation of the hand-painted wallpapers then fashionable. A 1690 inventory mentions 'hangings of gilt leather' in Mary Luttrell's closet at Dunster Castle, Somerset; these were later sent to her home, Milton Abbey in Dorset. An impressive set of pictorial leather hangings depicting the story of Antony and Cleopatra (possibly English-made), dating from the late seventeenth century, still survives in the gallery at Dunster. Margaret Luttrell (1726–66) proposed to repair them with 'a gilt leather border' in 1759, and they do have a floral border of a later date than the narrative panels.[7]

Like the wallpapers which gradually superseded them, leather hangings in Britain first took their designs from textiles, especially silk brocades. Following the invention of the embossing method, painters and silversmiths prepared designs specifically for the gilt-leather industry – these tend to be characterised by floral and foliate scrolls, birds, insects, cupids and other figures. In the early eighteenth century the designs became more formal and obviously symmetrical, a change which has been attributed to the influence of the designer Daniel Marot (1663–1752). In due course these heavier patterns gave way to a lighter, more informal style inspired by contemporary silks and chintzes.

The fashion for gilt-leather hangings was declining in England by the middle of the eighteenth century, as they were supplanted by wallpapers. They lasted a little longer in the Netherlands, and were still being used as late as 1756. An English traveller, Mrs Calderwood, recorded in her journal for this year: 'The Dutch have not come into the taste of paper in their houses; velvet and leather hangings are still much used.'[8]

In the late nineteenth century there was a revival of interest in leather wall coverings, both in Europe and America, particularly in Renaissance-style decorative schemes, and also for Aesthetic interiors. In some cases antique examples were used but these were both rare and expensive. Demand prompted the development of cheaper alternatives – the so-called 'leather papers' and imitations in other materials (plate 108). From the 1870s embossed and lacquered 'wallpapers' which were convincing imitations of tooled leather were produced in Japan for export to Europe. The first designs were thought to be too distinctively Japanese for the average English interior, but by the mid-1880s the Japanese product had been modified to suit

107. The Marble Dining Room, Ham House, Richmond, Surrey, with white and gold embossed leather wallhangings, c.1756
The National Trust, photo courtesy of V&A Picture Library

These embossed leather wallhangings replaced a more richly decorative set, with an elaborate design of cherubs, flowers and birds (see plate 105). The installation of this second set was a very late example of the fashion in England. Leather panels were thought to be particularly appropriate for dining rooms because leather did not absorb food smells as textile or flock hangings did.

European tastes, and was being imported in large quantities, notably by Rottmann, Strome & Co., a British firm who had even established their own factory near Yokohama. In Europe, imitation leather papers were produced by firms who were already making wallpapers, such as Jeffrey & Co. in England and Paul Balin in France, and in 1886 Sandersons set up a large department solely for the importation and sale of the Japanese leather papers.

These imitation leathers, with their lacquered and 'gilded' surfaces, were impressive and hard-wearing. They were also relatively expensive, costing between 20s and 80s per roll of 12 square yards (10m²). Many of the designs were based on sixteenth- and seventeenth-century originals; one of the Paul Balin papers in the Sanderson archive has a ticket inscribed: 'No. 4998 *Executé d'apres un cuir de Cordove*' [Made after a Cordovan leather].

Imitation leathers, and other kinds of embossed and relief decoration, were thought to be most suitable for halls, stairways, dining rooms, studies and libraries. Some recommended them for drawing rooms too; an illustration in the *Journal of Decorative Arts*, 1884, shows Rottmann's 'Japanese Leather Papers' combining a Japanese style in the dado with more obviously European patterns in filling and frieze. The overall effect is rich and heavy. Examples of the fill pattern were known to have been used in houses in Boston and Chicago.

Jeffrey & Co., known for their 'art' wallpapers, marketed a number of embossed and gilded imitation leathers, the work of designers such as Walter Crane and Morris. Edis proposes the use of embossed imitation leathers for their practical virtues, and recommends those from Jeffrey & Co. in particular (plate 109). Oscar Wilde rejected patterned wallpapers in favour of Japanese gold papers which he described as 'exceedingly decorative … no English paper can compete with them, either for beauty or for practical wear'.[9] At the Athenaeum, a London gentlemen's club, the Morning Room had 'walls of gold Japanese leather'; the *Art Journal* described the scheme as 'sumptuous and daring'.[10]

Various other relief decorations were developed in the last decades of the nineteenth century. The trade name 'Cordelova' was given to one of these made from pressed

108. Sample of paper imitating embossed leather, c.1890–1900
Produced for Liberty & Co. Embossed paper, with bronze pigment
E.436–1999
Given by Mr Paul Reeves

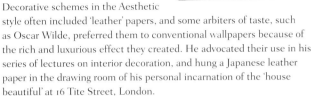

Decorative schemes in the Aesthetic style often included 'leather' papers, and some arbiters of taste, such as Oscar Wilde, preferred them to conventional wallpapers because of the rich and luxurious effect they created. He advocated their use in his series of lectures on interior decoration, and hung a Japanese leather paper in the drawing room of his personal incarnation of the 'house beautiful' at 16 Tite Street, London.

paper. In the Library at Dunster Castle, created by Salvin in 1870–1 in a Renaissance style, a Cordelova imitation leather was used, inkeeping with the overall style of the scheme. Scott Morton patented a material called Tynecastle Tapestry, a canvas material forced into patterned moulds to give an embossed surface. Embossing was also used to give a textured finish to printed papers which imitated textiles, making them more convincing.

The most popular and commercially successful of these embossed wall coverings were Lincrusta Walton (developed in 1877) and Anaglypta. Lincrusta, made of similar materials to linoleum (which was also invented by Frederick Walton), was welcomed because it was waterproof and washable (plate 110). It was also sturdy and lasted much longer than paper, even the washable sanitary wallpaper. Indeed it was advertised as 'the indestructible wall covering' and has been found in an extraordinary range of interiors, including old railroad cars, a log cabin (actually richly furnished and used as a hunting lodge and exclusive poker club by a wealthy mine owner) in Leadville, Colorado, and the New York mansion of millionaire John D. Rockefeller (the latter a richly gilded design in the Aesthetic style). A retrospective description of Oscar Wilde's Smoking Room in his house in Tite Street, Chelsea, as it was around 1891, includes the observation that 'The walls were covered with the peculiar wallpaper of that era, known as Lincrusta Walton, and had a William Morris pattern of dark red and dull gold.'[11] It lent itself to intricate

109. Wall covering imitating embossed and gilded leather, late 19th century
Produced by Jeffrey & Co.
Embossed paper with red and gold pigments
E.9–1945
Given by Mrs Margaret Warner

This design, with its putti and garlands in high relief, is closely related to the real leather hangings used in 17th-century Dutch interiors. It is richly coloured and lavishly gilded, as were the originals, although the gilding is tarnished and stained in places. Contemporary writers on interior decoration often recommended these luxurious but practical 'leather' papers for dining rooms.

designs, and a variety of treatments – it could be left plain, or painted, stained, varnished or gilded to resemble wood, plaster or leather most effectively. Avant-garde designers such as the Art Nouveau architect Hector Guimard produced designs for Lincrusta. Though cheaper than embossed leather or plaster reliefs, Lincrusta was still too expensive for the mass-market. A cheaper alternative, Anaglypta (made of cotton fibre pulp), was introduced in 1886 and by the 1890s was one of the most popular wall

coverings available. It was lighter and easier to install than Lincrusta, and it also took finer designs.

Though Lincrusta and Anaglypta have continued in production to the present, they have experienced long periods when they were out of favour. Their contrasting characteristics of durability and potential for ugliness are neatly encapsulated in a war-time anecdote. Writing in 1943, A.S.G. Butler acknowledged 'the triumph of Lincrusta. I do not mean aesthetically but quite the opposite, in a military sense. No material has … stood up to the blast so stoutly … It quite hurts me to think that something we have scoffed at for years has turned out a valuable ally in a fight. A pity it is so unattractive, especially when painted chocolate.'[12]

In the later twentieth century the use of 'wood-chip' papers was commonplace. Such papers were low-cost, practical and hard-wearing. The lightly textured surface created by incorporating wood chips or shavings in the paper had the advantage of disguising an unevenly plastered wall. There was no repeat to be matched so it was easy to hang, and like Lincrusta or Anaglypta it could then be painted. It has become a by-word for the bland and the boring, a 'safe', practical choice for decorating on the cheap.·

Shelf mark: PP.1803.kab

110. An advertisement for Lincrusta Walton in *The Journal of Decorative Art* (London), March 1884
Chromolithograph
By permission of the British Library

Made of linoleum, Lincrusta was a relief decoration giving the effect of embossed leather or carved wood panelling, but cheaper and more hardwearing. It was often used for the dado, with a wallpaper above, but here the entire scheme is composed of variant patterns in Lincrusta, from the dark-brown dado (in a design imitating wainscoting) to the filling, in a lighter all-over foliage pattern, and the frieze, highlighted with gold.

Health and Cleanliness

111. *(opposite)* **Sanitary wallpaper, 1895**
Produced by David Walker of Middleton, Lancashire
Colour print from engraved rollers
E.1943–1952
Given by Mr J. Robertshaw

Though technically innovative, most sanitaries were scorned by the design reformers because the fine detail permitted by the printing process – mechanised stipple engraving – encouraged the production of dense and 'busy' pictorial designs like this.

By the late nineteenth century it had become apparent that one of the drawbacks of wallpaper was its tendency to accumulate dirt, such as dust, soot and grease. Unlike wood-panelling ('wainscot') or distempered walls, it could not be cleaned, and once the grime began to show it had to be replaced. In his novel *Bel-Ami* (1885), Maupassant suggests the squalor and poverty of a Parisian lodging house of the period by describing the 'wallpaper, grey with a blue floral pattern [which] had as many stains as flowers, ancient, dubious-looking stains that could have been squashed insects or oil, greasy finger-marks from hair cream or dirty soap suds from the wash-basin'[1] (plate 112).

For an earlier period a papered room had been a sign of cleanliness and good housekeeping. In 1795 the *Journal du Lycée des Arts* declared 'For appearance, cleanliness and elegance, these papers [i.e. wallpapers] are to be preferred to the rich textiles of yesteryear.'[2] Hannah Solly's diary account of her family's summer holiday travels records their arrival at lodgings in Oban where they were 'highly delighted by the sight of a clean papered room. We were never more awake to the charms of cleanliness, having been in so many dirty stinking Holes for some days past.'[3] William Beckford, 'when about to sleep at an inn order[ed] it to be papered for him at the expense of £10', presumably as a precaution to ensure that it would be clean.[4] In fact and in fiction there are frequent references to whitewashing or re-papering to make an otherwise poorly built or damp room look fresh, clean and dry.

Before the introduction of washable wall coverings some manufacturers made a virtue of designs which simply didn't show the inevitable dirt too obviously. A 1786 advertisement in an American newspaper claimed: 'flies and smoke operate to soil paper in common rooms if the goods are too delicate; to prevent which I have pin-grounds that fly-marks will not be perceptible upon (plate 113). Also dark grounds which the smoke will not considerably affect in the course of twenty years, at such low prices will eventually be found cheaper than whitewash.'[5] This continued to be an important consideration, especially for public and commercial buildings. In a letter of 1902 a man fitting up a

Texas hotel wrote to his partner in New York: 'Paper should be strong, pretty and cheap. Patterns to reflect light as much as possible without too gaudily displaying dirt, tobacco juice, etc.'[6]

Much of the advice about wallpaper found in the many guides and manuals concerned with furnishing, decoration and household management in the later decades of the nineteenth century relates specifically to the problems of dirt and dust. Most of these publications were aimed at the residents of ordinary middle-class homes, often town houses. The authors address the day-to-day problems of the dirt, dust and grime that were so much a part of nineteenth-century urban life. Homes were heated by open coal fires and lit by smoky oil lamps, while an open window would let in air that was often a noxious smog, compounded of factory fumes, soot and smoke. Various suggestions were made about choosing wallpapers conducive to domestic health and cleanliness.

Preparing the walls prior to hanging the papers was also important. Eastlake says that papering over the old wallpaper is 'a slovenly and unhealthy practice',[7] while Edis advises against flock because of its inherent tendency to gather dust. Others objected to wallpapers being used in

112. (*right*) **Floral wallpaper; English, *c*.1850–75**
From Uppark, West Sussex
Colour print from engraved rollers
E.800–1969
Given by Mrs Jean Meade-Fetherstonhaugh

Before the invention of washable surfaces, and the practice of varnishing the surface, papers quickly became marked, stained or simply accumulated surface dirt. One of the advantages of machine-printed papers was that they were cheap enough to replace regularly, giving an appearance of cleanliness. However, in 1903 Arthur Seymour Jennings noted of American homes that it was customary among the 'common class' to repaper a room without removing the previous layers: 'The custom of papering over old paper is disgusting. It covers old dirt, disease, germs and insects.' [AJS, *Wallpapers and Wall coverings*, William T. Comstock, New York, 1903, p.105.]

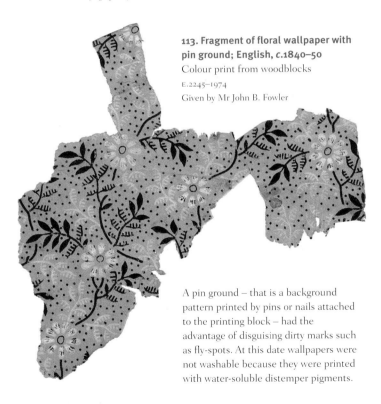

113. Fragment of floral wallpaper with pin ground; English, *c*.1840–50
Colour print from woodblocks
E.2245–1974
Given by Mr John B. Fowler

A pin ground – that is a background pattern printed by pins or nails attached to the printing block – had the advantage of disguising dirty marks such as fly-spots. At this date wallpapers were not washable because they were printed with water-soluble distemper pigments.

bedrooms because it was thought that they harboured insects such as bed bugs – a particular nuisance in inns and lodging houses. Elizabeth Wirt, in Washington, wrote: 'This *papering of chambers* is a dreadful business' of her struggle to eradicate bugs in the nursery. She tore off the paper and rubbed the wall cracks with spirit of turpentine, and declared, 'If after all this I do not get the mastery of *mine enemy* I shall give up.'[8]

This was still a problem in cheap hotels in the 1930s. In *Down and Out in Paris and London*, George Orwell described his lodgings in the Hotel des Trois Moineaux as 'a dark, rickety warren ... small and inveterately dirty ... the walls were thin as matchwood, and to hide the cracks they had been covered with layer after layer of pink paper, which had come loose and housed innumerable bugs'.[9] Lady Barker, in her book on the bedroom and boudoir, considers the treatment of walls at length, because they are 'the most important from a sanitary point of view'. She suggests painted or distempered walls, but says she prefers paper because it is important that these rooms should be 'extremely pretty'.[10]

Rhoda and Agnes Garrett recommended that the decorations on walls and ceilings be 'as inexpensive as possible' because 'they are certain to get dirty in our smoky atmosphere', and too often dirt is put up with because 'the decorations cost so much not so long ago', whereas a cheap paper can be replaced as necessary.[11] However, it is significant that none of these writers suggests using the new 'sanitary' papers which were specifically designed to be washable. Only Lady Barker, in an oblique reference, mentions papers 'made expressly, which do not attract dirt' and suggests that some are of 'lovely design'.[12] But for most authorities it seems that their practical advantages were vitiated by their poor colouring – either dull or garish – and their designs, which embodied all the faults of the popular patterns of the mid-century (plate 111). The earliest sanitaries were either pictorial, or made in imitation of other materials, often tiles or mosaics, in an obvious reference to their own claims to waterproof durability (plates 114, 115).

Nineteenth-century manuals do recommend other strategies to protect the wallpaper, such as the use of a panelled dado up to a height of three feet because it protects 'delicately-tinted paperhangings' from 'contact with chairs and careless fingers'.[13] Edis advocates the use of embossed imitation leather, lacquered and varnished, because it will not be affected 'by gas or smoke'; he recommends such papers as supplied by Jeffrey & Co.[14] But it seems that the sanitary papers themselves were thought fit only for the poor. The sternly didactic *Journal of Decorative Arts* published an article in 1887 entitled 'The homes of the Lower Classes; How to make them Sweet, Clean and Beautiful', which proposed the use of the economical hard-wearing sanitary papers for poorer houses.[15]

Distemper colours, used to print most wallpapers, were not waterproof, and manufacturers had been trying to produce a washable paper since the mid-century. In 1853 John Stather produced oil-printed papers, but it took another 20 years to develop a commercially viable process. In the meantime varnishes and other treatments were used to waterproof conventionally printed papers. In the early 1870s the Manchester company Heywood Higginbottom & Smith produced a monochrome washable paper printed in oil colours from copper rollers; this success was soon followed

114. (*below*) **Tile pattern sanitary wallpaper from a pattern book of sanitary and ingrain wallpapers, 1923–4**
Produced by Cole & Son (Wallpapers) Ltd
Colour machine print from engraved rollers, varnished
E.2651–1983
Given by Cole & Son (Wallpapers) Ltd

Sanitary papers, introduced fifty years earlier, remained popular for halls, passageways, kitchens, sculleries and bathrooms well into the 1930s. To emphasise the fact that they were washable, sanitary papers were often designed to imitate other hardwearing washable surfaces such as marble, wood panelling or tiling.

115. (*right*) **A bathroom – No.19 in *The Decorative Use of Wallpapers*, a volume of illustrations showing the use of wallpapers in a variety of domestic interiors; British, *c*.1910**
Colour half-tone
E.2017–1990

The room is decorated with panels of 'a plain blue varnished brick paper with a stile of varnished crackle paper and narrow border.' The ceiling has an Anaglypta border.

by other firms, such as Lightbown, Aspinall, who launched polychrome sanitaries in 1884. These were printed by engraved copper rollers with finely ground pigments to produce a fine, smooth surface which was then varnished.

From the 1880s tile patterns were a favourite style of decoration in the bathrooms of more modest homes (a good example can be seen in the Amy Miles' dolls-house, dated 1890, at the Bethnal Green Museum of Childhood). These economical strategies were disparaged by the critics who objected to their deceitful character. Warren K. Clouston, writing in the *Ladies Realm* in 1897 said, 'The poor bathroom is never allowed to be anything but a sham. The speculative builder has but two ideas: to cover the walls with a fearful mosaic paper … or else to content himself in the cheaper houses, with an equally hideous imitation of plain tiles … I hate imitations of all sorts, and if you cannot have real tiles do not have a copy.'[16] Some of these tile patterns were simple, but among examples produced by John Stather & Sons were elaborate designs copied from Turkish 'Iznik' tiles.

Naturally, bathrooms, kitchens and sculleries were the rooms most often papered with sanitaries, but such papers were also widely used in halls, passages and staircases. A showroom specimen from the London firm Dugdale, Poole & Co., of the 1880s, is labelled: 'A New Sanitary Decoration for Halls, Dining Rooms and Stairways'.[17] Some nursery papers were also produced as sanitaries. Kate Greenaway's drawings for her *Almanack* of 1893 were acquired by David Walker & Co. of Middleton, near Manchester, 'with especial and exclusive permission to reproduce them as designs for "sanitary wallpapers".'[18] Although there is little surviving evidence, it seems very likely that they were also used in pubs and hotels; a number of pictorial and commemorative papers were produced as sanitaries, notably for Queen Victoria's Golden Jubilee in 1887 – the pictorial design is much better suited to a pub than to a domestic setting, and washable papers would have been a great advantage in such a setting (plate 86).

Arsenic and lead in wallpaper pigments were other health hazards. In 1775 the Swedish chemist Scheele discovered a pigment containing arsenic (copper arsenite), thereafter known as 'Scheele's green'. By 1800 this was

116. A 'sanitary' wallpaper; English, *c*.1903
Designed by Arthur Gwatkin (worked *c*.1890–*c*.1903)
Produced by Wylie & Lochhead
Machine printed from engraved rollers
E.467–1967
Given by Miss Mary Peerless

The fashionable Art Nouveau-style has been applied here to the design of a sanitary or washable wallpaper. Since the 1870s most sanitary papers had been poorly designed and manufacturers had favoured pictorial patterns or imitations of mosaics, marble or tiles.

widely used in paints, fabrics and wallpapers. Mrs Beeton warned against 'Brilliant (emerald) green, which contains arsenic, and some kinds of glossy white, which is produced by the use of oxide of lead', both of which had a 'pernicious influence on the health'.[19] Rhoda and Agnes Garrett considered these bright greens to be 'aesthetically as well as physically poisonous'.[20] The often-cited story of Napoleon dying on the island of St Helena, poisoned by the arsenic in his wallpaper, has been disproved, though there was a paper printed with an arsenic green pigment in the Drawing Room of his residence, Longwood House, and the place was chronically damp, an aggravating factor.[21] However, it is certainly true that the vapour containing arsenic given off by this pigment on a damp wallpaper could be injurious to health, especially for children or the sick. Illnesses and even deaths were often attributed to wallpapers described as 'highly arsenical'[22]. This was yet another reason for avoiding wallpaper in bedrooms.

Jeffrey & Co. were one of the first manufacturers to respond to growing public concern about the levels of lead and arsenic in wallpaper pigments. In 1879 they invited Robert E. Alison, an eminent chemist at the Royal Arsenal, Woolwich, to examine their products; he declared them entirely free of poisonous substances, and from then on Jeffrey papers enjoyed an enhanced reputation for health and safety as well as for artistic qualities. In the mid-1880s they produced a range of 'Patent Hygienic Wallpapers', with designs by artists including Crane, William Burges and Bruce Talbert. These were shown at the International Health Exhibition in London in 1884 where one critic remarked 'with our walls covered with such papers we can gratify our artistic taste and at the same time may rest assured that we are not slowly being poisoned'.[23]

Though the earlier examples were dismissed by critics as aesthetically poor, by the 1890s sanitaries were being designed in fashionable styles by named designers. Arthur Gwatkin's Art Nouveau-style sanitary friezes, such as *Flaming Tulip*, 1901, for Wylie & Lochhead, were said to be very popular (plate 116). Certainly they employed richer colours and more elegant designs than those which preceded them. Some manufacturers of 'art' wallpapers, such as Essex & Co., sold huge quantities of sanitary papers, but the proprietor continued to abhor this popular taste and claimed he never sold them 'without a protest' because, in his view, they lacked artistic character.[24]

Manufacturers even co-opted medical opinion to support the use of wallpaper, and to guide customers' choices of colour and pattern. The pattern book *Backgrounds of Character* (1926), from T. Whatley & Son of Middlesbrough, is prefaced by quotes from an anonymous Harley Street doctor. He says, 'Wallpapers are the most important of all the furnishings of a room; because either they swallow up the light and make the room dark, or else they give the light back to our eyes and bodies. In the one case we live in "dark air", which is weakening; in the other case the air is filled with light, and so acts on our lungs as a tonic.' Mental

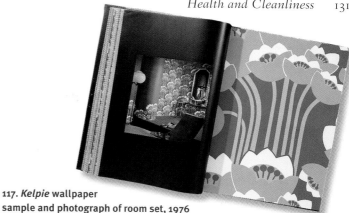

117. *Kelpie* wallpaper sample and photograph of room set, 1976
From *Studio One*, a pattern book of vinyl wallpapers in the Vymura range, produced by ICI (Ltd) Paints Division
Screen print
E.1102–1979
Given by ICI (Ltd) Paints Division

Large-scale patterns, first seen in the innovative *Palladio* range, continued to be popular in the 1970s. The colours and the stylised floral motif of *Kelpie* are reminiscent of the Art Nouveau-inspired style and colour schemes exemplified by the influential Biba range of clothes and accessories in the late 1960s and early 1970s.

health was also taken into consideration. Mrs Beeton warned that 'care should be taken in choosing bedroom papers to avoid any outré forms which the eye of a restless invalid, condemned to weary hours of solitude, could torture into the form or face of demon or grotesque horror'.[25] This concern continued, with an article in the US magazine *House Beautiful* arguing in 1915 against 'nervous discordant' colours that bred neurasthenia. By this date wallpapers were required to be 'quiet' and 'restful'.[26]

In the twentieth century new kinds of washable coatings were developed and applied to papers designed especially for the kitchen and bathroom. In the 1950s and 1960s, pictorial patterns relating to the function of the room were popular – fruit and vegetables in kitchens, soaps, toothbrushes and rubber ducks for the bathroom. Where the old sanitaries had soon yellowed to a dirty nicotine colour as the varnish was degraded by exposure to light, the new papers used vinyl resins or latex derivatives which stayed fresh and clean-looking. By 1961 ICI had developed 'Vymura', a paper coated with PVC and printed with specially developed inks. Such papers were no longer limited to kitchen and bathroom, but were promoted for use throughout the house (plate 117). A bold screen-printed vinyl, *Kenzan*, was presented as a classy decoration in the hallway of the home of actress Susan Hampshire[27] in Sandersons' successful 'VIP' campaign in the mid-1970s, and the rehabilitation of the 'sanitary' wallpaper was complete.

Wallpapers for Children

Children were generally housed in separate rooms or apartments in grand houses, although these rooms were not supplied with decorations or furnishings specific to children. But with the rise of an urban and suburban middle-class from the first decades of the nineteenth century, together with the separation of workplace and home, the houses of the middle-class also had, for the first time, sufficient space to dedicate rooms, even whole floors, to the accommodation of children and their carers – the nursemaid (later nanny) and the governess. This development was certainly fostered by writers on architecture, house decoration, and household management. For example, in *The Suburban Gardener and Villa Companion* (1838), J.C. Loudon told his readers that, wherever possible, rooms were being set aside for children, and that these rooms were to be called 'nurseries'.[1]

With the setting up of nurseries came the introduction of furnishings of all kinds designed specifically for children's use; these included wallpapers, though none have so far been discovered dating from any earlier than the third quarter of the nineteenth century. However, it seems to have taken some time for nursery wallpapers to become commonplace. In 1881, Col. R.W. Edis observed, 'In the dreariness of town houses, nothing has struck me as so utterly cruel as the additional dreariness which generally pervades the rooms especially devoted to children.'[2]

A number of the earliest papers, though drawing their subject matter and illustrations from popular literature, were clearly intended to have an improving influence, with mothers charged both with the moral education of their children and with decorating a home in accordance with those same moral principles. This accorded with the widely held view that children were uniquely sensitive to their environment, and must therefore be surrounded by things which were beautiful, 'honest' and inspiring, so the production of wallpapers which made this task easier was sound business sense. A popular poem in the 1840s by Suffolk Quaker Bernard Barton conflates the didactic role of furnishings with the mother's role as teacher; it was entitled 'The Mother of Dr Doddridge Teaching Him Scripture from the Dutch Tiles'.[3] It seems very likely that a similarly

118. (*opposite*) ***The Sleeping Beauty*, 1879**
Designed by Walter Crane (1845–1915)
Produced by Jeffrey & Co.
Colour machine print
E.60–1968

This nursery paper was included in the range of Patent Hygienic Wallpapers produced by Jeffrey & Co. in the 1880s, and promoted as being free from arsenic and also washable. The same design, without the figures, was reissued in 1880 as a block print called *The Briar Rose* (see plate 102).

didactic purpose was envisaged by parents who chose to furnish a nursery with wallpapers illustrating scenes from Bunyan's *Pilgrim's Progress* or Defoe's *Robinson Crusoe* (both from the period 1850–75), each an example of improving literature, though neither written specifically for children (plate 119). This idea, that children's wallpaper should serve to educate both in terms of informing, but also in terms of offering moral exemplars, is made explicit in the advice of Colonel Edis on the decoration of nurseries. He devotes several pages of his book *The Decoration and Furniture of Town Houses* (1881) to a discussion of the subject and suggests: 'Why not cover the walls of the nurseries with illustrations telling of the glories, and, if you please, the horrors of war – teaching peace and goodwill by illustrating the anti-type.' He goes on to list other suitable subjects such as 'the various birds, beasts and reptiles that went into the ark...flowers and all other things which are bright and beautiful', and says, 'All these would make the children's room a bright and cheery spot, and in pleasant guise teach them many things, better than all the lesson books in the world.'[4] He concludes that 'the writing on the wall' should be the earliest teaching of all that is beautiful in nature, art or science', and that 'illustrations of fairy lore [will] incline the thoughts of our little ones to all that is graceful and beautiful in imaginative faculties'.[5]

Edis makes no distinction between the sexes in the subjects he advocates for nursery wallpapers, but is clear that

119. (*right*) **Nursery wallpaper illustrating episodes from *Robinson Crusoe* by Daniel Defoe; English, *c*.1875–1900**
Printed from engraved rollers
E.714–1952
Given by Mr Wyndham Payne

120. (*above*) **Nursery wallpaper with representations of the Four Seasons; English, *c*.1850–75**
Colour print from woodblocks
E.1114–1921
Given by Mr Basil Ionides

although some wallpapers – such as nursery rhymes or 'Noah's Ark' subjects – were designed to appeal to young children of both sexes, others show a distinct gender bias. The neat, clean little girls who gather flowers and play with babies in *The Months* (machine print by David Walker & Co., 1893), a wallpaper derived from the hugely popular illustrations by Kate Greenaway, embody the distinctly feminine virtues expected of the middle-class female child (plate 121). (Nevertheless, this paper was used for the large day nursery at Erddig in 1903, although the nursery housed two boys.[6]) Lady Barker reiterates the point in *The Bedroom and Boudoir* (1878), where she says that boys should be given room to play without being constrained by their furnishings, but girls should be expected 'to keep their rooms

neat and clean'.[7] A boy might be expected to draw inspiration and a sense of his future role in the world by spending his formative years surrounded by a wallpaper which recasts Defoe's eponymous hero in the mould of a Victorian Empire-builder, subduing and civilising savage nations.

121. (*opposite*) **Nursery wallpaper, *The Months*, with illustrations taken from Kate Greenaway's *Almanack*, 1893**
Produced by David Walker, Middleton, Lancashire
Colour print from engraved rollers
E.1823–1934
Given by The Wall Paper Manufacturers Ltd

This was produced as a sanitary paper, as were many of the first nursery designs. It was issued with a matching frieze based on Greenaway illustrations representing the seasons.

From their wallpapers, Victorian children might learn the alphabet, but they would also get a lesson in the deportment appropriate to their class and gender. As Samuel Smiles wrote 'The nation comes from the nursery.'[8]

This pedagogic approach to furnishing a child's surroundings continued – in their influential book *The Decoration of Houses*, first published in 1897, Edith Wharton and Ogden Codman proposed that 'the child's surroundings may be made to develop his sense of beauty'. They compared 'poor pictures, trashy "ornaments" [i.e. patterns], and badly designed furniture' to 'a mental diet of silly and ungrammatical story-books'.[9]

From the 1870s onwards, many more nursery wallpapers appeared, the great majority with subjects adapted from children's books. Indeed some were the work of artists and designers who were themselves directly involved in book illustration, though others such as Greenaway and Caldecott simply allowed their illustrations to be purchased for the purpose. Perhaps the best known artist associated with the design of nursery wallpapers was Walter Crane, a prolific illustrator of fairy tales and toy books. His wallpaper designs, produced by the fashionable manufacturer and retailer of 'art' wallpapers, Jeffrey & Co., illustrate nursery rhymes – such as *The House That Jack Built* (1886) – or fairy tales – such as *Sleeping Beauty* (1879) (plate 118). Crane's wallpapers were bought by discerning customers concerned for their children's pleasure and comfort: in 1874 Samuel and Olivia Clemens built a splendid new house in Hartford, Connecticut, and a few years later, having more money, they decorated the nursery with Crane's *Miss Mouse at Home* (also known as *Ye Frog He Would A-Wooing Go*) (1877), newly available in America. In November 1879 Olivia Clemens wrote to her mother: 'The nursery is perfect ... When I remember the sense of being taken care of ... I feel I must give the same sense to the children.'[10] A Crane nursery rhyme paper was also used by the Earl and Countess of Carlisle at Naworth Castle, and in the top floor nursery of artist Linley Sambourne's London house. Both families favoured Morris papers elsewhere in their houses.

Crane's papers telling 'the tales of fairy land and nursery rhyme' were praised for their educational potential. A writer in the *British Architect*, 1884, suggested that 'With the aid of a little intelligent and sympathetic talk, nursery walls, covered with these designs, might be made to *live* within the lives of children. They would repay their cost many times.'[11]

On the whole, Crane's nursery wallpapers are flatter than his other designs, with simple obvious repeats that make them easier to 'read'. Indeed, they appear to be direct adaptations of book illustrations, with little modification. Only *Sleeping Beauty* employs a hidden repeat, which makes it more decorative than narrative, more pattern than picture. Another important point was that his nursery wallpapers, unlike his other papers for Jeffrey & Co., were all machine prints, and therefore significantly cheaper than the majority of his papers. Edis recommends Crane's papers as 'admirably adapted for the walls of day nurseries, and cheap ... enough to be frequently changed'.[12] It would no doubt have been considered an unnecessary extravagance to use expensive hand-block printed papers in rooms where their only adult audience would have been the servants, and where they would soon have become grubby and graffitied, and would therefore need to be regularly replaced. For the same reason, it seems that nursery patterns were amongst the earliest of the so-called 'sanitary' papers, which were printed with fast colours, or varnished, to render them washable (see 'Health and Cleanliness').

Edis also makes a novel suggestion which combines an educational element with economy. He suggests allowing children to cut what he describes as the 'really good illustrations' from the many monthly and weekly periodicals, and use them 'to paper over the whole of the lower portion of the walls'.[13] In similar fashion a decorative frieze could be devised using illustrations from the Christmas books illustrated by Henry Stacy Marks, Walter Crane and Greenaway, and pasting them up 'in regular order and procession'.[14] Children and teenagers have continued this DIY tradition, personalising their rooms by pasting up newspaper and magazine cuttings illustrating their hobbies, passions and 'crushes' – favourite subjects include horses, cats, aircraft, pop singers and actors.

Mrs Beeton, writing on the furnishing of the nursery in her *Housewife's Treasury of Domestic Information* (c.1865),

suggested that if children preferred the drawing room to the nursery, it was not simply that their parents were there, but that the room itself was attractive. Though she did not specify the use of wallpapers for the nursery, she did urge her readers to make the room pretty and pleasing, as did other writers, notably Lady Barker and Edis. Certainly as the nineteenth century progressed, there were more and more wallpapers for children that were simply pleasing rather than instructive.

And by the early twentieth century designs had become unashamedly entertaining, designed to please or amuse. This seems to have met with the approval of writers and critics such as Walter Shaw Sparrow, who maintained that 'obtrusive theories of education are out of place in a nursery'. He objected to nurseries where 'reading lessons were given from the words printed on a wall-paper, and where all the decoration was false just in order that children might be taught by silly pictures'.[15] No longer were children surrounded by images of moral fortitude and heroism, or even figures of fantasy and imagination; instead they were domiciled with idealised representations of themselves, in imagery that ranged from the chubby babies of Mabel

122. Page from *Décor*, a pattern book illustrating wallpapers in domestic interiors, published in France, *c*.1928

E.2021(1–54)–1990

A proposal for a decorative scheme for a nursery combines a simple floral stripe paper hung in framed panels (a fashionable wall treatment of the period) with a pictorial frieze entitled *La Cirque*, featuring clowns, dancers, jugglers and performing animals.

Lucie Attwell to the playful sturdy children in friezes by Cecil Aldin and Will Owen.

New subjects with innate child-appeal appear in the early decades of the twentieth century, some reflecting more spectacular forms of popular entertainment, ranging from the stylish sophistication of the frieze *La Cirque* (French, 1920s) (plate 122), to the lively depiction of the new Disney cartoon character Mickey Mouse (Sandersons *c*.1930) (plate 123). As well as printed wallpaper, the doting parent could also purchase cut-out stickers to create a do-it-yourself nursery frieze. Similar printed pictorial friezes had been recommended in an American advertisement of 1907 as introducing 'charm and … character' to a child's room and serving as a source of 'continual delight … to the little people'.[16]

123. (*above and below*) **Sections of 'Mickey Mouse'
wallpaper border and frieze, c.1930**
Produced by Arthur Sanderson & Sons Ltd
Flock, hand-painted
E.3100–1930
Given by the Arthur Sanderson & Sons' branch
of The Wall Paper Manufacturers Ltd
Design © Disney Enterprises, Inc.

The first animated film from the Walt Disney studio starring the cartoon
character Mickey Mouse appeared in 1928. This wallpaper, produced only
two years later, was testimony to the immediate popularity of the character,
and is also an early example of merchandising linked to films for children.

Very few nurseries survive intact with wallpaper in situ, but some evidence for the use of nursery friezes can be seen in dolls-houses of the period. The Amy Miles' house, dated around 1890 (now at the Bethnal Green Museum of Childhood), for example, is decorated with a scaled-down replica of a Cecil Aldin frieze of ducks and chickens (plate 124). Like so many other designers of nursery papers, Aldin (1870–1935) was better known as an illustrator. Another dolls-house, 3 Devonshire Villas, from about 1900, has a well-stocked nursery with a pictorial frieze. And in the 1930s-style Pamela Warne house, two replicas of full-size friezes can be seen in the nursery, including a panel from *The Hunting Frieze* designed by H. Watkins Wild for Sandersons, and first issued in 1904. The full-size version had been intended for an adult audience, probably in a billiard room or a smoking room. The decorations – of horses ploughing, and a hunting scene – were executed by different hands.

Of course, the choice of wallpapers for a nursery play-room or child's bedroom has not, until recently, been the choice of the child; instead, the decoration of the nursery reflected the parents' class, tastes and income, as well as expressing some of their assumptions about childhood in general and expectations for their child in particular. Increasingly, however, children have been allowed to choose their own furnishings, and their choice of wallpaper has reflected their hobbies and enthusiasms, but also the current popular culture, with space travel, television, films, pop music and various sports translated into wallpaper patterns. In America in the 1950s teenagers became a recognised demographic group and manufacturers of all kinds began to develop and market products aimed at this new market. Amongst the wallpaper patterns the teenager could choose were prom corsages, 45rpm records, football games and hot-rod cars.

Children of all ages are now a specific market targeted by the merchandising operation that inevitably accompanies the launch of films (*The Lion King*, *Pocahontas*, *Toy Story*, and so on) and the promotion of pop groups (Spice Girls), and football teams (Manchester United, Arsenal, etc.)

(plate 125). What remains common to all of these designs – for children from the 1850s to now – is that they are all baldly pictorial, with motifs repeated with little or no attempt at integration into a conventional pattern.

The gendering of choice in decoration is still apparent, even when children make their own selection. In an article on children's wallpaper in the *Independent* (25 October 1997) an 8-year-old boy said he liked the wild animal border he'd chosen, but went on: 'I'd love "Star Wars" wallpaper' and 'Indiana Jones' curtains. His 10-year-old sister, however, chose 'a border with unicorns, rabbits, fairies, and a castle – it was pretty and I like those kind of things'.[17] And a new kind of moral message appeared in children's wallpaper in the 1990s: now the middle-class child could express his or her interest in saving the planet by choosing Crown's *Go Wild!* wallpaper featuring endangered animal species.

124. Amy Miles' dolls-house, showing a detail of the nursery; English, *c.*1890

W.146–1921

The nursery is papered with an ordinary green and white leaf print design, and a scaled-down pictorial frieze of the kind designed for children around 1900.

125. *Quad Player 2* – wallpaper produced for Manchester United Football Club, 1995–6
Produced by Coloroll
Colour machine print
E.187–2000
Given by Michael Snodin

Many Premier League English football clubs and US sports teams produce a range of clothing and accessories, including bed linen and wallpapers, aimed at children and young people.

Nostalgia and Reproduction

An interest in the styles of the past has been a factor in the design and production of wallpaper from a relatively early date – the revival or continuity of patterns such as the 'Privy Council flock' is testimony to the longevity of individual designs. The pastiching or modification of earlier styles is apparent in, for example, the neo-Gothick designs of the 1830s and 1840s (plate 63), based on the architectural papers of the 1760s and 1770s, or in the Adamesque designs of the early twentieth century, reprising the decorative motifs and styles of the later eighteenth century (plate 126). Designers whose work has been regarded as radical and reforming have often done little more than adapt the styles of the past to suit the tastes of the present. Even William Morris, so often credited with reinventing wallpaper and restoring its credibility as an elegant artistic decoration, found his motifs and even the patterns themselves in medieval manuscripts, sixteenth-century herbals and Renaissance textiles. By the later twentieth century it was the anonymous patterns – the flower sprigs, ivied trellises and modest diaper patterns of the mid-nineteenth century which were lifted wholesale and relaunched in newly fashionable colours on a public increasingly keen to live post-modern lives in Victorian settings.

The majority of us, it seems, wish to live in houses which are either genuinely old, or which are modelled on older styles and incorporate their decorative features. In these circumstances it is hardly surprising that 'retro' styles of decoration – particularly for wallpapers, textiles and furniture – are favoured. This nostalgic impulse is a major force in the wallpaper trade in particular. From the 1920s onwards American firms such as Thomas Strahan Co. and M.H. Birge Co. specialised in reproduction papers. In the US and UK most wallpaper companies have continued to produce reproduction patterns and historical pastiches alongside their ranges of new designs. This long-established reverence for the styles of the past has more recently been supported by a new concern for historical authenticity in period decorative schemes, both public and private.

Museums – and the V&A in particular – have been implicated in this ransacking of past styles. The V&A's

126. (*opposite*) ***Portman* wallpaper, 1903**
Designed by Andrew F. Brophy (1846–1912)
Produced by Arthur Sanderson & Sons Ltd
Colour print from woodblocks
E.2148–1929
Given by The Wall Paper Manufacturers Ltd

Brophy was a freelance designer supplying designs to most of the major wallpaper manufacturers, including Jeffrey & Co., and Woollams. From 1900 until his death he supplied 140 designs to Sandersons, all in the period styles in which he specialised. This design is characterised by the use of neo-classic motifs in the style of Robert Adam. (The design is sometimes erroneously titled 'Adam'.)

collections were brought together with the specific aims of inspiring good design and offering the best of the past as well as the present to inspire and elevate the tastes of designers and manufacturers, and also of consumers. Morris himself adapted patterns from textiles which he saw in the V&A in the 1860s, and wallpaper designers have continued to use the museum's historic papers and textiles as a resource, copying or modifying them to produce period collections. Laura Ashley, Osborne & Little, and Colefax & Fowler have all put out collections which reproduce anonymous eighteenth- and nineteenth-century patterns (plates 128, 129). Manufacturers have enjoyed a collaborative relationship with historic houses, for example Zoffany at Temple Newsam, reproducing some of the papers found in the house, and supplying them for the reconstruction of certain of the interiors. The wallpaper collections at the Whitworth Art Gallery, English Heritage and the Silver Studio Collection (now MoDA) are similarly valuable sources of designs and of information about period colours and styles.

Wallpaper has a key role in schemes to restore or recreate historic interiors, especially domestic interiors. A whole range of reproductions are to be had, from the bespoke papers made with materials and by methods appropriate to the period (for example, the red flock for the restored

Uppark) (plate 130), to the pastiches and modernised versions of historic designs (the screen-printed Morris patterns from Sandersons; the 'new' patterns from Zoffany produced alongside the reproductions of document samples from Temple Newsam; or even, for the general market, Laura Ashley's recoloured versions of early nineteenth-century flower-sprigged papers).

Some of the greatest problems encountered in creating accurate reproductions of historic designs are matching colours (usually with inks and pigments which are different compounds to those used originally), and duplicating specific production techniques. Embossing and flocking can be difficult and expensive to copy, and projects such as Uppark, with the resources to reproduce (as far as possible) every aspect of the original, are rare. Some processes will have disappeared altogether and would be prohibitively expensive to recreate – for example, some of the Uppark papers, originally roller printed, had to be reproduced using screen printing as the nearest available equivalent. At Lorenzo, an 1808 house in Cazenovia, New York, the restoration team went to considerable lengths to reproduce a Zuber paper with a satin ground, ultimately involving wallpaper manufacturers and experts in France, Germany, England and the US.

The technique chosen for the reproduction has to approximate the characteristics of the original process, whether it is the variations in the application of the inks in a hand-block printed paper, the precision of a machine print, or the slightly off-register colours of a hand-stencilled print. And however carefully the processes are themselves reproduced, the inks and the paper will be very different from those used for the original wallpaper. The textures of hand-made rag paper, with its characteristic laid lines, or a cheap, thin machine-made woodpulp paper produce very different effects when printed, which it is difficult for the modern copy to reproduce effectively. However, for most

127. Design for a drawing room in a house in Holland Park, London, 1986
Designed by John Stefanidis
Watercolour over dye-line print
(drawn by Phillip Hooper)
E.200–1986
Given by the designer

This decorative scheme, in a sumptuous *grande luxe* style, draws on a range of historical precedents, predominantly French 18th-century fashions, and the court style of 16th-century Italy. The wallpaper is a classic pink and white stripe, in the style often known as 'Regency stripe'. This entire scheme, including the wallpaper, is characteristic of the taste for historicising styles in later 20th-century interior decoration. Here the look is appropriate to the interior of a mid-19th-century London townhouse. The 1980s saw a new interest in decorating in a style sympathetic to the age of the house, though the degree of period detail and authenticity varied.

128. *(left)* **Wallpaper adapted from William Morris's** *Willow* **design for printed cotton (c.1895), c.1975**
Produced by Osborne & Little for Liberty & Co.
Screen print
E.180–1978

129. *(right)* **Sample of wallpaper from the Laura Ashley Decorator Collection, 1989**
Colour screenprint
E.1219–1989
Given by Caroline Richardson
© Laura Ashley Limited 2001

The Laura Ashley style has always been characterised by a nostalgic prettiness, in clothing and for fabrics and wallpapers. The first wallpapers the company produced were modelled on document samples of 18th- and 19th-century wallpapers and fabrics in the V&A collection. This particular pattern was based on an 18th-century silk jacquard fabric.

purposes it is the overall effect of the paper when hung in conjunction with other furnishings that is important, and not whether the new paper is indistinguishable when set beside its original. At Clandon Park, a restoration carried out by John Fowler matched a red flock from the State Bedroom with a replica, but for general sales, and with costs in mind, Cole's produced a simple block-printed version.

Projects such as Uppark are exceptional in their precision and accuracy, and also in creating a further level of authenticity by fading the papers to match salvaged fragments of the originals in order to reproduce their aged appearance at the time of the fire. The Zoffany papers installed at Temple Newsam, on the other hand, were 'as new' and thus gave an equally deceptive but rather different impression – that the whole house had been redecorated at the same date, though with papers of varying dates belonging to different phases in the life of the house. In his catalogue to the exhibition, *Historic Paper Hangings from Temple Newsam and other English Houses* (1983), Anthony Wells-Cole examines the phases of redecoration that the house experienced under different owners, and laments the loss of several original papers in the 1940s when the house became a gallery for pictures removed for safe-keeping from the Leeds City Art Gallery. The project to rehang Temple Newsam with reproduction wallpapers after the original designs (or approximations of them) is

described as a 'rehabilitation', and Wells-Cole makes it plain that the appropriate wallpaper patterns and colours are the key elements in reawakening an awareness of the historical importance of the house itself.

At Uppark the restoration was much debated before the decision was taken to proceed. Key to this decision was the fact that a restored interior would be the most suitable setting for the salvaged contents, which had been designed or collected by the Fetherstonhaugh family over generations, especially for the rooms in which they lived. The wallpaper, restored, reproduced and artificially aged, was vital to this scheme; as the authors of *Uppark Restored* point out, 'the conserved wallpaper upholds the subtle harmony of the other contents of the room [the Red Drawing Room], notably the carpet and curtains, which have also undergone a similar ordeal by fire'.[1] In the Little Drawing Room the wallpaper was reproduced to copy its faded colour (rather than the brighter tone of the original, known from some preserved fragments) because this 'was more consistent with the patination of the contents of the room'.[2] Throughout the restored State rooms at Uppark, wallpaper is treated as the keynote to the colouring of the scheme as a whole, and as a unifying element. This painstaking process of ageing and matching old and new ensures that there are no jarring contrasts, no obvious anachronisms, and preserves the illusion of the house untouched by its ordeal, though the conservation of the Red Drawing Room wallpaper was seen by some as 'deranged perfectionism'.[3]

A purist 'good taste' approach to restoration in historic houses often gives a false picture of the past. At Wightwick, for example, successive redecorations have made the house more 'Morris & Co.' than when it was decorated for its first occupants in the 1880s and 1890s. Since 1937 more Morris work has been brought in by the Mander family and the National Trust, and several rooms have been redecorated with additional Morris papers. A restoration which strips away these elements because they do not fit *our* ideas of authenticity is inevitably ahistoric, and a falsification of the past. With some historic houses the process itself has become the product – the National Trust published a book about the decision to restore Uppark detailing the methods used to reproduce or restore the fabric and furnishing of the building. The same idea underlies the presentation of certain English Heritage buildings, for example Belsay and the house at Brinkburn Priory (both in Northumberland) make a virtue of their unrestored state, with walls stripped back to show the fabric of the building in places, and layers of discoloured wallpaper left in situ.

The restoration of a real documented interior takes wallpaper fragments found in situ, and, if possible, replaces them with an exact reproduction of the design, as was done at Temple Newsam. Where such evidence is lacking, a reproduction wallpaper of the period is installed, sometimes with the evidence of archives, diaries, inventories or old photographs to suggest colours or styles, but more often as the result of guesswork, as, for example, at Darwin's home, Down House, Kent, recently restored by the National Trust.

Period rooms in museums are often invented in their entirety, as at the Geffrye Museum, London, York Castle Museum (Victorian parlour) and at Beamish. In such cases invention is possible because its purpose is very different – the room represents 'typical' or 'fashionable' styles of a specific date and is furnished accordingly. The 'Aesthetic Room' at the Geffrye Museum for the period 1875–90 is papered with a modern reproduction based on a design by Christopher Dresser, while the 'Regency Room' has a blue and white replica of a paper found in Lauderdale House,

Highgate (now in the English Heritage collection). At Beamish a middle-class interior was invented with the help of photographs, pattern books and oral history, since this is a room of the fairly recent past with living witnesses to appropriate styles. The wallpaper and the other furnishings were chosen on the basis that they would have been affordable and locally available for a household of that type.

Projects such as Uppark and Temple Newsam, the rise of museums of social life which focus on domestic environments, and the growth of interest in antiques and collectibles beyond a traditional monied élite, have all contributed to a significant interest in furnishing one's home in a style appropriate to its date. The mania for ripping out original features and installing PVC window frames and other anachronistic fittings has led to a reaction amongst those people who are actively interested in the history of their own home. This interest has of course also been fostered by the rise in home ownership and the decline of public housing. Though it is largely middle-class, it is not exclusively so. It has been fostered and serviced by manufacturers of period furnishings – and here wallpaper manufacturers have led the way, perhaps because wallpaper can be the cheapest and easiest material to replace and to 'get right'. A number of firms deal exclusively or primarily in reproductions of historic patterns, working to commission for those who can afford it, but also maintaining a stock of period designs.

Country house visiting, a form of domestic tourism since at least the early nineteenth century, has in the last 30 years become a major leisure activity for all. The National Trust and regional history societies, with their preservations and restorations, have certainly played a part in exciting a wider interest in authentic, or at least historic décor. Several books have fed the fashion by recording high-profile restoration projects such as the Kennedy-period White House, Colonial Williamsburg, and Uppark. There are also manuals of resources such as Richard Nylander's exhaustive *Wallpapers for Historic Buildings: A Guide to Selecting Reproduction Wallpapers* (1983), the Silver Studio *Design and Source Book for Home Decoration*, by Turner and Hoskins (1988), (both reissued), and leaflets from the

130. The Red Drawing Room, Uppark, Sussex, 1995
© National Trust Photographic Library/Tim Stephens

View of The Red Drawing Room, showing wallpaper conservators
Allyson and Adrian McDermott at work on the reinstallation of the red
flock wallpaper. It is a patchwork of salvaged fragments and new paper.
The pattern of fading around pictures and mirrors has been carefully
reproduced, and joins between old and new portions camouflaged by
painting in pigment by hand.

Georgian and Victorian Societies on choosing wallpapers for
period houses. Magazines such as *Traditional Homes* (now
defunct) and *Country Homes and Interiors* have regularly
featured wallpapers, showing historic examples alongside
the modern reproductions, while the long-running *Country
Life* has from its earliest days featured articles on historic
interiors and decorations. Some of the first serious research
into wallpaper history appeared in the pages of the latter,
and it has certainly been a significant influence in the dis-
semination of the English country house style and the use
of reproductions of historic wallpaper designs as a suitable
setting for antique furniture and gracious living. New wallpaper ranges from firms such as Osborne & Little, Zoffany

and Colefax & Fowler emphasise their inspiration from, or
direct copying of papers in archives or fragments found in
situ in historic houses.

While revival styles and reproduction patterns have long
been a staple of the wallpaper industry, the obsession with
authenticity in the use of historic designs and colours is a
much more recent phenomenon. One of the most con-
tentious of recent refurbishments using reproduction
wallpapers was that of the Lord Chancellor's apartments in
the Palace of Westminster. The main argument in defence
of this expensive scheme (£59,000 for the wallpapers alone)
was that the various elements – carpets, upholstery, and in
particular the wallpapers – were authentic both to the
period and to the building. However, while it is true that the
wallpapers, printed by Cole's from the original Pugin
blocks, are authentic in that they were designed for the
Palace of Westminster, most were not originally used in the
rooms where they now hang, and indeed Lord Chancellors
have only been accommodated in the building since 1923.
The refurbished apartment, handsome though it is, is no
more authentic than the room sets in the Geffrye Museum.

New Directions

Wallpaper in the twentieth century had become very much associated with the 'country house' look, with chintzy florals, Morris revivals and historic patterns predominating. There was a brief flowering of new and original design directions in the 1950s and 1960s, when architects and artists revitalised the industry (plate 132); designers such as Lucienne Day initiated a trend for adventurous patterns inspired by contemporary painting and sculpture, while John Line's *Palladio* and *Modus* ranges were characterised by bold, large-scale contemporary designs, many by artists new to wallpaper (plates 11, 12, 133). However, this confident phase was soon overwhelmed by a taste for nostalgic patterns, reproductions and pastiches. And, as one journalist recently put it, wallpaper in the 1990s had been a 'no-no', out of fashion for so long 'we're almost scared to say its name'.[1]

A renaissance of sorts has been underway since the 1990s, as 1950s, 1960s and 1970s furnishings were rediscovered as design classics, and retro styles found a new and enthusiastic audience in the style-conscious generation: readers of the new aspirational interiors magazines, *Elle Decoration* and *Wallpaper**. Original 1960s and 1970s wallpapers got a new lease of life as collectibles, used on feature walls or framed as pictures and murals. At the same time, the very unfashionability of wallpaper, which had become associated with a certain kind of restrained middle-class 'good taste', prompted designers to reinvent it. One of the most striking aspects of the best contemporary wallpaper design is its rejection of traditional imagery and motifs, or the radical reworking of conventions. The new wallpapers take their cue from the best of the *Palladio* and *Modus* ranges, and use strong, uncompromising designs and colours.

David Oliver, who established a wallpaper range, the Paper Library, in 1998, claims he was inspired by the furore about 'the Chancellor's wallpaper' (the controversial refurbishment of the Lord Chancellor's apartments at the House of Lords in 1997). He said, 'I just thought wallpaper was getting such a negative press, it was a wonderful time to do something new and fresh and funky.'[2] Oliver deliberately avoided conventional motifs and certainly did not look to the history of wallpaper for inspiration. Instead, his first design was based on a drawing he had made, tracing the white space between the columns, pictures and headlines in a copy of the French newspaper *Libération* (plate 135). The result is a bold geometric pattern which has proved very popular; Oliver himself has used it in his hallway, where he says it has created a feeling of movement. It has since featured regularly as the backdrop to fashion and lifestyle features in magazines and newspaper colour supplements.

Minimalism, a decorating style which has largely coincided with an increase in 'loft-living' in converted industrial buildings or architect-designed urban developments, has tended to exclude the traditional use of wallpaper. Not only is there too much wall to cover, wallpaper itself still carries overtones of a cosy suburban domesticity which the urban loft-dweller is emphatically rejecting. However, artist and designer Sharon Elphick sees this shift towards living in larger open-plan spaces as an opportunity to use wallpaper in a new way. As she says, 'People have got the space for an interesting paper without it dominating everything.'[3] Again this is an acknowledgement of wallpaper's new place in the decorative hierarchy; it is not simply a background, but a

Sarah Lucas is one of the so-called Young British Artists who found fame in the early 1990s through work in various media which played with aspects of popular culture in images that were bold, vulgar and often confrontational. This wallpaper was designed by Lucas and first used as the backdrop to an exhibition of her work entitled *The Fag Show* at the London gallery Sadie Coles' HQ. Since the late 1980s a number of contemporary artists have made wallpaper for exhibitions and installations because it works so well as visual shorthand to suggest 'domestic space' in a gallery setting.

132. (*right*) **'Design 706', one of the Taliesin Line range; American, 1956**
Designed by Frank Lloyd Wright (1867–1959)
Produced by Schumacher & Co., New York
Screenprint
E.582–1966
Given by Schumacher & Co.
© ARS, NY and DACS, London 2001

Wright, a leading Modernist architect, also designed furniture, stained glass, and entire interiors – such as an office for the Kaufmann department store in Pittsburgh (now in the V&A). In 1956 he produced a range of patterns (also printed as textiles) for Schumacher, though he had earlier scorned the use of wallpapers in his own 'organic' houses. These designs, based on precise geometric ornament, and often characterised by optical effects, were of limited application; they were not successful commercially.

133. (*below*) **Wallpaper based on the crystalline structure of afwillite, for the Festival of Britain (detail); London, 1951**
Designed by William J. Odell (working from early 1950s)
Produced by John Line & Sons Ltd
Screenprint
E.885–1978

Mark Hartland Thomas of the Council for Industrial Design was responsible for choosing exhibits for the Festival exhibition. In 1949 he set up the Festival Pattern Group to develop designs on the theme of crystal structures, based on the work being done on crystallography by Dr Helen Megaw at Cambridge. In all, twenty-six manufacturers contributed to the project. It was a conscious attempt to devise contemporary patterns for wallpapers and textiles which had traditionally been dominated by floral and pictorial motifs. Hartland Thomas wrote of the crystal structure diagrams: 'they were essentially modern because the technique which constructed them was quite recent, and yet like all successful decoration of the past, they derived from nature – although it was nature at a submicroscopic level not previously revealed.' [Quoted in Lambert, S., *Pattern and Design: Design for the Decorative Arts 1480–1980* (V&A, 1983), p.37]. The furnishings devised by the FPG were used on the Festival site.

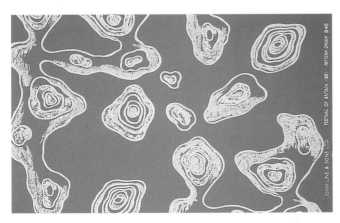

feature which complements other furnishings and fittings, or serves as a talking point in its own right, much as a painting or poster might do. Inspired by her own photographic limited edition wall-panels, Elphick has designed the quintessential wallpaper for the inner-city loft – *Prefab Stripe* is an all-over repeat of an image of a 1960s prefabricated tower block (plate 136). Printed in dull blues and greys with stripes of thinned colour veiling the image, it perfectly captures the stained concrete façade, with its monotony and anonymity embodying the alienation of urban life; it also looks like a typical urban landscape viewed through a pall of rain – a neat replication of the likely view from the loft's picture windows!

Several contemporary designs have been inspired by this idea that wallpaper should make some visual reference to the urban context, rather than reproducing the nostalgic fantasy of a rural lifestyle. In 1996 four wallpapers were commissioned by Glasgow's Centre for Contemporary Arts, and sold through the city's fashionable interiors store Nice House. These included David Shrigley's *Industrial Estate*, a cartoon vision of the anonymous uniformity of the contemporary urban landscape, with everything from carpet warehouse to garage, church and sauna inhabiting the same brick box or blank walled shed (plate 137). By his own admission, the paper would be 'very oppressive' to live with.'[4]

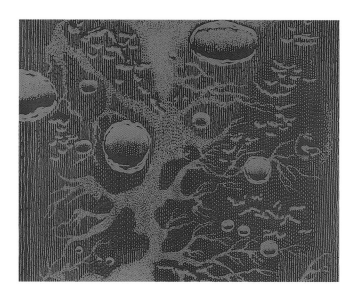

134. *(above)* **Lunar wallpaper (detail), 1964**
Designed by Michael Clarke (b.1920)
Produced by Cole & Son (Wallpapers) Ltd
Colour screenprint
E.952–1978
Given by Cole & Son (Wallpapers) Ltd

Just as some later 19th-century wallpaper designers and manufacturers had found inspiration in popular culture and topical events, so the 1960s saw wallpaper design incorporating 'new' imagery inspired by subjects such as space exploration. This was one of the earliest examples, an abstract image derived from photographs of the moon's surface, and clearly related to the fantasy imagery of contemporary psychedelic graphics. By 1969, the year of the first manned landing on the moon, it was possible to buy a variety of fabrics and wallpapers patterned with rockets and other lunar imagery printed in vivid 'Pop Art' colours.

136. *(above)* **Prefab Stripe wallpaper, 1998**
Designed by Sharon Elphick (b.1968)
Size colour hand-printed screenprint
E.261–2000

Elphick's urban imagery is inspired by her photo-collage wallhangings of tower blocks and sky-scrapers. The wallpaper is printed to order.

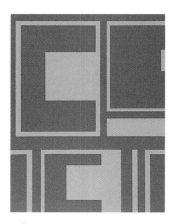

135. *(left)* **Libération wallpaper (detail), 1998**
Designed by David Oliver, Paper Library
Screenprint
Courtesy of David Oliver

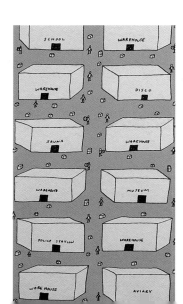

137. *(left)* **Industrial Estate wallpaper (detail), c.1996**
Designed by David Shrigley (b.1968)
Commissioned by the CCA, Glasgow and printed by Sileby Prints, Leicestershire
Screenprint

Martin Boyce designed a geometric black, grey and white grid, *From Now Until Night*, intended to evoke the pattern of darkened office-block windows. He designed the paper for public spaces where people were simply passing through – hotel lobbies, waiting rooms, corporate foyers – rather than domestic settings. Domestic life itself provides the motif for Hayley Tomkins' design: a 'messy'[5] collage of babies' heads in shades of pink, *Cry Baby* suggests that there can be a claustrophobic aspect to the domestic ideal (plate 138).

Limited editions, commissions and unique prints have produced wallpapers with the kind of exclusive status previously enjoyed by flocks, Chinese papers and French scenics. One of the finalists in the Peugeot Design Awards for 2000 was Deborah Bowness with her *Hooks and Frocks* wallpaper (plate 139). Each version of the design is unique to the client, whose furniture and possessions are photographed and reproduced in pictorial montages on lengths of wallpaper. When hung, real hooks are added so the client can, if they wish, hang the actual frock, shirt or bag over its two-dimensional counterpart. Ella Doran has also broken with the tradition of repeating pattern and conventional mural decoration in wallpapers such as *Gloriosa*, with its bold single image of a lily blown up to wall-size. She does produce more conventional repeating designs of photographed objects – shoals of fish, asparagus, artichokes and pebbles – but the images are manipulated on computer and can be printed so that every piece is different. This is expen-

139. *Hooks and Frocks* wallpaper, c.2000
Designed by Deborah Bowness
Screenprint and heat transfer
Photo: Karen Hatch

This is a contemporary version of the bespoke wallpaper, personalised for the client by incorporating images of his/her own clothes and accessories. The images are photographed and montaged, enlarged and printed onto lining paper, with selected areas hand silk-screened in colour and details added using heat transfer paper.

sive, about £700 ($1000) for one average living room wall, but the appeal lies in the fact that the decoration would be unique; as she says, 'nobody else would have exactly what you've got'.[6] And though these limited edition designs and one-off commissions are relatively dear, the cost is offset by using the paper on only one wall, in a corner or an alcove. Indeed, Doran sees her papers as being too assertive to be used for a whole room and says the result 'would be a nightmare'.[7] In fact, the new generation of designs are generally limited to use on one wall – a 'feature' wall, as in the 1950s and 1960s. Advertising agency Mother has used original 1960s papers in this way in their Clerkenwell premises; textile designer Neisha Crosland likewise used her own wallpapers (for Paper Library) in her Fulham Road shop.

Wallpapers like these continue the trend which began in the late nineteenth century for the home and its furnishings to be seen as self-expression, an extension of the owner's personality and taste. 'Good taste' is no longer the issue – the kitsch, eccentric or ironic are all valid characteristics of personal taste, and are 'read' and appreciated as such by others.

138. *Cry Baby* wallpaper (detail), c.1996
Designed by Hayley Tomkins (b.1971)
Commissioned by the CCA, Glasgow and printed by Sileby Prints, Leicestershire
Screenprint

Notes

Introduction

1. William Morris, 'The Lesser Arts of Life' in Reginald Stuart Poole, *Lectures on Art: Delivered in Support of the Society for the Protection of Ancient Buildings* (London: Macmillan & Co, 1882), p.220.
2. John Houghton, *Collection for Improvement of Husbandry & Trade*, extract dated 30 June 1699.
3. John Gwynn, *London and Westminster Improved – Observation on the State of the Arts*, London, 1766. Quoted in Entwisle, *Literary History* (1960), p.38.
4. Thomas Hardy, *Far From the Madding Crowd*, 1874 (Penguin ed., 1975), ch.35, p.295.
5. Mrs Gaskell, *Wives and Daughters*, 1866 (Penguin ed., 1969), ch.16, p.219.
6. Comtesse de Genlis, *Dictionnaire critique et raisonné des étiquettes de la Cour* (Paris: 1818), I, 163.
7. Quoted in Andrew Anthony, 'What about the workers?', *The Observer Review*, 13 December 1998.
8. Charlotte Perkins Gilman, 'The Yellow Wallpaper', *The New England Magazine*, May 1892.
9. Lucy Lippard, 'Out of Bounds', in *Susan Hiller* (exhibition catalogue, London: Institute of Contemporary Arts, 1986), unpaginated.
10. See *Apocalyptic Wallpaper*, Wexner Center for the Arts, Columbus, Ohio, 1997. Essay by Gill Saunders, pp.31–47.
11. Shelter campaign literature, March 2001.
12. See Bibliography, especially Entwisle, E.A., *The Book of Wallpaper* (1970); Hoskins, L. (ed.) *The Papered Wall* (1994); Oman, C.C. and Hamilton, J., *Wallpapers: Catalogue of the Collection of the Victoria & Albert Museum* (1982).
13. See Louise Ward, 'Chintz, swags and bows: the myth of English country-house style' in *Things*, 5, Winter 1996–7, pp.7–37.
14. See for example Lisa G. Corrin (ed.), *Mining the Museum: an installation by Fred Wilson* (Baltimore/New York, c.1994).

1 Who Used Wallpaper and Where?

1. Both quoted in *Literary History*, p.14.
2. Quoted in Sugden and Edmondson, p.45.
3. *Covent Garden Journal*, 27 June 1752. Quoted in *Literary History*, p.29.

4. Domino is a French term for single-sheet decorative papers, with various uses, which were precursors of wallpaper proper; *papiers de tapisserie* were patterned or pictorial papers, produced as single sheets to be joined in hanging, for wall decoration.
5. Quoted in *The Papered Wall*, p.25. The Act was 10 Anne c.18. For a full account see Dagnall, H., *The Tax on Wallpaper* (Edgware, Middlesex, 1990), the standard work in English on this subject.
6. Quoted in *Literary History*, p.24.
7. Mortimer, T., *The Universal Director: or the Nobleman and Gentleman's True Guide to the Masters and Professors of the Liberal and Polite Arts and Sciences* (London, 1763), p.54. Quoted in *Literary History*, p.37.
8. Samuel and Joseph Newsom, *Picturesque California Homes*, no.2 (San Francisco: S. and J. Newsom, 1885), p.5.
9. Adolf Loos, 'Ornament and crime', 1908, reprinted in Münz, L. and Künstler, G. (eds), *Adolf Loos* (New York: Praeger, 1966).
10. Quoted in Lynn, op.cit., p.115.
11. John M. Dickey, *Research and Planning Studies for the Restoration of the Proprietary House, Perth Amboy, New Jersey*, Media, Pa., unpublished report, 1 July 1973. Quoted in *The Papered Wall*, p.118.
12. Guy de Maupassant, 'Madame Tellier's Establishment', in *Selected Short Stories* (Penguin ed., 1995), p.210.
13. Contemporary advertisement quoted in *Historic Paper-Hangings*, p.4.
14. Charlotte Brontë, *Jane Eyre*, 1847 (Penguin ed., 1987), ch.11, p.125.
15. See *Sanderson 1860–1985*, Sandersons of Berners Street, 19 July–4 October 1985, cat. no.92.
16. Everett, *Observations on India* (London 1853), p.22.
17. *Hartly House, Calcutta. A novel of the days of Warren Hastings*. Reprinted from the edition of 1789 (London, 1908), ed. J. MacFarlane, p.147.
18. Emily Eden, *Up the Country*, 1866 (Virago ed., 1983), p.128.
19. *The Wall-Paper News and Interior Decorator*, December 1908.

20. Quoted in Sugden and Edmondson, p.116.
21. Jacques Rancière, *La Nuit des prolétaires: Archives du rêve ouvrier* (Paris: Fayard, 1981); [*The Nights of Labour: The Worker's Dream in Nineteenth-Century France*, trans. J. Drury, Temple University Press, Philadelphia, p.30].
22. See Gere, *Nineteenth Century Decoration*, p.53.
23. A.J. Downing, *The Architecture of Country Houses*, 1850 (reprinted New York: Dover Publications, 1969), pp.369–70.
24. Mrs Gaskell, *Mary Barton*, 1848 (Penguin ed. 1996), ch.2, p.15.
25. Quoted in Gere, op.cit., p.120.
26. *The Australian*, 23 June 1883.
27. Henry Mayhew, *London Labour and the London Poor*, 1851, vol.I, p.47.
28. Photo by Huestis Cook, Valentine Museum, Richmond, Virginia. Illus. as fig.9.14 in Myrna Kaye, *There's a Bed in the Piano* (Boston, 1998).
29. *How to furnish a House and make it a Home* (Economic Library, London, 1851). Quoted in *Literary History*, p.97.
30. *Official Catalogue of the 1880 Melbourne International Exhibition*, Melbourne, 1882, p.81.
31. *A Popular Art. British Wallpapers 1930–1960* (Silver Studio exhibition catalogue, Middlesex Polytechnic, 1990), p.9.
32. *The Architect & Building News*, 1 June 1945, p.123.

2 Shopping for Wallpaper

1. All trade cards referred to above in British Museum.
2. Ill. in Lynn p.314.
3. Ill. in Lynn p.230.
4. Treve Rosoman, *London Wallpapers*, pp.54–57.
5. R. Hills, *A Short History of Paper Making in Britain 1488–1988*, (Athlone, 1988). Quoted in Rosoman, op cit., pp.2–3, 54–7.
6. Letter to Henrietta Louisa, Countess of Pomfret, *Correspondence* 11.254, H-P 19/2/1741. Quoted in *Historic Paper-Hangings*, p.2.
7. See *Encyclopaedia of Interior Decoration* under Chippendale.
8. Thomas Sheraton, *The Cabinet Dictionary*, 1803, p.281.

9. *Daily Advertiser*, New York, 11 April 1787.

10. P. Toynbee and L. Whibley (eds), *Correspondence of Thomas Gray* (Oxford: Clarendon Press, 1935), letter dated 13 November 1761.

11. Duppa, Slodden & Co., Letter Book, *c.*1800–20, V&A, NAL 86.AA.14.

12. Quoted in Sugden and Edmondson, p.78.

13. Quoted in *Historic Paper-Hangings*, p.47.

14. Quoted in *The Papered Wall*, p.34.

15. *Leeds Intelligencer*, 10 April 1787. Quoted in *Historic Paper-Hangings*, p.48.

16. *Norfolk Chronicle* and *Norwich Gazette*, 4 February 1815.

17. Advertisement for William Marchent in *Boston Gazette*, 9 April 1754. Quoted in *Literary History*, p.31.

18. *Letters and Works of Lady M.W. Montagu*, Lord Wharncliffe (ed.) (London, 1837). Quoted in *Literary History*, p.24.

19. Ill. in Rosoman, op.cit., p.6.

20. *Memoirs of Rev. Sydney Smith*, by his daughter Lady Holland. Quoted in *Literary History*, p.81.

21. *The Leeds Mercury*, 20/3/1847 and 3/4/1847.

22. L.N. Tolstoy, *Anna Karenina*, 1878 (Penguin ed., 1978), part 6, ch.20, p.647.

23. Quoted in R. Kelly, 'Getting the blues in Washington, D.C.' in *Wallpaper History Review*, 1995, p.22.

24. C.L. Eastlake, *Hints on Household Taste*, p.107.

25. Walter Shaw Sparrow, *Hints on House Furnishing*, 1909, p.130.

26. *Sandersons* exhibition catalogue, op.cit., 1985, p.18.

27. *Magazine of Art*, 15, 1897, p.165.

28. *Lady's World*, 1887, p.240.

29. *Journal of Decorative Art*, 1891, p.157.

30. Quoted in Elizabeth Donaghy Garrett, *At Home: The American Family 1750–1870*, New York: Abrams, 1989, p.267.

31. Thomas and Caldcleugh, in the *Baltimore Federal Gazette*, 29 May 1801.

32. See Garrett, op.cit., p.267.

33. Produced by J. Morgan & Co., Cleveland, Ohio, *c.*1900. In Whitworth Art Gallery, w.2.1976.

34. Ruskin, 'Of Queen's Gardens', in *Sesame and Lilies*, 1865, in Cook, E.T. and Wedderburn, A. (eds) *The Works of John Ruskin*, 18 (London, 1903), pp.121–22.

35. Elsie de Wolfe, *The House in Good Taste*, 1913, p.5.

3 Paperhanging

1. Quoted in Rosoman, *London Wallpapers*, pp.10–11.

2. See Peter Thornton, *Authentic Décor: The Domestic Interior 1620–1920* (London, 1984), p.132.

3. John Walsh Jr, Letter Book, MS 766, 1781–86, w462, p.30. Baker Library, Harvard Business School, Cambridge, Mass. Quoted in *The Papered Wall*, p.120.

4. Casey Papers, 22:317. Society for the Preservation of New England Antiquities Archives, Boston, Mass. Quoted in *The Papered Wall*, p.120.

5. GW to Clement Biddle, 30 June 1784. Fitzpatrick (ed.), *Writings of George Washington*, 27:430.

6. Quoted in Rosoman, op.cit., p.11.

7. Sheraton, *The Cabinet Dictionary*, 1803, p.281.

8. Quoted in Sugden and Edmondson, p.51.

9. *Autobiography and Correspondence of Mary Granville, Mrs. Delany*, Llanover (ed.), 1861–2, vol. II, p.562.

10. Gustave Flaubert, *Madame Bovary*, 1857, part 1, ch.5. Quoted in *Literary History*, p.102.

11. Quoted in Rosoman, op.cit., p.32.

12. *Pennsylvania Packet*, Philadelphia, 5 October 1786.

13. See Lynn, p.501, note 14.

14. James Arrowsmith, *The paper-hanger's and upholsterer's guide* (London, 1851), p.16.

15. Deborah Franklin to Benjamin Franklin, October 6–13?, 1765, *The Papers of Benjamin Franklin*, Leonard Labarre (ed.) and others (New Haven and London, 1968), 12:294-8. Quoted in Lynn, p.154.

16. James Fenimore Cooper, *The Pioneers*, 1823 (Penguin ed., 1988), ch.v, p.64.

17. Anon., 'Interview with Mr. Charles F. Voysey, architect and designer', *The Studio*, vol.1, 1893, p.233.

18. See Christopher Gilbert, *The Life and Work of Thomas Chippendale* (London, 1978), p.246–7.

19. Heal Collection, British Museum. Ill. in Rosoman, op.cit., p.8.

20. *Encyclopaedia of Interior Design* (1994), p.271.

21. *Universal Advertiser* 13/2/1753, 6/4/1754.

22. Ada Longfield suggests that this was a reference to the new fashion for pasting directly on the wall. See 'History of the Dublin Wallpaper Industry in the 18th Century' in *The Journal of the Royal Society of Antiquaries of Ireland for the Year 1947*, pp.101–16.

23. Mersham Le Hatch correspondence, January 1771. Quoted in the *Encyclopaedia of Interior Design*, 1994, p.271.

24. Duppa, Slodden & Co., Letter Book, *c.*1800–20, V&A, NAL, 86.AA.14.

4 Textile Influences on Wallpaper

1. *Letters of Sir Horace Walpole, Earl of Orford, to Sir Horace Mann*, Lord Dover (ed.) (London, 1833), III, pp.44–45.

2. In the Heal Collection, British Museum. Ill. in Rosoman, *London Wallpapers*, p.9.

3. Quoted in Entwisle, *Literary History*, p.11.

4. *The Postman*, No.1059, 10 December 1702.

5. In Bagford Collection, British Museum. Ill. in Entwisle, *Literary History*, p.18.

6. First ed., 1728. Quoted in Entwisle, *Literary History*, p.23.

7. In V&A, E.373A–1940. This is lettered *Roger Hudson Trunk Maker in Coney Street York*.

8. Quoted in John Irwin and Katharine B. Brett, *The Origins of Chintz* (London: HMSO, 1970), p.24.

9. Quoted in Rosoman, op.cit., p.17.

10. Account dated 14 March 1774. Quoted in Gilbert, *Chippendale*, p.273.

11. Account dated 7 June 1774. Ibid., p.274.

12. This watercolour is in the Swedish Royal Collection, Stockholm. Ill. in *The Papered Wall*, pp.68–9.

13. Ill. in *The Papered Wall*, pp.70–71.

5 Flock Wallpapers

1. Both in the Department of Textiles & Dress at the V&A.

2. Quoted in Rosoman, *London Wallpapers*, p.32.

3. Quoted in *Historic Paper-Hangings*, p.46.

4. Manuscripts of Lord Kenyon. Hist: MSS: Commission 14th Report. Quoted in Entwisle, *Literary History*, p.50.

5. C. Gilbert, *The Life and Work of Thomas Chippendale* (1978), pp.139–147. Quoted in Rosoman, *London Wallpapers*, p.37.

6. Lady Margaret Heathcote to her father, 1st Earl of Hardwicke, 13 September 1763. Add. MSS. 35356, f.356.

7. See C. Rowell and J.M. Robinson, *Uppark Restored* (National Trust, 1996), p.121.

8. Quoted in Douglas Goldring, *Regency Portrait Painter* (London, 1951), pp.247–8.

9. Skipwith Papers, Earl G. Swem Library, The College of William and Mary in Virginia. Quoted in Lynn, *Wallpaper in America*, p.72.

10. A.W.N. Pugin, *The True Principles of Christian or Pointed Architecture*, 1841, pp.25–26.

11. Richard Redgrave, *Report on Design* (London, 1852), p.26.

12. C.L. Eastlake, *Hints on Household Taste*, 1868, p.111.

13. R.W. Edis, *The Decoration of Town Houses*, 1881, pp.17–20.

14. Mrs Beeton, *Housewife's Treasury of Domestic Information* (London: Ward Lock & Co., c.1865), p.211.

15. *The Builder*, 6 October 1877, p.1002.

6 Chinese Wallpapers and Chinoiserie Styles

1. *Letters and Journals of Lady Mary Coke*, Hon. J.A. Home (ed.) (Bath, 1970), 4 vols. Quoted in *Literary History*, p.38.

2. V&A, FED, E.412, 413, 1924.

3. Letter dated 8 April 1771. Quoted in Gilbert, op.cit., p.179.

4. See *Chinese Export Art and Design*, Craig Clunas (ed.) (Victoria & Albert Museum, 1987), p.112.

5. Recorded in the receipt book of the voyage. Quoted in *The Papered Wall*, p.49.

6. Madame du Bocage, *Letters concerning England, Holland and Italy*, (first published 1750; trans from the French, London 1770).

7. James Cawthorne, *Essay on Taste*, 1756. Quoted in T.N. Foss and D.F. Lach, 'Images of Asia and Asians in European Fiction, 1500–1800', in *China and Europe*, Thomas H.C. Lee (ed.) (Hong Kong, 1991), p.181.

8. Quoted in John Cornforth, 'A Role for Chinoiserie?', *Country Life*, vol.CLXXXIII, no.49, 7 December 1989, p.147.

9. See Craig Clunas in *Dreams of the Dragon: Visions of Japan and China* (exhibition catalogue), University of Essex, 18 April–6 May 1994.

10. Quoted in Cornforth, op.cit., p.151.

11. John Macky, *Journey Through England*, 1722. Quoted in *Literary History*, p.24.

12. Cornforth, op.cit., pp.146–7.

13. See *Passages from the Diaries of Mrs Philip Lybbe Powys of Hardwick House, Oxon.*, Emily J. Climenson (ed.) (Longmans, 1899), p.139.

14. See Climenson, ibid., pp.146–7.

15. Quoted in Stella Tillyard, *Aristocrats: Caroline, Emily, Louisa and Sarah Lennox 1740–1832* (London: Vintage, 1994), p.200.

16. *Letters and Journals of Lady Mary Coke*, Hon. J.A. Home (ed.). Quoted in *Literary History*, p.38.

17. Quoted in *China and Europe*, p.182.

18. Quoted in *Dreams of the Dragon*, p.14.

19. Quoted in *China and Europe*, p.177.

20. J.B. Jackson, *An Essay on the Invention of Engraving and Printing in Chiaro Oscuro* (London, 1754), p.8.

21. J. Shebbeare, *Letters on the English Nation* (London, 1756). Quoted in *Dreams of the Dragon*, p.3.

22. William Parrat, *World*, 20 September 1753.

23. *Journal of Rt Hon Sir Joseph Banks, 1768–71.*

24. *Letters and Journals of Lady Mary Coke*, Quoted in *Literary History*, p.50.

25. Cornforth, op cit., p.149.

26. See *Leeds Art Calendar*, 61, 1968, pp.14–17.

27. *The Letters of Walter Scott*, Herbert J.C. Grierson (ed.), 12 vols, 1932–7, letters VII, pp.279–80.

28. 21 August 1693, quoted in Entwisle, *The Book of Wallpaper*, p.57.

29. The V&A, the Museum of London, and Whitworth Art Gallery, Manchester.

30. Foss and Lach, 'Images of Asia and Asians in European Fiction, 1500–1800', in *China and Europe*, p.178.

31. *New York Evening Post*, 17 February 1804. Quoted in Lynn, p.106.

32. Quoted in Lynn, p.106.

33. George Washington to Robert Morris, 2 October 1787. Quoted in Lynn, p.106 and note.

34. Quoted in Sugden and Edmondson, pp.49–50.

35. *Beautiful Houses*, 1882, p.81.

36. Galsworthy, *The White Monkey*, 1924 (Penguin ed. 1968), p.22.

7 Architectural Wallpapers

1. Quoted in Sugden & Edmondson, p.111 (leaflet is in the Print Room of the British Museum).

2. Quoted in *The Papered Wall*, p.72.

3. *Faulkner's Dublin Journal*, 13/4/1762. Quoted in Longfield, op.cit., p.110.

4. *Letters of Sir Horace Walpole, Earl of Orford, to Sir Horace Mann*, Lord Dover (ed.) (London, 1833), vol.III, pp.44–5.

5. *Passages from the Diaries of Mrs Philip Lybbe Powys of Hardwick House, Oxon.*, Emily J. Climenson (ed.) (Longmans, 1899), p.115.

6. For a full account of this wallpaper see Emma Hardy, 'Fresh fashions from London', *Wallpaper History Review*, 1996–7, pp.12–18.

7. *History and Antiquities of Norfolk*, 1781. Quoted in Hardy.

8. *Gentleman's Magazine*, vol.LXIX, pt.1, January 1799, p.62. Quoted in Hardy.

9. A.W.N. Pugin, *The True Principles of Christian or Pointed Architecture*, 1841, pp.25–26.

10. *The Boston Newsletter*, 17 May 1764 and 24 January 1765; *The Boston Postboy and Advertiser*, 30 July and 3 September 1764.

11. *Connecticut Courant*, 25 January 1796.

12. P. Toynbee and L. Whibley (eds), *Correspondence of Thomas Gray*, (Oxford: Clarendon Press, 1935), letter 342, dated 8 September 1761.

13. Ill. in Lynn, p.86.

14. James Fenimore Cooper, *The Pioneers*, 1823 (Penguin ed., 1988), ch.v, p.64.

15. J.C. Loudon, *Encyclopaedia of Cottage, Farm and Villa Architecture* (London, 1836), p.583.

8 Print Rooms

1. C.E. Aïssé, *Lettres de Mademoiselle A à Madame C[alandrini]*, Paris 1787. Quoted in Jourdain, 'Print Rooms', *Country Life*, 1948, 104, pp.524–5.

2. Letter of 12 June 1753; *Letters of Horace Walpole, Earl of Orford, to Sir Horace Mann*, Lord Dover (ed.) (London 1833).

3. Quoted in Stella Tillyard, *Aristocrats*, op.cit., p.202.

4. Ibid., p.204.

5. Quoted in D. Guinness, 'The Revival of the Print Room', *Antique Collector*, June 1978, 48, pp.88–91.

6. *Sayer and Bennett's Catalogue of prints*, 1775 (reprinted Holland Press, 1970), p.110.
7. Quoted in *Literary History*, p.49.
8. Tillyard, op.cit., p.204.
9. Ibid., p.204.
10. Quoted in *Upark Restored*, p.131.
11. Quoted in Susan Lambert, *The Image Multiplied* (London, 1987), p.183.

9 Scenic Wallpapers

1. Honoré de Balzac, *Old Goriot* [Le Père Goriot], 1834 (Penguin ed., 1951), p.31.
2. Joseph Dufour, *Livret explicatif sur les Sauvages de la mer Pacifique*, Mâcon, an XIII (1804/5), p.11.
3. Quoted in Entwisle, *French Scenic Wallpapers*, (Leigh-on-Sea, 1972) p.34.
4. Quoted in Entwisle, ibid., p.48.
5. Odile Nouvel-Kammerer, in *The Papered Wall*, p.102.
6. See Sabine Thümmler, 'The Battle of Austerlitz Scenic Wallpaper: New Dating and Old Politics', in *Studies in the Decorative Arts*, The Bard Graduate Center, vol.IV, number 2 Spring–Summer 1997, pp.22-62.
7. Friedrich Blaul, *Träume und Schäume vom Rhein: In Reisebildern aus Rheinbayern und den angrenzenden Ländern* (Speyer, 1838–9; reprint Speyer, 1982). Quoted in Thümmler, op.cit., p.59.
8. C.A. Halstead, *Investigation, or Travels in the Boudoir* (London, 1837), p.70.
9. Sir Charles Oman, *Memories of Victorian Oxford*, 1941, ch.xx, p.220.
10. A single panel of which was given to the V&A in 1914.
11. In very poor condition, the paper was removed and eight panels given to the V&A in 1938.
12. From Henry Smithers' account of Liverpool (1825). Quoted in John Cornforth, 'Vitality and Variety. The Musée du Papier Peint at Rixheim near Mulhouse, France', *Country Life*, 9 April 1987, p.142.
13. 7 June, p.598.
14. See Lynn, p.225.
15. Both quoted in Lynn, p.229.
16. *Retrospect of Western Travel in 2 Volumes* (London and New York, 1838), 1:83–4.
17. Illustrated in *Wallpaper** magazine, September 2000, p.290.

18. Charles Dickens, *Little Dorrit*, 1857 (Penguin ed., 1998), part II, ch.13, p.550.
19. Tate Britain.
20. Issue dated 20/10/2000, p.12.

10 Design Reform

1. *Household Words*, 4 December 1852.
2. Wilkie Collins, *Basil*, 1852, (Oxford University Press, 1990), part I, ch.x, p.61.
3. Quoted in Entwisle, *The Book of Wallpaper*, p.111.
4. C.L.Eastlake, *Hints on Household Taste*, 1868, p.102.
5. *Catalogue of the Select Specimens of British Manufacture and Decorative Art* (London, 1847), p.4.
6. *Great Exhibition of 1851, Jury Reports*, vol.IV, p.745.
7. *Art Journal*, 1861. Quoted in Entwisle, *The Book of Wallpaper*, p.112.
8. *House Furnisher*, 1871.Quoted in Entwisle, *The Book of Wallpaper*, p.118.
9. 'Art and its producers', *Collected Works of William Morris*, vol.XXII (London, 1914), p.352.
10. *The Builder*, XI, 1851, p.422.
11. See Entwisle, *The Book of Wallpaper*, p.13.
12. *Ladies Realm*, 1897, p.616.
13. Eastlake, *Hints*, p.103.
14. Richard Redgrave, *Report on Design* (London, 1852), p.26.
15. Charles Dickens, *Hard Times*, 1854 (Penguin ed., 1967), pp.51–2.
16. Richard Redgrave, op.cit., p.25.
17. GHL Journal, 13 November 1863. Quoted in Gordon Haight, *George Eliot A Biography* (London, 1985), p.372.
18. George Eliot, 'Mr. Gilfil's Love-Story', in *Scenes from Clerical Life* (Penguin ed., 1973), ch.4, p.116.
19. Catherine Beecher and Harriet Beecher Stowe, *The American Woman's Home* (New York, 1869), p.84.
20. R.W. Edis, 'Internal Decoration', in *Our Homes and How to Make Them Healthy*, S.F. Murphy (ed.) (London 1883), p.356.
21. Walter Crane, 'The English Revival in Decorative Art' in *William Morris to Whistler* (London, 1911).
22. Nikolaus Pevsner, *An Enquiry into Industrial Art in England* (Cambridge, 1937) p.11.

11 William Morris

1. BL MS 4380, fol.1.
2. William Morris, *Some Hints on Pattern Designing* (London, 1881), p.6.
3. 'Lesser Arts' in *Collected Works*, vol.22, p.260.
4. Quoted in J. Banham et al, *Victorian Interior Style*, p.94.
5. Quoted in ibid., p.98.
6. Lady Mount Temple, *Memorials*, 1890, pp.64–5. Quoted in *William Morris* (exhibition catalogue), Linda Parry (ed.) (V&A/Philip Wilson, 1996), pp.200–2.
7. J.W. MacKail, *The Life of William Morris* (London, 1899). Quoted in Linda Parry (ed.), *William Morris* (London: Philip Wilson Publishers in association with the Victoria & Albert Museum, 1996), p.202.
8. Metford Warner, paper to the Art Workers' Guild, 1896.
9. Mrs Orrinsmith, *The Drawing Room: Its Decoration and Furniture* (London, 1877), p.12.
10. Quoted in Linda Parry, *William Morris Textiles* (London, 1983), p.129.
11. Mrs Humphrey Ward, *A Writer's Recollections (1856–1900)* (London, 1918), pp.123–4; p.119.
12. John Galsworthy, *The Man of Property*, 1922 (Penguin ed., 1970), p.68.
13. Shirley Nicholson, *A Victorian Household* (London, 1988), p.211.
14. Letter dated 17 October 1873, MSL/1995/14/109/1, V&A, NAL.
15. JDA, 1882, p.273.
16. R.M. Watson, *The Art of the House* (London, 1897), p.10.
17. E.M. Forster, *Howard's End*, 1910 (Penguin ed., 1969), p.153. The paper referred to might be Walter Crane's prize-winning *Macaw* design (1908), or the earlier *Peacocks and Amorini* (1878), a gilded leather with a pattern that included cockatoos.
18. 'The home and its dwelling rooms', in *The British Home of Today*, Walter Shaw Sparrow (ed.), 1904, cii.
19. Although most were hand-block prints, their prices (in 1888) ran from 3s to 16s, with some machine-printed patterns at 2s 6d. At the other end of the scale a gold-ground embossed paper cost 40s. In the

1870s, Sandersons were distributing French hand-printed papers at prices between 4s 6d and 16s a piece, and in 1880 selling their own single colour block prints for 3s or 3s 6d.

12 Embossed Wall Coverings

1. Hans Huth, 'English Chinoiserie Gilt Leather', *Burlington Magazine*, July 1937.
2. Quoted in Peter Thornton, *Seventeenth-Century Interior Decoration in England, France and Holland* (London, 1978), p.45.
3. In Rijksmuseum.
4. Metropolitan Museum, Robert Lehman Collection, 1975.1.144.
5. Quoted in Entwisle, *The Book of Wallpaper*, p.31.
6. Quoted in Maurice Tomlin, *Ham House* (V&A, 1986), p.14.
7. See National Trust guide to Dunster Castle, Somerset (1993).
8. Margaret Calderwood, *Letters and Journals of Mrs Calderwood from England, Holland and the Low Countries* (Edinburgh, 1884). Quoted in Entwisle, *The Book of Wallpaper*, p.35.
9. Quoted in Gere and Hoskins, *The House Beautiful*, p.103, note 98.
10. A.L. Baldry in *The Art Journal*, 1898. Quoted in Bruce Boucher, 'Alma-Tadema, Poynter, and the Redecoration of the Athenaeum Club', *Apollo*, CL, 1999, pp.21–29.
11. Vyvyan Holland, *Son of Oscar Wilde*, 1954. Quoted in Gere and Hoskins, *The House Beautiful*, p.103.
12. *Recording Ruin*, 1943, p.139.

13 Health and Cleanliness

1. Guy de Maupassant, *Bel-Ami*, 1885 (Penguin ed., 1975), p.61.
2. Quoted in *The Papered Wall*, p.57.
3. Quoted in R.M. Anthony, 'A Diary of 1803' in *History Today*, 16, 1966, pp.476–83 (482).
4. Quoted in *Works of Bentham*, John Bowring (ed.), 1843, vol.x, p.285.
5. Quoted in *Literary History*, p.55.
6. Quoted in Cynthia A. Brandimarte, *Inside Texas: Culture, Identity and Houses, 1878–1920* (Texas Christian University Press, Fort Worth, 1992), pp.245–7.
7. Eastlake, op.cit., p.103.

8. Quoted in *At Home: The American Family*, p.138.
9. George Orwell, *Down and Out in Paris and London*, 1933 (Penguin ed., 1940), p.2.
10. Lady Barker, *The Bedroom and the Boudoir* (Art-at-Home series, London, 1878), p.8.
11. Rhoda and Agnes Garrett, *Suggestions for House Decoration* (Art-at-Home series, London, 1876), p.89.
12. Lady Barker, op.cit., p.9.
13. Eastlake, op.cit., p.109.
14. Edis, op.cit., p.66.
15. *JDA*, 1887, p.33. Quoted in Christine Woods, 'Those Hideous Sanitaries: Tracing the Development of Washable Wallcoverings', in *The Quarterly* [*Journal of the British Association of Paper Historians*], no.26, April 1998, pp.1–5.
16. *Ladies Realm*, 1897, p.726.
17. Whitworth Art Gallery, w.1967.285.
18. See *A Decorative Art: 19th Century Wallpapers in the Whitworth Art Gallery* (exhibition catalogue, 1985), p.63.
19. Mrs Beeton, *Housewife's Treasury*, p.211.
20. R. and A. Garrett, op.cit., p.70.
21. See David Jones, 'The singular case of Napoleon's wallpaper', *New Scientist*, 14 October, 1982, pp.101–4.
22. Ibid., p.102.
23. *The Buyer's Health Guide*, July 1884. Quoted in *A Decorative Art*, p.60.
24. *JDA*, 1893, p.377. See C. Woods, op.cit., part 2, *The Quarterly*, no.27, 1998, pp.17–19.
25. Mrs Beeton, op.cit., p.211.
26. *House Beautiful*, 37, no.6, May 1915.
27. Ill. in *The Papered Wall*, p.229.

14 Wallpapers for Children

1. J. C. Loudon, *The Suburban Gardener and Villa Companion*, 1838, p.680.
2. R. W. Edis, *The Decoration and Furniture of Town Houses* (London, 1881), p.227.
3. L. Barton, *Selections from the Poems and Letters of Bernard Barton* (Woodbridge, 1849) p.270.
4. Edis, op.cit., pp.228–9.
5. Ibid, p.230.
6. See Merlin Waterson, *The Servants' Hall: A Domestic History of Erddig*, 1980, p.92.
7. Lady Barker, *The Bedroom and the Boudoir*, 1878, pp.13–14.

8. Samuel Smiles, *Self Help*, 1859.
9. Wharton and Codman, *The Decoration of Houses*, 1978 (reprint of 1902 ed.), pp.173, 175, 187. Quoted in Kaye, *There's a Bed in the Piano*, p.222.
10. Letter to her mother Olivia Langdon, Mark Twain/Clemens Papers, Stowe-Day Library and Foundation, Hartford, Connecticut.
11. *British Architect*, 25 May 1884.
12. Edis, op.cit., p.229.
13. Ibid., p.228.
14. Ibid., p.228.
15. Walter Shaw Sparrow, *Hints on House Furnishings*, 1909, p.285–6.
16. Ill. in Lynn, p.453.
17. *Independent*, 25 October 1997.

15 Nostalgia and Reproduction

1. C. Rowell and J.M. Robinson, *Uppark Restored* (National Trust, 1996), p.126.
2. Ibid, p.126.
3. *Guardian*, 27 April 1995. Quoted in ibid., p.126.

16 New Directions

1. Andrea Childs [in feature on Neisha Crosland] in *Red* magazine, May 2001, p.33.
2. *The Observer Magazine*, 22 October 2000, p.86.
3. Quoted in *The Independent Weekend Review*, 10 April 1999, p.17.
4. See Marian Pallister, 'Art decor is back on a roll', *The Herald*, 6 September 1996.
5. Her own description. See note 4 above.
6. Quoted in *The Guardian Weekend*, 16 January 1999, p.37.
7. Quoted in *The Independent Weekend Review*, 10 April 1999, p.17.

Bibliography

A Decorative Art: 19th Century Wallpapers in the Whitworth Art Gallery (exhibition catalogue, 1985)

A Popular Art: British Wallpapers 1930–1960 (exhibition catalogue, Silver Studio Collection, Middlesex Polytechnic, 1989)

Calloway, S., *Twentieth-century Decoration: The Domestic Interior from 1900 to the Present Day* (Weidenfeld and Nicolson, London; Rizzoli, New York, 1988)

Cooper, N., *The Opulent Eye: Late Victorian and Edwardian Taste in Interior Design* (with photographic plates by H. Bedford Lemere) (The Architectural Press, London, 1976)

Crick, C., *Historic Wallpapers in the Whitworth Art Gallery* (Manchester, 1972)

Entwisle, E.A., *A Literary History of Wallpaper* (B.T. Batsford Ltd, London, 1960)

Entwisle, E.A., *The Book of Wallpaper: A History and An Appreciation* (Kingsmead Reprints, Bath, 1970)

Entwisle, E.A., *Wallpapers of the Victorian Era* (Leigh-on-Sea: F. Lewis, 1964)

Entwisle, E.A., *French Scenic Wallpapers 1800–1860* (Leigh-on-Sea: F. Lewis, 1972)

Fowler, J. and Cornforth, J., *English Decoration in the 18th Century* (London, 1974; 2nd ed. 1978)

Garrett, E. Donaghy, *At Home: The American Family 1750–1870* (Harry N. Abrams, Inc., New York, 1990)

Gere, C., *Nineteenth-Century Decoration: The Art of the Interior* (Weidenfeld & Nicolson, London; Harry N. Abrams, Inc., New York, 1989)

Gere, C. and Hoskins, L., *The House Beautiful: Oscar Wilde and the Aesthetic Interior* (Lund Humphreys in association with Geffrye Museum, London, 2000)

Hapgood, M. Oliver, *Wallpaper and the Artist from Dürer to Warhol* (Abbeville Press, New York, 1992)

Hoskins, L. (ed.), *The Papered Wall: The History, Patterns and Techniques of Wallpaper* (Thames & Hudson, London, 1994)

Jacqué, B. (ed.), *Les Papiers Peints en Arabesques* (Editions de la Martinière, Paris/Musée du Papier Peint, Rixheim, 1995)

Koldeweij, E., 'The Marketing of Gilt Leather in Seventeenth-century Holland', *Print Quarterly*, XIII, 1996, 2, pp.136–48

Kosuda-Warner, J., *Kitsch to Corbusier: Wallpapers from the 1950s* (exhibition catalogue, Cooper-Hewitt National Design Museum, Smithsonian Institution, New York, 1995)

Kosuda-Warner, J., *Landscape Wallcoverings* (Scala Publishers, London, in association with Cooper-Hewitt, National Design Museum, Smithsonian Institution, New York, 2001)

Lynn, C., *Wallpaper in America from the Seventeenth Century to World War I* (Norton, New York, 1980)

Nouvel, O., *Wall-papers of France 1800–1850* (Zwemmer, London; Rizzoli, New York, 1981)

Nouvel-Kammerer, O., *Papiers-Peints Panoramiques 1795–1865 / French Scenic Wallpaper 1795–1865* (Paris: Musée des Arts Décoratifs/ Flammarion, 1990; English edition, 2000)

Hapgood, M. Oliver, *Wallpaper and the Artist from Dürer to Warhol* (Abbeville Press, New York, 1992)

Oman, C.C. and Hamilton, J., *Wallpapers: A History and Illustrated Catalogue of the Collection of the Victoria and Albert Museum* (Sotheby Publications in association with the V&A Museum, London, 1982)

Parry, L. (ed.), *William Morris* (Philip Wilson Publishers in association with the V&A Museum; Harry N. Abrams, Inc., New York, 1996)

Rosoman, T., *London Wallpapers: Their Manufacture and Use 1690–1840* (English Heritage, 1992)

Saumarez Smith, C., *Eighteenth-century Decoration: Design and the Domestic Interior in England* (Weidenfeld & Nicolson, London, 1993)

Sugden, A.V. and Edmondson, J.L., *A History of English Wallpaper 1509–1914* (B.T. Batsford Ltd, London, 1926)

Teynac, F., Nolot, P. and Vivien, J.D., *Wallpaper: A History* (Thames and Hroson, London; Rizzoli, New York, 1982)

Thornton, P., *Seventeenth-century Interior Decoration in England, France and Holland* (Yale University Press, New Haven and London, 1983)

Thornton, P., *Authentic Décor: The Domestic Interior 1620–1920* (Weidenfeld and Nicolson, London, 1984; Seven Dials, 2001)

Turner, M. and Hoskins, L., *Silver Studio of Design. A Design and Source Book for Home Decoration* (Webb & Bower/Michael Joseph, Exeter/ London, 1988)

Une Aventure de Papier Peint, La Collection Maunay (exhibition catalogue, 21 June–21 September 1997)

Wells-Cole, A., *Historic Paper Hangings from Temple Newsam and Other English Houses* (Temple Newsam Country House Studies Number 1, Leeds City Art Galleries, 1983)

Woods, C. (ed.), *Sanderson 1860–1985* (exhibition catalogue, Arthur Sanderson and Sons Ltd., 1985)

Index